Prostate Health *in* 90 Days

LARRY CLAPP, Ph.D., J.D.

Hay House, Inc.
Carlsbad, California • Sydney, Australia

Book design by Sara Patton, Maui, Hawaii
Printed in Canada

ISBN #1-56170-460-1
Library of Congress Catalog Card #97-90589

The information in this book is presented solely for educational purposes. It is not intended to serve as medical advice or a prescription, or to replace the advice and care of your doctor. Be sure to check with your doctor before beginning any aspect of the program. It's also a good idea to check with your doctor before beginning, altering, or ending any health, lifestyle, or diet program.

Some respected authorities feel that prostate massage can cause existing prostate cancer to spread. If you have prostate cancer or an infection of the prostate, check with your health advisor before having prostate massage.

03 02 01 00 15 14 13 12
First printing, Hay House edition, July 1997
12th printing, August 2000

CONTENTS

CHAPTER 1

FROM DISEASE COMES A PLAN

Life was great back in the fall of 1990. At age 58, I was in a wonderful new relationship, awash with the excitement of a new love and sex life. I was living in my beautiful estate in Hawaii. Business was both exciting and profitable. As Chairman of the Public Transit Authority and numerous other public bodies, I was heavily involved in political and social issues, enjoying a high public profile. And my health seemed to be excellent.

But one day, out of the blue, urination became painful, and I found myself wanting to urinate a lot. My urologist quickly diagnosed the problem as prostatitis, a common infection of the prostate gland that can lead to inflammation, pain, fever, an excessive urge to urinate, and other problems. The doctor had me take antibiotics for three to four weeks, which immediately cleared up the symptoms, and slowly eliminated the infection.

It was pretty standard to have a blood test called *the PSA* following prostatitis, so I had one. The PSA test was fairly new back then so, like most people, I didn't know that it stood for "prostate-specific antigen." The PSA measures the blood levels of the agent that thins the ejaculate immediately after ejaculation in order to make the sperm more aggressive swimmers as they head for the ovum. Prostate-specific antigen is manufactured both by the prostate and by cancerous cells within the prostate. A score of 0 to 4 is considered normal and healthy. Anything over that is cause for investigation, suggesting either a very large prostate, prostate inflammation or infection, or prostate cancer. My PSA result was relatively high: 7.6.

I was frightened and upset by the result. I was also puzzled because my urologist, who had been examining me at least once a year for eighteen years, had been telling me all along that my prostate was quite enlarged and irregularly shaped. But he had also said this was very common. I reminded him that I had undergone an urgent prostate biopsy eighteen years ago, at his insistence. I asked him why, if my prostate had been enlarged and oddly shaped all this time, and if something had worried him enough to call for a biopsy, he had kept telling me that everything was OK. He replied, in effect, that he had been waiting for my prostate to deteriorate to the point that it would have to be surgically removed, because there is nothing else to do. This seemed incredible; moreover, it was unacceptable to me.

An elevated PSA only *suggests* that cancer may be present. In order to make a diagnosis, the urologist scheduled a prostate biopsy—my second. A biopsy is an uncomfortable procedure which, in 1990, was performed in the hospital on an outpatient basis, without anesthesia. (Today it

How could I suddenly have cancer when I had been pronounced one of the healthiest men in Honolulu?

is usually done in the urologist's office.) An ultrasound probe is placed into your rectum; you can see the image of your prostate created by the ultrasound on a monitor. Then a long, thin biopsy needle is inserted into your rectum. Guided by the ultrasound, the doctor places the biopsy needle at suspicious spots on the prostate. Then, when he pushes a button, a spring-loaded, hollow needle jumps out to grab and cut away a tiny piece of the prostate. The ultrasound probe felt uncomfortable, but the biopsy was downright painful. With each "grab," the pain grew cumulatively worse. Most doctors want six samples of prostate tissue in order to map the prostate, although I've read of others who take 30 to 75 samples. I'm glad I had only three; I don't think I could have tolerated more.

The biopsy only took about twenty-five minutes. I left the hospital feeling greatly relieved that it was over, although I had gnawing discomfort in my prostate. There was blood in my ejaculate for the next two weeks, but the doctor had told me to expect this.

Then came the long wait for the biopsy results—longer than normal because the local pathologists couldn't agree on whether or not my samples were malignant. So the slides of my prostate tissue samples were sent to Johns Hopkins, which was then considered to be the final arbiter of prostate samples. I called my doctor often during the next, suspenseful ten days, hoping for good news. Finally, his nurse called me to make an appointment to come in—with my family—to discuss the results. I chose to go alone, which upset the doctor. I preferred, however, to manage whatever news I might receive in my own way at first, without concern or pressure from others. I knew I would eventually want my loved ones to be involved, but I wanted to examine my own feelings and make some tentative decisions on my own first. I wanted to be alone should the results be bad.

And they were bad. The pathologists at Johns Hopkins had decided my biopsy samples were malignant, giving my prostate cancer a Gleason score of 6. The Gleason scale rates a tumor's aggressiveness on a scale of 2 to 10, with 10 being the highest, and most aggressive. A 6 on the Gleason scale is definitely not good news.

The next diagnostic step was to determine whether or not the cancer had spread beyond the prostate. If it was confined to the prostate, my doctor told me the odds of "getting it out" were good. But if it had metastasized out of the prostate and spread, then there was nothing to do except prepare for an extremely painful death. I went in for a bone scan and CT scan. The tests themselves, which took two to three hours each, were minor inconveniences. But the cold, bureaucratic attitude of the hospital staff and their deeply fearful, guarded demeanor, suggesting imminent death, was annoying and pretty frightening. The staff was unable or unwilling to answer any of my questions, or to discuss the side effects of the tests I was undergoing. I asked whether the radiation I was subjected to would have an effect on my body. Didn't I have the right to know what these effects might be? The staff didn't seem to think so, and clearly resented my questions.

Again, I had to make an appointment with my urologist to get the test results. And again he wanted me to bring my family with me, but I went alone. The conference was shocking. The doctor began by telling me that I was scheduled for surgery the next day. But that was good news, he insisted. The test results were negative; the cancer had not spread beyond my prostate, so the entire thing, prostate and cancer, could be "scooped out." He quickly added that immediate surgery would save my life. I *had* to have the surgery, he insisted, and right away. This is "the big one, the Big C," my doctor of eighteen years told me. "You will die unless I cut it out tomorrow." There was a risk of side effects, he admitted. I could wind up impotent and unable to hold my urine, but there were solutions to those problems—there were more surgeries and special devices. And I would be off work for "only" six to eight weeks while convalescing.

He kept telling me that this was the Big C, that I *had* to have surgery right away! Everything was set, the surgery was scheduled. All I needed to do was sign the consent form and show up—all costs would be covered by my insurance.

Many men are understandably stunned when they receive this fait accompli recommendation. Unprepared, not knowing their options, not knowing if there *are* any alternatives, they typically sign on the dotted line, wanting to just get it over with, to save their lives by excising the cancer as quickly as possible. Fortunately, I had already done some research and begun assembling a team of expert advisors. I knew that prostate cancer tends to be slow-growing, and I didn't have to undergo surgery the next day. I had time to think, time to investigate my options. Although very unhappy that I declined his offer to save my life by surgically removing my prostate, my doctor agreed when I suggested that I should get a second opinion, and he recommended radiologists who specialized in "killing" cancer with radiation. He seemed to feel that I would return to him for the surgery within a few days.

OPTION TWO: RADIATION

I thought that talking to a radiologist would clarify matters for me. Instead, it further muddied the waters. The radiologist suggested that I undergo immediate radiation treatment, not surgery. Destroying the cancer with beams of radiation "accurately aimed at my prostate," he said, would do the job. There was an 80% chance that the procedure would kill the cancer or send it into remission. And the risk of side effects was only 20%, with less chance of impotence or incontinence than is typical with surgery. He said that the side effects were minor. I would lose some hair, but I wouldn't have too much radiation sickness until toward the end of the ten-week treatment period, and I would feel great when it was over. I would probably lead a normal life, and might have an almost-normal sex life.

Should I have surgery or radiation? The urologist championed surgery as the "gold standard," while the radiologist touted the benefits of radiation. Each insisted that theirs was the best therapy: more effective and with fewer side effects than the other. Frustrated by my inability to find simple, authoritative answers despite exhaustive questioning, I began researching even more intently, going to medical libraries and creating a global network of healers, both traditional and alternative.

My extensive research led me to the Pacific Tumor Institute in Seattle. There I spoke with Dr. Ragde, the principal of the institute who was considered by many top professionals to be on the cutting edge of prostate treatment. His special interest was an old treatment, newly computerized, called *internal seed radiation.* After in-depth interviews with the doctor, I forwarded my medical records, scheduled an appointment, and flew from Honolulu to Seattle for tests. After reviewing my tests and personally feeling my prostate, Dr. Ragde said that immediate treatment was required.

His treatment was simple and elegant, he explained. Instead of beaming radiation onto the body around the area of the prostate and damaging surrounding tissue, tiny radioactive pellets, or "seeds," are inserted through needles, in a precise, computer-controlled grid, right into the little gland. These seeds literally kill the cancer from within the prostate. I was given the names and phone numbers of other patients who were pleased with their progress after seed implantation. They all reported that they had normal PSAs and digital rectal examinations (DREs), they had suffered no side effects, and they had returned to work the day after their procedures, feeling great. They also reported normal sex lives and bodily functions.

Seed radiation seemed to be the best medical option: the least objectionable way to remove the cancer within my prostate. But good as seeding was, I considered it to be only a half-measure. The medical doctors said my cancer was a "one-shot" disease, that I was sick because my prostate happened to have been "mugged" by cancer. But I felt it went deeper than that, much deeper. I knew that even if the cancer were successfully radiated or excised, whatever had caused the disease in the first place would remain within my being. This underlying problem would sooner or later cause another problem, perhaps in my prostate, perhaps elsewhere, unless it was addressed.

A THIRD WAY: HEALING THE PROSTATE NATURALLY

Diseases are signs of greater problems. They're messages telling us to change our ways. Sometimes the message is related to diet; perhaps we're eating too many processed foods, jam-packing ourselves with preservatives and other dangerous chemicals. Other times, disease tells us we're not taking care of ourselves, that we've failed to rest, to handle our stress, or to wash away the impurities that we knowingly and unknowingly absorb into our minds and bodies. Prostate cancer, I felt, was a pretty loud, screaming message.

I also believed that surgery and radiation were not the best responses to the message of disease. They might sometimes be necessary in an emergency situation, but they would not solve the underlying problem. Not only do they overlook the deeper ailment, they place additional stresses on the body, weakening its ability to heal. The entire idea of surgery and radiation is somewhat arrogant. It assumes that we humans know more than nature, which designed our wonderful and very, very complex bodies.

Acting against medical advice, refusing to allow the eager doctors to begin radiation treatments or surgically remove my prostate, I began developing my own healing plan, one that would get to the root of the problem, not just treat the symptoms (the cancer). Peter Grimm, D.O., the oncologist at the Pacific Tumor Institute, encouraged my emerging plan to heal the cancer metaphysically and spiritually, while monitoring the malignancy with monthly PSA tests and digital rectal examinations. Meanwhile, I studied with many traditional and alternative healers, adopting and adapting their ideas to my situation. I knew that I was taking chances, but it was vital for me to interpret the message my body was sending me via this cancer, and to respond accordingly. I decided to give my plan six months. If it wasn't successful, I would have the seed radiation.

Between January 8, 1991, the day of my diagnosis, and March 8, 1991, I earnestly put my healing plan into action. I was both confident and frightened. Confident, because I had devised and implemented many complex business, social, and political strategies before, often in the face of great opposition. I was accustomed to succeeding. But I was frightened because I knew I was challenging modern medical science. I was telling myself that I knew more than physicians who had spent years studying and treating illness. Frightened though I was, I stuck to my guns.

I prayed, meditated, and visualized myself healed. I expanded my exercise program. I took kelp, zinc, and saw palmetto, and eliminated all dairy foods and nearly all fats from my diet. I mixed eucalyptus oil and oil of lavender, 50-50, and massaged my wrists and ankles twice a day. I did a lot of psychological work. I got in touch with and released—by "re-feeling"—the anger and major feelings of sexual inadequacy affecting my prostate. My love and sex life became more fulfilling and supportive.

By April 1991, my PSA was down to 4.2. Not too long after that it dropped even further, safely below 3, and stayed there. Several physical exams proved that my prostate had shrunk to a more normal size and shape, and had softened. There were none of the nodules or hard spots indicative of a tumor. I was delighted: I had healed my cancer without having to undergo the surgery or radiation that my doctors had told me was absolutely necessary.

HEALING IS ONE THING, STAYING HEALTHY IS ANOTHER

Several happy, prosperous, and productive years passed by quickly. I had relocated to San Francisco, then to Boulder, Colorado, and in 1994 to Santa Monica, California, researching and working with ever more aware doctors and other resources to continue my own healing and to research this book. Periodic PSAs and physical examinations showed that my prostate remained healthy.

By Thanksgiving of 1995, the details of my bout with prostate cancer were but a dim memory. I was feeling better than ever before. I was proud of my success and health, which was constantly improving beyond the levels measured by traditional medicine. I had defied the doctors while beating cancer. I had developed a worldwide network of doctors and healers to call upon for advice. I was practicing and teaching tantra, bringing spiritual relating, healing, and sexuality to others. I was counseling men with prostate cancer, finding great enjoyment in teaching and helping others.

But on the Monday after a great Thanksgiving weekend in Hawaii, 1995, I got another loud, painful message: Things were not okay. I awoke that morning to mild pain in my lower abdomen/prostate area. By 10 A.M. the pain was excruciating and I was at the nearest hospital, listening grimly as the doctor explained that I had a kidney stone. I was stunned. After all, I had been a vegetarian for fifteen years. I jogged, worked out, and rollerbladed regularly. I meditated and otherwise took great care of my health. I was a spiritual teacher of tantra. And I had beaten cancer. How could I get a kidney stone? The experience was both painful and humiliating.

We tried all the standard procedures to move the stone. If it had still been in my kidney they could have destroyed it with ultrasound, but it had moved into my ureter. So instead they gave me drugs to dull the terrible pain, and exercises designed to move the stone out of its position. But the stone was strategically lodged in the narrowest part of my ureter, in the neck of the ureter between the kidney and the bladder, making any movement very difficult and extremely painful. Surgery was recommended as the only option. So the following day I flew home to Santa Monica, heavily medicated against the pain, to seek other advice and to try to move the stone.

On December 9, after two weeks' worth of drugs and exercise were unsuccessful, I went to Cedars Sinai Hospital for surgery, under general anesthesia, to remove the stone. I asked the urologist, Dr. Leslie Kaplan, to do yet another prostate biopsy while I was anesthetized and couldn't feel it. I had received a clean bill of health back in 1991 and in subsequent evaluations, but my PSA had been edging up slightly over the past year, registering as high as 5. (Up to 4 is considered normal, with anything above that considered a sign of possible danger.)

While my PSA was 3.5 at the time of the surgery, my albumin level had been declining for several months. The albumin level is a good reflection of immune-system function. People with albumin levels below 4.0 oftentimes get cancer, while those with 4.2 or greater usually do not.

Unfortunately, my albumin had been down at 3.9 for a couple of months, and I now had the kidney stone. I knew something was stressing my immune system. I wanted my prostate re-biopsied just to be sure.

The surgery to remove the kidney stone, including the biopsy, took only 45 minutes from the time I was wheeled into the room until the time I opened my eyes, and went extremely well. The procedure is fairly simple. The body isn't cut into; instead, a pair of long, slim "tongs" inserted up through the tip of the penis into the ureter is used to pull out the stone. The surgery was successful (I was given the little stone) but the results of the biopsy were not so happy: I again had a small tumor in my prostate. The pathologists gave the tumor a Gleason score of 7—higher and more aggressive than in 1990.

Dr. Kaplan explained what I already knew about the various invasive methods of treating and removing prostate tumors—the surgeries and radiation treatments I had successfully avoided the last time around. I listened as yet another top urologist explained in detail how he could remove my prostate but "spare" the nerves that run along the outside of the prostate gland, the ones that make it possible for a man to have an erection. He said that I would have normal erectile function and could enjoy orgasms, but they would be dry, without ejaculate.

As I weighed my choices, feeling pretty overwhelmed, I asked myself: Why did I get this kidney stone? Was it so that I would re-biopsy my prostate? What message was the stone and cancer trying to tell me? After examining all of the possible factors that could lead to the creation of the kidney stone, I realized that a major part of the problem was my colon, which I had assumed my physicians were monitoring. But they were not. In fact, we had overlooked it entirely.

Traditional doctors tell us (and most people believe) that your intestines are healthy as long as your bowel movements are regular. The truth is, unfortunately, quite different. Doctors focus very little on intestinal health until it gets so bad that the organs have to be cut out. They pay no attention to the large and small intestines, which are so vital to nutrient absorption and cleansing, two of the body's most basic and essential functions. Yes, there's a procedure called *proctoscopy* that helps detect polyps and cancers in the intestines. I had had a favorable proctoscopy every year since age 35, with stool samples quarterly, as part of my annual executive physical examination, but these examinations only looked for indications of cancer; they did not focus on the health of the intestine.

The standard lab analysis of stool samples could focus more on intestinal health, but medical doctors seem to be simply not interested in this. In fact, I learned that back in the 1930s and 1940s, physicians had colonics and other procedures designed to keep intestines healthy banished from the hospitals. The idea that the intestines had anything to do with health or were anything more than a "railroad" for waste was ridiculed.

Although it's hardly mainstream (and it is professionally risky) for physicians and other healers to believe that the colon plays a larger role in health, some do. A few brave practitioners have authored papers and books on colon health. In recent years, Dr. Bernard Jensen has written much on intestinal health, proving that even though your bowel movements are "regular," thick layers of toxic debris may have built up on the walls of your intestines, leaving just enough space for excrement to pass through the colon. But the built-up toxic matter does more than simply clog the passageway. It prevents the normal function and movement of the intestines, and interferes with the absorption of nutrients from food. It also creates a breeding ground for parasites, which have a habit of eating right through the colon, allowing powerful toxins to spill out onto other organs and into the bloodstream. When this happens, the liver and kidneys shift into overdrive trying to eliminate the poisons spreading through the body. But they can only do so much. And the prostate, which sits right next to the colon, is a frequent and easy target for the toxins.

The theory—that toxins spewing from unhealthy intestines caused my kidney stone and prostate cancer—made sense. (Dr. Kaplan, a noted urologist, concurred.) Unlike surgery or radiation, intestinal cleansing was fast, easy, and inexpensive therapy, with no side effects. I decided to cleanse my intestines and otherwise work toward a healthy colon as the cornerstone of a new health regimen before allowing the doctors to take any invasive action.

Acting against medical advice, I devised and began my now-proven *Ultimate Fast* and continued developing the other elements of my plan. My doctors and many friends kept urging me to have surgery for the cancer, raising the frightening specter of a painful death if I refused. But I stuck to my guns. Six months later my cancer was gone. And it wasn't just my imagination.

- The AMAS (a non-invasive blood test that measures for cancer antibodies, which has become well known and accepted in recent years) showed that there was no cancer in my body.

- In addition, the level of toxicity in my body had dropped from 24 (the highest and worst possible rating) all the way down to a very healthy—and rare—3.
- My albumin level was 4.5, the highest and healthiest it had been since 1984.
- My cellular pH level, which had been chronically acidic since I began monitoring it in 1991, was within a few one-hundredths of the optimum level.
- My dental problems were cleared up. Readings of my teeth had indicated hidden infections that were affecting my pancreas (which controls the prostate). They now read nearly normal, indicating that the homeopathics combined with the cleansing regime had been successful.
- Toxins around the site of my 1959 appendix removal were gone.

These were dramatic, scientifically measurable improvements that occurred between December 1995 and May 1996!

HEEDING THE MESSAGE

Some of my doctors have applauded my success, while others are somehow unaccepting and do not believe these results. I do. I firmly believe and have now personally experienced that every illness is a message. If we understand the message and make the necessary improvements—physically, and in our thoughts, diet, and lifestyle—the illness goes away. This happens regularly in clinics successfully treating cancer. (See the appendix for a list of practitioners using alternative medicine, and read the monthly magazine *Alternative Medicine*, which features a clinic every month). The approach has worked well for doctors such as Bernie Siegel, whose many books describe his success in using group therapy to help treat cancer.

Of course, if we don't get the message, we're given another, stronger, message. The messages *keep getting stronger* until we "get it." I consider a kidney stone and prostate cancer to be a very loud message: so loud I finally had to listen to my body. And the process of becoming ill and finding myself at the mercy of the medical system, though painful, led me to develop a new understanding of disease and a new approach to handling prostate cancer.

I can honestly say I'm glad I developed cancer. I am much healthier and happier as a result—although part of me wishes I had gone through life blissfully unaware of my poor health habits until I reached extreme old age, then suddenly died in my sleep. But since I did become ill, I'm glad my illness led me to a whole new level of health, and to developing an approach for treating prostate cancer so that I can help others.

My message is simple: If you have been diagnosed with problems with the prostate, including cancer, you don't have to let the doctors give you radiation or surgically remove your prostate. There is an alternative, one that will not only eliminate your disease but also increase your general level of health. What you'll find in this book is the plan I created to heal myself naturally from prostate cancer, and attain the outstanding levels of health and vitality I enjoy today. My hope is that you (or your loved ones) will use my experience to become yet another example of the body's innate ability to heal itself through cleansing, fasting, and eliminating toxins.

YOUR BODY MUST BE CLEAN TO BE HEALTHY

Internal cleansing is the basis of health. Even the best nutritional and supplement program is largely wasted if the colon is too dirty and clogged to absorb nutrients, if emotional blockages are harming body tissue, if hidden dental infections are poisoning the body, or if parasites are stealing the best nutrients. That's why my *Nine-Point Cleansing Program* is so important. The program:

1. Thoroughly cleans the colon and intestines.
2. Purifies the lymph system.
3. Begins to flush parasites from the body.
4. Eliminates many of the toxins that plague us so.
5. Removes excess, dangerous acidity or alkalinity from the body.
6. Releases the emotional blocks that harm body tissue.
7. Eliminates dental sources of poison and ill health.
8. Re-energizes the mind, body, and spirit by "cleaning" the chakras and aura.
9. Clears the organs, including the prostate, allowing them to function in "high gear."

The cleanse will jump-start your healing regime, and the rest of the program will lead you to a healthy prostate in 90 days.

If you are "dirty"—if your colon is filled with impacted fecal matter and parasites, if you are the unwitting host to toxins and emotional blockages—you cannot be healthy. Simply treating the symptoms, which are the results of these impurities, isn't helpful. In fact, doing so is downright harmful, for it turns your attention away from the real problem. Slapping a Band-Aid on the symptoms temporarily hides the problems, but they continue to grow until one day they burst from behind the Band-Aid, threatening your health or life. Not only that, but most symptom-based treatments have side effects, some of them quite severe. *You cannot be healthy if you are unclean.* But if you cleanse yourself—physically, emotionally, and spiritually—good health is all but guaranteed.

THERE'S ALWAYS HOPE

Upon diagnosing prostate cancer, the typical physician will tell you that you must act fast, before the cancer spreads beyond the prostate, or else you will die. That's typical of Western medicine, a "science" based on fear and resignation. And that's why cancer, which thrives on fear, is so prevalent in Western society. Many people are coming to realize that fear-driven medicine, which ignores the messages the body brings to us, is not healthful. Instead, it encourages further disease, as well as lifelong dependence on doctors, drugs, and surgery. That's why many people are looking for an alternate approach to healing, one that gently accepts the body's message and makes the necessary changes.

The differences between Western medicine and the alternative approach represented by my *Cleansing Program* are stark:

- Western medicine sees disease as something that just happens to you, caused either by germs or genes. *The Cleansing Program views disease as a message, urging you to change your life.*

- Western medicine is based in fear, sternly warning you of the serious consequences that will follow if you do not immediately follow directions. But fear invariably leads to disease. *The Cleansing Program encourages you to overcome the temporary problem, and to grow stronger and healthier as a result.*

- Western medicine allows small problems to grow large before doing anything. *The Cleansing Program strives to avoid big problems by heeding the little messages and building perfect health.*

- Western medicine looks only for a limited number of signs and symptoms of disease, ignoring countless others, limiting its tests and "cures" to the physical body only. *The Cleansing Program searches for evidence of ill health in every part of the body, mind, and spirit so you can heal every level of your being.*

- Western medicine relies almost exclusively on the "heavy artillery" of drugs and surgery. *The Cleansing Program uses herbs, massage, nutrition, meditation, spirituality, and other gentle touches to nudge the body and mind toward health.*

- Western medicine offers few solutions for an enlarged prostate, other than "reaming it out" (described in

Chapter 2), surgically removing it, or using drugs of debatable effectiveness and side effects. *The Cleansing Program utilizes cleansing, herbs, and massage to restore the prostate to a normal size, texture, and shape, which are indications of prostate health.*

- Western medicine wants to treat cancerous prostates with surgery or radiation. *The Cleansing Program heals by cleansing the body of physical and emotional toxins.*

- Western medicine makes you the passive victim, quietly accepting the drugs and surgery which, in many cases, make you weaker and *less* healthy. *The Cleansing Program encourages you to take the responsibility for healing your body, and offers proven tools and techniques to achieve optimum, radiant health.*

The complete *Nine-Point Cleansing Program* will be explained in detail, beginning in Chapter 4. First, however, let's look at the prostate, and why it becomes sick.

CHAPTER 2

THE PROSTATE: ITS DIAGNOSIS AND TREATMENT

Imagine a little bucket sitting inside your belly—that's your bladder. Now picture, right below the bucket, a tiny chestnut—that's your prostate. There's a tube running out the bottom of the bucket, right down through the middle of the chestnut, top to bottom—that tube is your urethra. Water continually collects in your bladder (bucket). Every so often the muscles at the bottom of your bladder open up, while the muscles surrounding the bladder contract, squirting the urine into the urethra (tube), which runs through the prostate (chestnut) and continues through the penis, all the way to the tip and out of the body.

The chestnut-shaped prostate sits right below the bladder and is wrapped around the urethra, but it has nothing to do with a man's urinary apparatus. The prostate happens to be where it is only because it's needed for ejaculation, and the ejaculate passes through the same urethra as the urine does. That's why the prostate sits below the bladder, and that's why prostate problems interfere with a man's ability to urinate and to have sex.

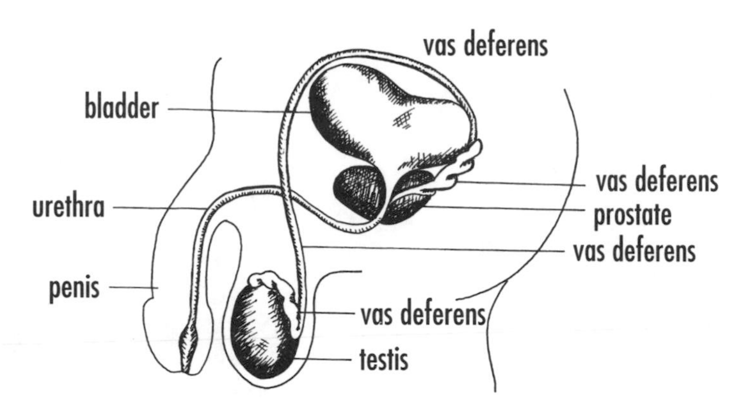

Figure 2-1. Male anatomy.

Situated right under the bladder, wrapped around the urethra, the prostate gland's primary job is to add special fluid to the sperm before it shoots out the penis during ejaculation. Sperm is produced in the testicles. From the testicles it moves up into the epididymis, where it matures, then into the two small, muscular tubes called *the vas deferens*, which coil up and around the bladder, to the seminal vesicles. Finally, the sperm moves into the prostate—its last stop before being shot out of the body by the contractions of muscles in the testes, epididymis, vas deferens, seminal vesicles, prostate gland, and the base of the penis.

A LOOK AT THE PROSTATE

One of the prostate's main duties is to create the seminal fluid that mixes with and carries sperm out of the penis upon ejaculation. The prostate also helps to pump the semen and sperm with sufficient power out of a man's body on its way to fertilizing a woman's egg. This means that the prostate functions as both a gland and as a muscle.

The prostate is also the nerve and emotional center of a man's sex life and sexuality. It is the feeling center for sexual pleasures, disappointments, stresses, feelings of inadequacy, immorality, hates, and dislikes. Unreleased emotions of this nature, stored in the prostate, are an important source of prostate problems.

WHAT GOES WRONG

Three main types of problems—infection, enlargement, and cancer—can afflict the prostate. Prostate infections, called *prostatitis*, are fairly common in men from the teen years on. These infections can be brief or long-lasting, mild or severe, easy or difficult to treat. Symptoms of prostatitis can include frequent and/or painful urination, other urinary difficulties, or pain during sex.

Prostate enlargement, called *benign prostatic hypertrophy*, or *BPH* for short, is an unwanted but non-cancerous enlargement of the prostate. Although men in their twenties can suffer from BPH, it usually surfaces later in life. It's estimated that half of all men have BPH by the age of 60, and 90% will suffer from it by age 85. If the prostate enlarges outward, a man probably won't know he has BPH (unless it grows upward and pushes into the bladder). But if it swells inward, squeezing the urethra which passes through the center of the gland, he will know there's a problem. With the prostate squeezing down on the urinary tube, a man can suffer from hesitancy in urinating, straining to start the stream, a weak urinary stream, starting and stopping of the urine, dribbling of urine before and after urinating, frequent urination, getting up several times at night to urinate, or urgency of urination (a feeling that he has to go *right now*). He may also suffer from incomplete

The prostate is a particularly vulnerable organ.

urination, which means that he can't completely empty his bladder, and possibly incontinence as well.

The principal medical "solution" to BPH symptoms is the non-invasive surgery called *TURP* (transurethral resection of the prostate), also referred to as *reaming out the prostate.* The urologist inserts an instrument through the penis (while the patient is under anesthesia). This allows the urologist to see and remove enough of the tissue to open the urethra passage through the prostate and restore normal urine flow. For a clear and comprehensive explanation of the TURP process, its successes and problems, read *Your Prostate* by Chet Cunningham, an excellent resource.

There are proven medical and alternative cures for BPH (benign prostatic hypertrophy).

There are drugs such as Proscar to shrink the prostate, but they have not been very effective and have objectionable side effects. The one quasi-medical approach that really does work was banned by the FDA in 1990. This approach was pioneered in a 1958 study by Drs. Feinblatt and Gant,[1] and subsequent studies confirmed its effectiveness. BPH was shown to be reduced in 77 to 92% of cases by capsules containing amino acids, glycine, alanine, and glutamic acid. This combination is available in several prostate supplements found in health food stores. There are no known side effects. If you have BPH symptoms, find one of these formulas that works for you while you do the cleansing to become truly healthy so that you won't need these formulas anymore.

---

[1] Drs. Feinblatt and Gant, *AMA Journal,* March 1958, Vol. 58, No. 3.

Although prostatitis and BPH can, in advanced cases, be quite dangerous, the most serious prostate problem is cancer. Cancer of the prostate is the second most frequently diagnosed cancer in males (after skin cancer), and the second most frequent cause of cancer death in males (after lung cancer).[2] Approximately 200,000 American men will get the unhappy diagnosis of prostate cancer this year alone—and 38,000 will die of the disease. No one is quite sure how many other men have prostate cancer and are not aware of it. Autopsy studies of men who died of other causes suggest that by age 50 or so, 30% of all men have undetected prostate cancer. And autopsies show that by age 90, the majority of men have it; it simply never grew or didn't grow large enough to get their attention.

Comedian Jerry Lewis has prostate cancer. So do Senator Bob Dole, General H. Norman Schwarzkopf, philanthropist-financier Michael Milken, and Andrew Grove, CEO of Intel Corporation. The disease has killed singer Frank Zappa, Nobel Prize-winning scientist Linus Pauling, and actors Telly Savalas and Bill Bixby. I've had prostate cancer twice, in separate areas of my prostate, both times without symptoms.

As was true in my case, men usually don't know that they have prostate cancer for quite some time after the

[2] Silverberg, E., Boring, C.C., Squires, T.S. Cancer Statistics, 1990. *CA* 1990; 40:9–26: Scott, R., Mutchnik, D.L., Laskowski, T.Z., Schmalhorst W.R. 1969. Carcinoma of the prostate in elderly men: incidence, growth characteristics and clinical significance. *J Urol* 101:602–7: Montie, J.E., Wood, D.P., Pontes, J.E., Boyett, J.M., Levin, H.S. 1989. Adenocarcinoma of the prostate in cystoprostatectomy specimens removed for bladder cancer. *Cancer* 63:381–5.

malignancy takes root, because it produces no symptoms in its early stages of growth. In fact, often there are no symptoms at all, or only very minor ones that can easily be overlooked. The early symptoms of prostate cancer are very similar to those of BPH, including getting up frequently at night to urinate (called *nocturia*); urinating frequently, but often only in small amounts (referred to as *frequency*); having to wait longer for the urine flow to begin (*hesitation*); and a urinary stream that starts and stops (*intermittency*).

Having these symptoms does not mean that you have prostate cancer. But if you do have these or other symptoms, it's best to get yourself checked.

Despite the fact that it's the number-two cancer killer in men, prostate cancer ordinarily grows slowly and is not, by itself, a deadly disease—if it stays in the prostate. It will likely cause mild to severe urinary problems, but will not, in most cases, be deadly. Unfortunately, the cells that make up prostate cancer like to travel. Like boiling water in a pot bubbling over, prostate cancer "pours" out of the prostate gland into the surrounding tissue. Once free of the prostate, the cancer cells can find new homes in the bones, liver, brain, lungs, spinal cord, or elsewhere. When that happens, the cancer that was simply annoying becomes deadly. And it often becomes deadly long before anyone knows it exists, for more than 40% of all prostate cancers have moved beyond the prostate gland before they are detected.[3]

---

[3] Murphy, G.P., et al. 1982. The National Survey of Cancer in the United States by the American College of Surgeons. *J Urol* 127:928–934.

WHAT CAUSES PROSTATE CANCER?

Many things can turn a healthy prostate cancerous, including poor diet, emotional distress, muscular pressure, stress, family history, exposure to various toxins, environmental factors, radiation, sex life, general lifestyle, and even the type of clothing you wear. BPH is often a precursor to prostate cancer, and should be treated as quickly as possible. All these possible causes share one thing in common: *They restrict the flow of blood and oxygen to the prostate.* Without life-giving oxygen and the numerous nutrients in the blood, prostate cells are bound to go bad.

Diet, long ignored by modern medicine, was finally recognized as a major cause of prostate cancer in 1982 when the National Research Council's report, *Diet, Nutrition and Cancer,* strongly linked dietary factors to prostate, breast, and colon cancer. Fat was identified as the major culprit, causing hormonal imbalances that are known to clog the tiny blood vessels of the prostate and encourage cancer.

The most convincing information concerning the diet/prostate cancer link comes from comparing large groups of people with different diets. For example, black males living in Africa have little or no prostate cancer, while those living in the U.S. have the highest rate of prostate cancer in the world, an incidence 50% greater than that of white American males. Why are blacks in America more likely to get prostate cancer than blacks in Africa or white men in the United States? In an attempt to answer that question, an intriguing study[4] looked at a total of 284

---

[4] Ross, R., et al. 1987. Case-control studies of prostate cancer in blacks and whites in Southern California. *J Natl Cancer Inst* 78(5):869–874.

black and white men in California who had been diagnosed with prostate cancer. It found that the risk of the disease:

- Increased significantly (1.8 to 2.8 times) among black men who frequently ate pork, beef, and eggs.
- Decreased significantly among those who frequently consumed carrots, spinach, collards, and poultry.

Among both black and white men studied, the major dietary risk factor for prostate cancer was a high intake of fat, especially among black men. Histories of sexual behavior, cigarette smoking, and occupational exposure to cadmium were not found to be significant predictors of increased risk. A history of venereal disease (gonorrhea) yielded a slightly increased risk. (Although there is a link between venereal disease and prostate cancer, there is no causal link. *Prevention* magazine's *Practical Encyclopedia of Sex and Health* reported a link between multiple sex partners and prostate cancer,[5] but the popular theory that prostate cancer is caused by an infectious sexually transmitted agent seems to have been disproved by a study of 1,400 Catholic priests. The celibate priests were found to have a high incidence of prostate cancer and a significantly increased risk of dying from prostate cancer, as compared to age-adjusted controls.[6])

[5] Bechtel, S., ed. 1996. *The Practical Encyclopedia of Sex and Health.* Emmaus, PA: Rodale Press.

[6] Ross, R.K., et al. 1981. A cohort study of mortality from cancer of the prostate in Catholic priests. *Br J Cancer* 43:231–235.

This theory, that a high-fat diet puts men at an increased risk of prostate cancer, is supported by a comparison of black men living in America, with the highest rate of prostate cancer in the world, and black men living in Africa, with one of the lowest rates of prostate cancer in the world. Clearly, the American and African blacks have the same genes, so we can't blame genetics. But their diets are different. The U.S. diet is very high in fat; the African diet is much lower. And when black men in Africa move to the United States and adopt the standard American diet, their risk of developing prostate cancer jumps tenfold.

Japanese men with a yen to move have helped to strengthen the proof of a link between diet and cancer. A study of 8,000 men of Japanese ancestry who moved from Japan to Hawaii showed that their risk of prostate cancer increased substantially as they adopted Western ways—especially the Western diet.[7] While no firm relationship was found between intake of total fat or total protein and the development of cancer, an increased risk was detected in men who consumed large amounts of butter, cheese, eggs, and margarine, all of which are much more characteristic of the American diet. And those who consumed traditional Japanese foods such as rice and bean curd (tofu) on a regular basis throughout their lives, even after emigrating, statistically had a significantly lower risk of developing cancer. As the traditional low-fat Japanese diet is becoming more "Americanized" and the Japanese have been eating more beef and dairy products in the past 15

---

[7] Severson, R., et al. 1989. A prospective study of demographics, diet, and prostate cancer among men of Japanese ancestry in Hawaii. *Cancer Res* 49:1857–1860.

to 20 years, the incidence of prostate cancer has progressively increased.

Fat is not the only part of the diet that plays a role in the development of prostate and other cancers. In Japan, where the incidence of prostate cancer has historically been very low, the dietary patterns of Japanese men with the disease were compared to those of healthy people. These investigators found that while elevated dietary fat consumption (as measured by food frequency questionnaires) did not increase the risk of cancer, the specific consumption of large amounts of butter and margarine did. And consuming small amounts of foods containing vitamins A and C, such as fresh fruits and vegetables, reduced the risk of developing prostate cancer.

Emotions are another largely ignored cause of prostate cancer. Our unreleased or "stuck" emotions create energy and eventually physical blockages, called *adhesions,* in the body, which hamper circulation. The muscles become rigid in order to keep the emotions suppressed. This process is evident in sore and nonfunctional muscles that eventually become calcified if circulation is not restored. Such calcified areas can be very difficult to clear. The deep tissue bodywork of Ida Rolf and many others over the years has shown that releasing stuck emotions improves general health and acts as a medicine for specific ailments.

How do our emotions restrict the flow of blood and oxygen to the prostate? This gland is the center of male emotions concerning sexuality. All of our emotions and judgments around sexual inadequacy, immorality, feelings of guilt, anger, and stress are stored in the tiny muscles and other tissues of the prostate, restricting blood flow. If these emotions are released, the restrictions are "washed away." But if they are allowed to remain, unreleased, they become semi-permanent and can set the stage for cancer.

As if poor diet and emotional distress weren't enough, the prostate must also contend with damage done by nearby muscles. The prostate, which is a muscle as well as a gland, becomes congested when surrounding muscles, most prominently the abductors that pass alongside it, tighten down. (You can find your abductors by feeling up your thigh into the groin.) The abductors are tight in many men due to stress, underuse, and/or emotional blockage. When these muscles become too tight, they clamp down on the tissue surrounding the prostate, preventing the normal expansion and contraction necessary for optimum blood flow through the gland. Pressure from the abductors can also cause the prostate to become quite hard, further restricting the blood flow. As you'll learn later in this book, rectal massage and release of tension from the abductors in the prostate area produces an immediate, significant softening of the prostate, as well as a reduction in size. This softening and reduction has been observed to last for weeks and months, and is believed to be cumulatively permanent.

Stress, particularly chronic or long-lasting stress, is especially damaging to the prostate. Stress causes all areas of the body to tighten up, restricting the flow of blood and energy. As the stress continues, the tension and restriction grow cumulatively worse. The prostate, an emotional center that relies on tiny blood vessels for nutrition and cleansing, is severely damaged by tension caused by years of stressful living. This damage sets the stage for prostate enlargement and eventually cancer. So releasing any pent-up stress is integral to maintaining a healthy prostate. In addition, many men are amazed at how much better they function sexually when they finally learn to relax.

Family history has been shown to play an important role in the development of prostate cancer. The scientific evidence suggests that if your father or brother has or had the disease, you probably will; and if your mother has or had breast or reproductive cancer, you are more likely to have prostate cancer. The evidence may seem pretty convincing and is valuable for encouraging preventive measures, but discretion is warranted. Don't fall into the trap of believing that if your father had prostate cancer or your mother had breast or reproductive cancer, you are doomed. For one thing, it's often the shared environment, lifestyle, and emotional patterns that caused the problem, not genetics. And you can change your environment, lifestyle, and emotional patterns. Second, accepting as fact the idea that you will get cancer is nearly guaranteed to be a self-fulfilling prophecy. If your parents had or have cancer, focus on developing a happy, healthful lifestyle. Exercise regularly, visualize yourself as being healthy, and practice prevention. You don't have to be a victim—you *can* take charge of your life and health.

Various toxins can harm the prostate, including the many chemicals we're exposed to at home and work: in pesticides, smog, tap water, coffee, tobacco, alcohol, and food preservatives. Parasites, bacteria, and viruses can also add to our toxin load. Ideally, the liver, kidneys, lungs, skin, colon, and lymph glands expel toxins from the body. But when these internal garbage disposals are overwhelmed, the toxins pile up in the body, weakening the immune system, interfering with endocrine glands, hampering the body's ability to utilize vitamins and minerals, upsetting body chemistry, and setting the stage for disease. (Most medical doctors aren't concerned with toxins, primarily because they know little or nothing about them or the harm they do, and because they don't register on standard medical tests.)

General lifestyle also contributes to the health or illness of your prostate. Exercise promotes circulation and relieves tension in the body, which greatly facilitates a healthy prostate. "Uptight" men have a higher incidence of prostate cancer, again related to the flow of blood in those tiny arteries. These varied causes suggest many choices that will be discussed later in the chapters on prevention.

Even the type of clothing worn can be a contributing cause of prostate cancer. Tight clothes can lead to poor blood flow to the prostate by restricting circulation. Tight briefs, which do not allow the testicles to move freely and regulate their own internal temperature by moving up and down, alter the critical hormone balance necessary to a healthy prostate by interfering with the testicles' ability to produce hormones. Nickel—either carried consistently in the pocket or worn in a large, cowboy-style belt buckle—is believed to create an energy blockage that restricts the flow of blood to the prostate. It may be significant that cultures without such clothing have little prostate cancer. Any belt buckle, whether it's made of nickel or another material, should be worn slightly to the side of center. Otherwise, the buckle will block the flow of energy through the critical center meridian that flows through the belly button, or *conception center*, to the prostate and the rest of the body.

Environmental factors must also be carefully considered. Alternating electrical currents from high-voltage power lines, electric blankets, and other sources of alternating current have been found to cause cancer.

The late pioneer healer Hanna Kroeger, of Boulder, Colorado, demonstrated that the microwave is particularly damaging to the male reproductive system, including the prostate. She reported that even the presence of a microwave oven in the home, unused and unplugged, is damaging, particularly to the male reproductive system.

Ley lines—the lines representing the earth's magnetic forces — are also sources of concern. Areas where north/south ley lines intersect east/west lines are thought to cause cancer and other diseases. Ley line dowsers use dowsing rods to detect areas of danger. You can survey your own house and workplace by making your own dowsing rods from #8 or #10 copper wire. Bend two pieces of wire in the shape of an "L" with the short part about 6 inches long and the long part about 18 inches long. Hold the short end of the rods in each hand, and point forward with the long ends. When you get to the harmful areas, the rods will point strongly inward, crossing, on their own. If you're sleeping on one of these harmful confluences of ley lines, or if your desk or favorite chair happens to be on one, you need to relocate your bed, desk, etc. Coil springs in normal mattresses and inner spring sets amplify these harmful magnetic currents. They should be replaced by a futon or other mattress that does not have coiled springs.

The aluminum in cooking utensils and commercial deodorants is another environmental factor to watch for. Aluminum is very toxic to the body, and an unnecessary stress on the immune system. This metal is thought to be a primary cause of Parkinson's disease. It is recommended that you discard any aluminum cooking utensils and read the labels of your deodorants carefully. Most herbal deodorants sold in health food stores do not contain aluminum, but most popular varieties do.

As you can see, there are numerous ways in which the prostate can be deprived of a steady supply of blood and oxygen. The tiny blood vessels in the prostate are easily dammed up by physical or emotional blockages. But while healthy prostate cells choke when deprived of oxygen, cancer cells flourish. That's why the solution is to ensure a steady flow of health-giving blood through the prostate.

DIAGNOSING PROSTATE PROBLEMS

There are three simple tests used to diagnose prostate cancer: (1) the digital rectal examination, (2) the PSA, and (3) the biopsy. These are relatively simple tests that can be performed in a doctor's office.

■ *The digital-rectal examination*, called *the DRE* for short, is a low-tech test. The process is simple. The doctor puts on a thin, nearly transparent glove, then inserts his or her index finger into your rectum as you stand, leaning against the examination table. The probing finger can feel the right and left lobes of the prostate, checking for size, shape, texture and hardness. (Ideally, the prostate is smooth, symmetrical, slightly moveable, soft but not squishy, and of normal size, with no bumps or hard spots.) If any irregularities are found, more tests are called for. If the prostate is simply enlarged, you may be suffering from BPH, an uncomfortable but non-cancerous condition. If, however, the doctor finds that your prostate is rock hard, or feels firm nodules on the gland, cancer must be suspected.

Although the DRE has long been considered the "gold standard" exam for the prostate, it does have some drawbacks. The doctor can't feel the entire prostate. Unless the cancer happens to be growing on or near the parts the doctor can feel, it may escape detection. If the cancer is still small, the doctor may not feel it at all—even if it's growing right where it can be felt. And some cancers don't "feel cancerous"; rather, they feel normal.

The problem is complicated by the fact that not all prostates feel the same. Some are harder, rounder, larger, bumpier, or more mobile than others. How is a doctor to know if yours is diseased or naturally that way? Finally, doctors can only make a subjective judgment about what they feel. What feels hard or squishy to one doctor may feel fine to another. The DRE is not a perfect test, but it is a simple way to look for many of the warning signs of prostate cancer.

- *The PSA,* a test that became available in the early 1980s, measures the amount of prostate-specific antigen (PSA) in the blood. A substance naturally produced by the prostate, the PSA rises when one has cancer because (1) cancerous prostates (which tend to be larger than normal ones) produce more PSA, and (2) the cancerous cells themselves produce more PSA than non-cancerous cells. Generally speaking, a PSA level below 4.0 is considered to be safe, while a level above 4.0 is felt to be suspicious—and anything above 10.0 can be dangerous, often indicating that cancer has spread beyond the prostate.

Age	Safe PSA Level
<40	<1.4
40–45	<1.8
45–50	<2.2
50–55	<2.6
55–60	<3.0
60–65	<3.4
65–70	<3.9
70–75	<4.4

Recently, prostate research has allowed us to refine the notion of a "good" PSA level, adjusting it to reflect the changes in a man's body as he ages. Since younger men tend to have smaller prostates and lower PSA levels, waiting until the level surpasses 4.0 may be dangerous in some cases. Adjusting the "safe" level for age helps compensate for this problem. The age-adjusted safe PSA levels are shown at left.

Unfortunately, the PSA is not foolproof. If, for example, you naturally have a very small prostate, your PSA level will start out at an unusually low number. On the other hand, if your gland is naturally large or you have BPH, your PSA may be above 4.0 even though you don't have cancer. The PSA can also be elevated by prostate infections, while drugs such as Proscar (finesteride) can push it down.[8] And if your cancer is still very small, it may not be producing enough additional PSA to push the total above 4.0. Bladder infections can also upset the PSA, as can recent prostate massage or the medical use of a catheter or cystoscope. Overall, the PSA is quite reliable over time; however, a single PSA should not be the basis for any invasive action. Instead, consider immediately beginning the *Nine-Point Cleansing Program* and having a follow-up PSA in 30 days (or sooner if your PSA is 10 or higher).

[8] *Abstracts. Geriatrics*, Vol. 49, No. 7, July 1994, p. 52, notes that "using finesteride for BPH can decrease PSA by 50% after 6 to 12 months of treatment."

■ A *biopsy* may confirm the suspicions of prostate cancer raised by the digital rectal examination and/or the PSA. Usually performed right in the urologist's office, the biopsy allows the doctor to cut out very small pieces of prostate tissue and send them to the laboratory for analysis. Guided by an ultrasound probe, the urologist inserts a needle through your rectum up to the thin lining that separates the colon from the prostate. After pushing the needle through the barrier, they can take one or more "cuts" of prostate tissue. The samples can also be taken via a small incision made in the area between the anus and testicles, or through the urethra (if you are already undergoing cystoscopy or another procedure involving the insertion of a tube into your penis). Although the biopsy is a useful tool, it is not perfect. The doctor may simply miss the cancerous spot(s) in your prostate, and many feel that the biopsy itself can spread the cancer.

The DRE, PSA, and biopsy are usually enough to diagnose prostate cancer or rule it out. But these are not the only tests a man should undergo before setting out to heal himself, because they only indicate if cancer is in the prostate, and not if that cancer has spread beyond the gland. That's why physicians call for other tests after a diagnosis of prostate cancer, including:

■ *Reverse transcriptase polymerase chain reaction,* or *(RT)–PCR:* A new blood test which shows whether or not the cancer has spread to other parts of the body. The test checks for the presence of cancerous cells in the blood, a strong indication that the cancer has spread.

■ *Serum acid phosphatase (ACP):* A blood test that has been used for many years to help determine if the cancer has spread. With results presented on a scale of roughly 0.5 to 1.9 U/L (units per liter), depending on the methods and laboratory used, an elevated ACP generally suggests that the cancer has spread. The test is not foolproof, however, for ACP levels may rise due to Guacher's disease, prostatic infarction, and other conditions. The results may also be skewed if the patient has recently had a rectal examination or prostate massage, or been catheterized for urinary tract problems.

■ *Alkaline phosphatase (ALP):* Looks at an enzyme related to the liver, bones, and other parts of the body to help the doctor discover whether the cancer has spread to the bones. ALP levels range typically range from 90 to 239 U/L (units per liter) in men, with higher values suggesting that cancer has invaded the bones. But the test is only suggestive, not conclusive; it can be upset by broken bones, drugs that affect the liver (such as barbiturates), and other conditions.

■ *Bone scans:* Help determine the spread of the cancer. The patient is given an intravenous injection of a radioactive substance. Then, a few hours later, a "camera" takes specialized "pictures" of him while he is lying on a table. The radiologist later examines the pictures, looking for "disturbances" that suggest the presence of cancer in the bones. (The disturbances are not specific; they may be cancer, arthritis, or other problems.)

■ *MRI,* or *magnetic resonance imaging:* Gives the doctor a "look" inside the patient's body. The patient lies on a special tabletop inside a cocoon-like apparatus. The test, which takes as long as 40 minutes, is painless but boring, which is why many MRI devices are set up so that the patient can watch television, listen to music, or talk with a friend. Like the bone scan, the MRI is used to check for the spread of prostate cancer.

"STAGING" THE CANCER

Having discovered that you have prostate cancer, your doctor will then *stage* and *grade* it. To "stage cancer" is to determine how far it has spread. Using tests such as the MRI, bone scans, ACP, and ALP, the doctor will determine which stage your cancer has reached. There are several systems for staging cancer. The simplest is the one used by the American Cancer Society:[9]

- *Very early:* The cancer is confined to the prostate gland and cannot be felt during a rectal examination. Very early prostate cancers are often discovered when a man has a biopsy for what is believed to be BPH. Physicians typically offer no treatment at this point, preferring to wait until the cancer has grown large enough to "warrant treatment."
- *Localized:* This cancer is large enough to be felt during a rectal examination, but is still confined to the prostate.
- *Regionalized:* The tumor has spread from the prostate to surrounding tissue.
- *Advanced:* The cancer has spread well beyond the prostate, leading to one or more tumors in the lymph nodes in the pelvis or beyond, or to the bones or other parts of the body.

[9] From the American Cancer Society Cancer Response System, #462557.

The National Cancer Institute favors a more detailed, and complex, "A-B-C" staging system:

- *Stage A:* The cancer is causing no symptoms, and cannot be felt during the DRE or seen with the unaided eye. It is found when a biopsy of the prostate is taken for other reasons, such as BPH, and sent to the laboratory for examination.
- *Stage A1:* Microscopic cancer cells in one area of the prostate.
- *Stage A2:* Microscopic cancer cells in more than one area of the prostate.
- *Stage B:* The cancer, which can be felt during a DRE, is confined to the prostate.
- *Stage C:* The cancer has pushed through the covering of the prostate, growing into nearby tissue. It may have invaded the neck of the bladder or the seminal vesicles.
- *Stage D:* The cancer has spread to lymph nodes, organs, or tissues.
- *Stage D1:* The cancer has spread to lymph nodes near the prostate.
- *Stage D2:* The cancer has spread to lymph nodes far away from the prostate, or to the bones, liver, lungs, or other parts of the body.
- *Recurrent:* Treated and thought to have been eliminated, the cancer has returned to the prostate or another area of the body.

There are variations of this A-B-C staging system, but in every case "A" is the mildest form of the disease.

The TNM (tumor-nodes-metastasis) system is also used by doctors to stage prostate cancer. This system focuses on tumor anatomy by looking at first the tumor itself, then at the regional lymph nodes, and finally at the metastasis (or spread).

T *The primary tumor:* Evaluates whether the cancer has spread.

TX Tumor cannot be assessed

T0 No evidence of tumor

T1 Tumor is not clinically apparent, is not palpable, cannot be visualized ("seen") with imagining devices

T2 Tumor is confined to the prostate

T3 Tumor has broken through the prostatic capsule

T4 Tumor has invaded or affixed itself to adjacent tissue (other than the seminal vesicles)

N *The lymph nodes:* Evaluates whether the cancer has begun to spread to the local lymph glands.

NX Cannot be assessed

N0 No evidence of spread to regional lymph nodes

N1 Spread to a single lymph node

N2 Larger spread to a single lymph node, or to more than one node

N3 Larger spread to a regional lymph node

M *The metastasis:* Evaluates whether the cancer has spread to distant parts of the body.

MX Cannot be assessed

M0 No evidence that the cancer has spread to distant areas

M1 The cancer has spread to distant areas

All three systems are helpful ways for staging prostate cancer. Whichever your doctor uses, make sure it is fully explained to you.

"GRADING" THE CANCER

Knowing that you have a tumor and how far it has spread is a good start. You can also learn how "aggressive" or malignant the cancer is by looking at your Gleason scale number.

The Gleason grade is given by a pathologist in the laboratory, who studies a tissue sample taken from your prostate during surgery or a biopsy. Cells in the tissue are rated 1 to 5, depending on how well formed (differentiated) they are. Healthy cells are well formed, cancer cells are not. The more aggressive the cancer, the more poorly the cells are formed. Well-formed, healthy cells are given a 1, while very poorly formed, aggressive cancer cells are rated 2 to 5.

After dividing the cells into the five different groups, the pathologist looks to see which two groups are most prevalent. If, for example, you have lots of 1's and 2's, a few 3's, and no 4's or 5's, then 1's and 2's are most prevalent in your sample. The pathologist adds the two most prevalent groups (1 + 2) together to get a Gleason score of

3. If your two most prevalent groups are 3's and 4's, your Gleason score will be 7. If your two most prevalent groups are 4's and 5's, your Gleason score will be 9.

The best Gleason score is 2. You can get a 2 only if all of your cells are healthy 1's. The most dangerous score is 10, which you get if you have an overwhelming number of 5's.

As a rule of thumb, a Gleason score between 2 and 4 means your cells are considered to be fairly well formed; 5 to 7 means the are moderately well formed; and 8 or higher suggests poorly formed cells, and very dangerous cancer.

WHAT NOT TO LET YOUR DOCTOR DO—AND WHY

When your doctor gives you a diagnosis of prostate cancer, he or she is also likely to tell you that you must have treatment immediately or you will die.

If you're being treated by a urologist, a surgery called *radical prostatectomy* will probably be recommended. Also known as *open prostatectomy,* or simply *the radical,* radical prostatectomy is a major surgery which calls for your belly to be cut open and your entire prostate cut out. The theory behind the radical prostatectomy is deceptively simple: pluck out the entire prostate, cancer and all, before the cancer has a chance to spread.

If you're not careful, your doctor will have you believing that the radical prostatectomy is as simple and effective as using your spoon to scoop a little piece of hair out of your soup. If only it were true!

The surgery works only if the cancer is totally confined to the prostate, and *not a single cancer cell has spread beyond it.* Despite advances in testing, doctors cannot guarantee that a few cells haven't escaped the prostate. Many thousands of prostates have been surgically removed without curing the patients, for tiny bits of the cancer had already escaped. The surgeries were for naught—and for many came at great sacrifices in quality of life.

Most men who undergo a radical prostatectomy end up suffering from varying degrees of impotence and incontinence. That's not surprising, given that the nerves controlling erection run right along the outside of the prostate. Even with the newer, "nerve-sparing" approach to the surgery, these precious nerve are often damaged or destroyed. Although some men recover to some degree, half or more of all men whose prostates have been surgically removed will never regain the ability to get and maintain an erection. And of course, there's a chance that you will die from the surgery itself.

But even if the radical prostatectomy worked more often and more effectively, it would still be ill-advised and dangerous. Why shock the body by cutting it when you can regain health without going under the knife? And the prostate is the center of a man's sexual energy—when it's gone, his total energy is bound to lag. Look at and listen to men who have had the surgery. Ask your doctor for names of men who have had the surgery—or, better yet, find a support group such as PAACT (Patient Advocates for Advanced Cancer Treatments).

If, on the other hand, you happen to wind up in the hands of a radiologist, you'll get an entirely different recommendation. Since they've been trained to use radiation, these specialists urge their patients to undergo radiation therapy, also called *radiotherapy* or *irradiation.* The idea is to radiate cancerous cells to death, hoping to shrink and possibly eliminate the cancer. The radiation doesn't kill the cancer cells right away; instead, it "gets" them when they attempt to divide in two. *If, however, the cancer has spread beyond the prostate, radiation therapy can only slow its growth. It will not cure you.*

The standard approach has been to apply the radiation externally by "beaming" radiation right into your abdomen as you lie on a table. Radiologists will usually apply the radiation beam to an area larger than the actual cancer, just in case they've underestimated the size. If the cancer is localized in the prostate or the areas immediately adjacent, radiation treatment generally takes between six and eight weeks, five days a week. Common side effects of external beam radiation include incontinence, nausea, fatigue, diarrhea, radiation skin burns, and skin irritation. If the radiation damages the nerves that control erections (which run right by the prostate, touching the gland) you may wind up impotent. Of course, you can never be sure that the radiation "got" every single cancer cell in the body. If even *one* cell remains, the tumor can regrow, the cancer can spread, and all will have been for naught. And if the cancer does come back you can't turn to radiation again, for too much radiation can actually *cause* cancer.

A newer approach to radiating prostate cancer, called *internal seed radiation,* uses tiny radioactive "seeds" surgically implanted in the prostate. Internal radiation refines the approach by getting the radiation right up against the cancer cells instead of passing it through the body and possibly harming other tissue along the way. The radiation seeds, which look like rice or bird seeds, are pushed through small needles right into your prostate. Fifty or more radiation seeds may be used on a typical patient.

Internal seeding has some advantages over external beam radiation. It's an outpatient procedure that takes only an hour to two. The seeds are placed right at or close to the cancer site, delivering their radiation "on target." Because the radiation is more focused than the external beam, there appears to be less risk of impotence and incontinence, and recovery takes only a day (or less). Andy Grove, CEO of Intel, elected to have seed radiation after researching the issues quite carefully. He wrote an outstanding article on the subject, called "Taking On Prostate Cancer," in the 5/13/96 issue of *Fortune* magazine—must reading for anyone considering treatment of prostate cancer!

Most men with cancer that is still confined to the prostate wind up undergoing either surgery or radiation. But if the cancer has spread, doctors will typically suggest hormone therapy. Hormone therapy is based on the idea that prostate cancer cells are especially hungry for testosterone, the male hormone. Take away this "food," and the cancer cells die. Most of the testosterone in a man's body is produced in the testicles, which is why doctors used to simply cut them off to "cure" prostate cancer. (The surgery to remove the testicles is called *orchiectomy.*)

But it's not enough to surgically remove a man's testicles, because the adrenal glands go into action to produce even more testosterone. So even after the testicles have been removed, a man suffering from prostate cancer must still take medicines to block the flow of testosterone from the adrenal glands. Another approach, which allows men to keep their testicles, is to use powerful drugs to block the flow of testosterone.

Whether a man keeps his testicles or not, hormone therapy deprives him of his usual testosterone. This slows the cancer somewhat, but has unpleasant side effects and undesirable psychological consequences. Men find themselves unable to get or keep erections, they lose muscle mass and gain breast tissue, and they suffer from fatigue, hot flashes, reduced brain function, and other problems. Hormone therapy can be a helpful temporary measure to arrest or shrink the cancer.

Although surgery, radiation, and hormone therapy are the medical system's favored approaches to treating prostate cancer, there are others. For example:

- *Cryosurgery* is a relatively new procedure in which cancer cells, and the prostate they are in, are frozen to death. It is still considered to be an experimental procedure by many authorities. Although it's a "lesser" surgery than the radical prostatectomy, cryosurgery is still a major surgery that is a shock to the body. Impotence and incontinence are common. Other side effects include bleeding, infection, hypothermia, urethral-rectal fistula (which may lead to a colostomy), injury to the bladder or urethra, urgency and frequency of urination, and urinary retention. Cryosurgery is an effective alternative medical treatment that is far less invasive and just as effective as a radical prostatectomy.

- *Hyperthermia*, the opposite of cryosurgery, is utilized separately and in conjunction with radiation. With hyperthermia, heat is applied to the prostate via microwaves coming from a cigar-box–like device placed between the man's legs or over his abdomen. No one knows quite how heat kills cancer. Some authorities argue that the heat damages the blood vessels leading to cancerous cells, without affecting normal cells, or that it kills the cancer cells weakened by radiation. Still others believe that heat interferes with the cancer cells' ability to make proteins or keep themselves "clean," but it is effective.

■ *Chemotherapy* uses powerful drugs to kill cancer cells. But the drugs don't specifically target cancer cells. Instead, they look for any rapidly growing cell. Cancer cells grow rapidly, but so do hair cells, cells lining the stomach, cells of the immune system, and cells in the bones. They, too, are killed by chemotherapy, causing a host of terrible side effects. Chemotherapy is not effective against prostate cancer per se; it's typically used only when the cancer has spread. And it's not a cure; it only helps relieve some advanced cancer symptoms.

■ *Watchful waiting* is recommended by some doctors (usually for older men) in the early stages of prostate cancer, before the tumor is big enough to "warrant" attack by surgery or radiation. Watchful waiting has the benefit of not assaulting the body, but it does nothing to stimulate the body's defenses. Many studies have found that watchful waiters match or slightly exceed the life spans of those who opt for surgery, and that the quality of their lives is far superior. (For more on this subject, read "Still Waiting, Watchfully" in the 5/13/96 issue of *Fortune* magazine.)

These interesting approaches may be useful adjuncts or substitutes for the traditional surgery, radiation, and hormone therapy, but they all miss the boat. None of them cleans the body of toxins and blockages, or strengthens the body's ability to heal itself—and this process is the *only* way to successfully deal with prostate cancer.

WHAT SHOULD YOU DO?

Urologists argue passionately for surgery, while radiologists sing the praises of radiation therapy. Other physicians may insist that hormone therapy is the only salvation. Each specialist urges you to opt for their approach, insisting that it's absolutely the best thing to do, and that you should do it right now.

If your doctor tells you they have you scheduled for surgery or radiation tomorrow, or if they want to remove your testicles, start grilling them. Ask them to describe the side effects of these treatments, and the likelihood of suffering associated with each. Verbally pin them to the wall; make them defend their approach and *show you* the statistics that prove theirs is the best approach. Ask the doctors if their approaches help the body heal itself. If they are honest, they'll admit the answer is no. Ask for comparative analyses with other possible treatments. Get second and third opinions. Learn all you can.

After you've discovered the limitations of standard Western medicine, look into ways of cleansing your body and removing the blockages that encourage disease. Think about and visualize strengthening your body's ability to heal itself. Doesn't that make the most sense? If you agree that the best approach is to make your body strong enough to naturally and completely dispense with the cancer, keep reading. Then spring into action!

Implement your own healing plan. It *can* work, and it can work *quickly:* in 90 days! Remember, healthy bodies successful ward off cancer every day! Regularly monitor your progress. You can always fall back on your medical treatment of choice if necessary. (My unused fall-back choice was seed radiation.)

Now we know what goes wrong with the prostate. We've heard all the bad news. Let's begin the good news with a look at how we can tell what's really happening inside our bodies.

CHAPTER 3

LET SCIENCE SHOW YOU WHAT'S *REALLY* GOING ON INSIDE YOUR BODY: THE BTA TEST

According to our physicians, most of us are in pretty good shape. And they can "prove" we're healthy by pointing to blood tests that show that the blood count, glucose, BUN, creatinine, and twenty or so other body indices are within normal limits.

But if we're so healthy, why are so many of us tired, hit again and again with vague diseases that sap our energy, and taking several medications at once? If we're as robust as our doctors claim, why are millions of us suddenly surprised to find we have cancer, heart disease, diabetes, or some other terrible—and possibly terminal—disease? Why do we as a nation spend far more on health care than any other, but have more health problems than the people of any other country?

The answer is simple: Most of us are not as healthy as our doctors want us to believe.

Why do our physicians mislead us? Not because they are mean people who want us to suffer. No—they're not cruel, they're not out to get us. The problem is simply that they don't focus on real health. Instead, they are taught to treat the symptoms. They get paid for diagnosing and treating symptoms; and the more threatening the symptoms, the better the pay. According to Western doctors, *if you don't have* an immediate, obvious disease, then you *must* be healthy.

Western physicians tend to have a very black-and-white, "either/or" approach to health. Either you're healthy or you're ill; there's no in-between. To doctors, health and disease is like a light switch: Either the switch is up and you're healthy, or it's down and you're sick.

If only life were that simple. Unfortunately, health and disease are not like a light switch. They are more like a dimmer, the round dial you turn to make a light get slowly brighter or dimmer. There's a clear and obvious difference between turning the dimmer all the way to the left or the right, between having the light blazing at full strength or being completely off. But the countless stages of brightness in between all the way on and all the way off are subtle.

Suppose you were sitting in a room reading a book, when someone quietly turned the dimmer down just a little bit, perhaps enough to dim the light by only 1%. You probably wouldn't notice the difference. Instead, your eyes would immediately adjust to the new lighting and you would continue reading. Now suppose that same someone turned the light down another 1%, then another 1%, on and on, ever so slowly dimming the light. The loss of light would be so gradual you wouldn't notice anything had happened for a long time, not until the light was way down.

So it is with our health: It often weakens slowly, each little loss being too small to notice. But our physicians think of disease as something that's either all the way on or all the way off. That's why they don't monitor the in-between stages. They don't know how to see when someone's "health dimmer" has been turned down just 1 or 2%. That's why they tell us we're healthy when we're not. And that's why so many of us are shocked to discover that we've "suddenly" developed a terrible disease. We wonder how we could be perfectly healthy one day, then deathly ill the next.

Clearly, we need to move from the light switch to the dimmer concept of health and disease. And we need tests that will allow us to detect tiny, 1% changes in health, whether for better or worse. Most Western physicians don't have such a test. The numerous tests they do have are very useful in other ways, but are not designed to monitor our health dimmers.

"GROWING" GOOD HEALTH

Fortunately, there's a relatively new test in the United States called the *Biological Terrain Assessment,* or *BTA* for short. The BTA does the highly accurate measurements we've been waiting for. There are only about 70 thus far among physicians and other practitioners in the United States, so you may have to search to find one. One of the test's developers, Dr. Robert Greenberg, can refer you to the nearest practitioner. He can be reached at (520) 474-4181.

The BTA is an entirely new approach to health testing. Instead of randomly checking numerous unrelated items, the BTA measures the "deep health" of the body by monitoring the pH, redox (reduction-oxidation), and resistivity of the blood, saliva, and urine. These three measures, taken in each of three different fluids, provide nine views of the body's true health.

The BTA monitors health at a level far beyond that even contemplated by traditional Western medicine, eliminating surprises.

The BTA goes way beyond the important but surface measures of blood count, glucose level, etc., that physicians normally monitor. The BTA serves as a supersensitive light meter that tells us when our health dimmers are being turned down—or up.

The concept of biological terrain is based on the work of European professor Louis Claude Vincent, who was hired by the French government to explain the varying incidences of cancer in different areas of France. The professor concluded that the underlying problem had to do with the quality of the water supply in different areas of the country. He went on to pioneer the BEV, a measurement system for the biological terrain of the body, which has since been refined to become the BTA today.

To understand the BTA, imagine a farmer whose corn isn't growing well. He or she might try to medicate or bandage each individual ear of corn, or perhaps they would search for the root of the problem by examining the soil in which the corn is growing. The clever farmer would work to make the growing terrain as healthy as possible by balancing the pH of the soil, and also add minerals and other substances to the ground to ensure that the various

By precisely tracking the biological terrain, practitioners can pinpoint weaknesses in a person's health and then fine-tune corrective therapy with regular BTA feedback.

nutrients and parts of the soil work together to produce healthy crops.

Shouldn't we, who want to "grow" good health for ourselves, make our basic terrain, our bodies, as healthy as possible? Wouldn't that be the best way to ensure a great "crop" of health, year after year?

The BTA is based on a simple premise: *Good health can only grow if the terrain is strong, and strong terrain will always produce good health.* Conversely, if the terrain is bad you cannot be healthy, and if you are unhealthy it is because your terrain is weak. That's why it is so important to measure, fine-tune, and strengthen your biological terrain.

Various standard laboratory tests can tell us if we have enough of this or that substance in our bodies, but only the BTA shows us whether certain keys to building health are working together. It does so by measuring three different things in three different body fluids: the pH, redox, and resistivity of the blood, urine, and saliva. These three items, checked in three body fluids, reveal whether or not our body's "soil" can support great health.

BTA MEASUREMENT #1: THE pH

The pH, commonly referred to as the *acid base balance,* is measured on a scale of 0 to 14, with 0 being extremely acidic, 7 being neutral, and 14 being extremely alkaline (or basic). The blood, saliva, stomach acid, bile, urine, and numerous other body fluids and tissues operate at very specific optimum pH balances. For example, stomach acid must be very acidic, running between 1.0 and 3.5 on the pH scale. Most body fluids, however, straddle the middle ranges between 6.0 and 8.0, running from somewhat acidic to somewhat alkaline.

Table 3-1. Optimal pH balances for certain body fluids.[1]

Tissue or fluid	pH
Gastric secretion	1.0–3.5
Urine	6.8
Saliva	6.5
Venous blood	7.3–7.35
Capillary blood	7.35–7.4
Small intestinal secretion	7.5–8.0
Arterial blood	7.4–7.45
Bile	7.8
Pancreatic secretion	8.0–8.3

The body continually struggles to keep the pH of various tissues and fluids at the proper levels. Unfortunately, normal metabolic reactions tend to produce acids. So do stress and overexercise, as well as the incomplete digestion of proteins, carbohydrates and fats from the food we eat. The body "deactivates" as many of the harmful acids as possible, storing the rest in "safe spots." But if you're too stressed or your diet is poor, acids may spill out of the safe

[1] Adapted from "Biological Terrain," R2 Medical Technologies, Inc., Manhattan Beach, CA, 1996.

storage spots to disrupt cellular metabolism, interfere with enzyme systems, upset body chemistry, and harm your health.

Health suffers as the cells become more and more acidic. The liver is the first organ called upon to deacidify the body. When overworked, it passes the acid load down to the kidneys. The stomach, skin, lungs, and colon are also involved in the ongoing struggle to deacidify the body. By monitoring the pH of the blood, saliva, and urine, the BTA allows us to see if our terrain is becoming too acidic *before it becomes a problem.*

BTA MEASUREMENT #2: THE REDOX

Did you ever mix chemicals together in a test tube during science class? Perhaps you watched two clear liquids turn blue when they were mixed together. It wasn't magic that made the clear liquids blue; it was the exchange of electrons between molecules in the fluids that did the trick.

Chemical reactions in the body are driven by the ability of the electrons in its fluids to attract and repel. Electrons are the negatively charged particles circling around an atom's nucleus (which contains positively charged protons and uncharged neutrons). Atoms constantly pass electrons back and forth in order to reach stability (neutrality).

Good health can only grow if the terrain is strong.

If a substance loses an electron, it has been oxidized. If it gains an electron, it has been reduced. (Though it may sound backwards that gaining an electron causes reduction, it makes sense, because when the substance gains an electron, its positive charge is lessened.) The constant reducing and oxidizing is called *reduction-oxidation,* or *redox* for short.

Redox is vital, for it helps the body create and store energy in the form of ATP (adenosine triphosphate), and it oxidizes ("burns up") certain "germs" and pollutants that find their way into the body. Measuring the redox tells us how many of the electrons needed for these reactions are available to the blood and the body cells.

The redox is measured in rH2 units on a scale of 0 to 42. Ideally, the redox should be:

22.0 in the blood
22.0 in the saliva
24.0 in the urine

Knowing one's rH2, or *redox potential,* is important. When body fluids have sufficient numbers of electrons available, life-giving chemical reactions can occur. But if all the electrons in the fluid are "tied up," if there are few or none available for exchange, then there is little potential for "action" in the fluid, little ability to carry out the reactions essential for a healthy life. The BTA allows you to assess your health by gauging the "liveliness" of your blood, saliva, and urine.

BTA MEASUREMENT #3: RESISTIVITY

You've undoubtedly heard it said that a metal pipe is a good conductor of electricity, while a brick is not. A pipe is a good conductor of electricity because it puts up little resistance to the flow of electrons. Bricks, on the other hand, put up a lot of resistance.

The BTA looks at the body's resistance to electrical currents, which is called *resistivity*. As the concentration of bodily minerals increases, the resistivity goes down and the conductivity increases, meaning that it is easier for electrical currents to flow. As the concentration of the minerals decreases, the resistivity increases and the conductivity decreases, meaning that electrical currents flow with more difficulty, resulting in reduced energy flow and deteriorating health.

The BTA measures the resistivity of the blood, urine, and saliva (i.e., their ability to conduct electricity), giving the result in *r* units (ohms). As with the pH and rH2, the resistivity of various body fluids and tissues must be kept within certain ranges in order for essential chemical reactions to occur. If the concentration of mineral salts rises or falls beyond normal limits the resistivity will change, contributing to illness.

Ideally, the resistivity should be:

190–210 in the blood
180–220 in the saliva
30 in the urine

Using the BTA to measure resistivity can tell a practitioner a great deal about the blood, digestive enzyme levels, and kidneys, as well as the effects of the diet and supplements on the body, and assist with making fine adjustments to bring the body toward precise balance.

PUTTING IT TOGETHER: pH + rH2 + *r* = BTA

It takes nine measurements to make up a BTA:

- The pH, redox, and resistivity of the blood.
- The pH, redox, and resistivity of the urine.
- The pH, redox, and resistivity of the saliva.

The BTA *does not* diagnose specific diseases, nor does it tell you which therapies are necessary. Instead, the anal-

> **Once we know what's out of balance, we can begin to make it right again.**

ysis of the pH, redox, and resistivity helps the doctor to assess your biological terrain. The three tests performed on three body fluids give your doctor a look at your body's ability to handle the chemical and biological reactions vital to health and life.

The BTA provides information about your enzymes, amino acids, molecules, and electrons, along with how well the enzymes are doing their jobs, and whether the nutrients from your food are being properly absorbed. A skilled healer can use the BTA results to learn about the health of your digestive system. The test also clearly shows whether the kidneys are cleansing the blood by excreting acids and toxins via the urine. This is important, for as we're exposed to more and more toxins from our air, food, and water, our kidneys are in danger of being overloaded and unable to eliminate all of the toxins assaulting our bodies. If the body is unable to eliminate them, it must store the toxins and, depending on where they're stored (which varies from person to person), they can cause different diseases. In the joints, toxins may produce rheumatoid arthritis; in the muscles, fibromyalgia; in the connective tissues, lupus; in the prostate, BPH or prostate cancer.

By precisely tracking the biological terrain, the BTA enables practitioners to find any weaknesses in a person's health, to fine-tune the therapy and quickly discover whether or not the patient is getting better. In other words, the BTA provides very precise feedback information for any health regime. The accurate feedback provided by the BTA assists the practitioner in guiding patients from illness to health, usually within 90 days to 12 months.

Below are some sample BTA results. The ones on the left are optimum, while those on the right suggest ill health. As you can see, small changes in some categories can make a big difference in health.

	Optimum Results				Unhealthy Results			
	pH	rH2	*r*	uW	pH	rH2	*r*	uW
Blood	7.35	22.0	200	240	7.55	28.0	180	240
Saliva	6.50	22.0	200	365	7.35	28.0	174	268
Urine	6.80	24.0	30	3245	6.80	34.0	120	635

uW stands for micro watts. This measurement, which is derived from other three, reflects the total charge of the specific biological fluids.

STRENGTHENING THE TERRAIN

No matter how ill you may be, it *is* possible to improve the soil in which you "grow" your health. If you follow the program laid out in this book (with the help of skilled practitioners), as I did, you'll find your biological terrain becoming a rich soil, one that ensures vigorous, radiant health. My BTA went from unhealthy to near optimum in 69 days.

HOW THE BTA IS PERFORMED

The BTA procedure is quite simple—it's just like the standard tests you have probably undergone at a physician's office.

Your doctor will ask you to fast for 12 to 14 hours before having the test. This may sound difficult, but it only means eating nothing after dinner, then going to the doctor's office for the test *before* having breakfast.

When you wake up on the morning of the test, don't eat or drink, and don't use toothpaste, lipstick, or anything else that might get into your mouth. Your doctor will have given you a small container in which to collect your first urine after 4:30 in the morning (the approximate time your kidneys finish their daily cleansing). Then you bring your urine to your doctor, who will also take a small sample of your blood (0.5 mg) and saliva (0.5 ml). That's all there is to it. The computer calculates the results in a few minutes, and your doctor goes over the results with you right then.

To make sure the BTA goes smoothly, your doctor will give you an instruction sheet that explains the procedure, and what you should do beforehand, in detail.

THE STARTING POINT FOR ALL TESTING

The BTA provides early evidence of biochemical imbalances in the body. It does not diagnose disease; instead, it pinpoints weaknesses in the body's *milieu* (terrain). The BTA can also be used to assess the effectiveness of any therapy, and to assess objectively whether or not a patient is improving. This is the test that catches the tiny changes in the dimmer switch of health that traditional Western medicine overlooks. This is the test that lets us know what's really going on inside our bodies. And once we know what is out of balance, we can begin to make it right again.

CHAPTER 4

THE NINE-POINT CLEANSING PROGRAM

Out of the anguish of my cancers, and the fear flung at me by the medical establishment, came the *Nine-Point Cleansing Program*. It draws upon the best from traditional medicine, Oriental medicine, nutritional healing, spiritual healing, herbology, homeopathy, and other disciplines. It's a plan that draws upon and focuses your own inner strength to cleanse and heal your body. The nine areas cleansed by the program are:

1. Colon/intestine walls
2. Lymph system
3. Parasites
4. Toxins
5. Acidity
6. Emotions
7. Dental
8. Energy/aura/chakras
9. Organs, including the prostate

A key point to remember is that every illness is a message. We don't just "happen" to get sick. We aren't randomly "attacked" by nasty germs. *Disease tells us that something is amiss physically, emotionally, and/or spiritually.*

In order to heal, we must seek to understand the message, and then correct the underlying problem. Despite its incredible store of knowledge and diagnostic capabilities, Western medicine fails in the long run because it treats or suppresses symptoms without addressing their underlying causes, ignoring the message as well as the patient's physical, mental, emotional, and spiritual aspects. Western health practitioners believe that cancer, heart attacks, diabetes, etc., are the real diseases, and never dig deeper to discover and repair the true imbalance. And the treatments physicians give us often weaken our ability to heal—or to even hear the message our body is trying to send us. Since the message of disease is routinely ignored, the illness often remains or reappears, carrying the same message over and over again, louder and stronger, causing us to suffer and often to die prematurely.

The *Nine-Point Cleansing Program* teaches you how to listen to the message of the illness and then respond, utilizing the body's built-in cleansing and healing mechanisms. Although there are many possible variations of this program (depending on who you are and how your prostate problem has manifested), the program can be broken down into three steps.

1. *Cleanse* the body while beginning to balance cellular pH.

2. *Strengthen* the body's natural defenses (such as the immune system).

3. *Maintain* lifelong, radiant good health, far beyond that measured by traditional medicine.

Let's take a brief look at each of these steps.

PHASE ONE: CLEANSING THE BODY WHILE BEGINNING TO BALANCE CELLULAR pH

Most of our diseases, including prostate cancer, are usually caused by a *build-up of toxins within the body.* The average person can't help being filled with these dangerous substances; after all, our air, food, and water are filled with pesticides, hormones, lead, and countless other toxins, including those that leak from unhealthy colons. There are toxins produced by the parasites that live in our intestinal tracts and other parts of our bodies. There's mercury and other metals leaking out of our dental fillings, plus legions of substances used in cosmetics, deodorants, hair sprays, and the other substances we put on our bodies.

Pesticides are among the most harmful of the toxins, for they are specifically designed to cripple insects' reproductive systems. Over time, the pesticides we inadvertently eat, drink, and inhale affect our own reproductive systems, including the prostate in men and the uterus and ovaries in women. The result is more than simply disease that is confined to our prostate, uterus, or ovaries, because our sexual centers are responsible for our creative energy and drive in all areas of life. Disease in these areas of the body inevitably weakens the entire person. (The same result occurs when these parts of the body are treated with radiation or surgically removed.)

Physical toxins are not the only ones that damage the body. The negative emotions we store in our bodies are just as dangerous. Our suppressed angers, fears, and hurts don't dissipate into the air. Instead, they're stored in our muscles, organs, and other tissues, where they create tightness that impedes the flow of blood and energy, and invite disease by decreasing blood flow in those areas. There aren't specific storage areas for different types of negative emotion; in fact, we humans are very clever about subconsciously stuffing them into the most remote areas of the body! While there are no firm rules, men do tend to store their emotions about sexuality—both happy and unhappy —in their prostates.

Together, these physical and emotional toxins cause constrictions (blockages) at various places in the body, impeding the flow of blood and energy through various organs and tissues, weakening our natural defenses and encouraging disease. The prostate, which has some of the smallest blood vessels in the body and is in the path of toxins leaking from the colon, is often hit hard by toxins from both sources.

True healing cannot take place until the parasites and toxins, including dental toxins, have been cleared out of the body.

If the constrictions caused by physical and emotional toxins were all we had to worry about, it would be enough. But there's more. The liver and kidneys frantically work overtime in an attempt to clear up the "garbage" that accumulates in the body as a result of physical and emotional toxins. When, as so often happens, these organs become overwhelmed, the acid-base (pH) balance of blood, saliva, urine, and body cells is thrown out of whack, further damaging the body's ability to cleanse and defend itself. If your pH levels are balanced, you won't become ill. But when the pH becomes unbalanced—either too alkaline or too acidic—serious disease is the inevitable result. Cancer can't live in a balanced pH environment but thrives in one with an unbalanced pH. My own cancer disappeared when my pH came into balance.

It's not known exactly how many people are too acidic, for traditional medicine ignores the cellular pH. Indeed, it's not even part of the typical blood test. However, it's been estimated that 90% of Americans are acidic. In large and polluted cities like New York or Los Angeles, the estimates are as high as 99%! Even those of us who eat a vegetarian diet, exercise regularly, and otherwise take care of ourselves are likely to be toxic and acidic. That's why *healing begins with cleansing.* Proper cleansing eliminates physical and emotional toxins as well as constrictions from the body, while helping to balance cellular pH. Cleansing does not directly balance the pH, but the cleansed body naturally inclines toward a balanced pH, and is ready to be further cleansed and strengthened by homeopathics. Furthermore, you probably cannot get into pH balance without first cleansing the body.

During the fast, the 35% of the body's energy that is normally devoted to digestion becomes available for healing.

True healing cannot take place until the toxins and parasites have been cleared out of the body, and the cellular pH has been restored to near normal. That's why Phase One of the nine-point program cleanses the body, with an eye toward balancing the cellular pH. During the eight days you're on Phase One, you'll clear accumulated debris out of your colon, cleanse your lymph system, begin to release stored emotions that have been encouraging disease, and relax your groin and other muscles as you build toward optimal circulation and health.

The following eight steps are the cleansing phase of the cure. You may choose to work into them and do those that seem to benefit you.

1. The *Ultimate Cleanse*
2. Lymph drainage
3. Homeopathic remedies
4. Dental purification
5. Prostate massage
6. Chelation
7. Microwater
8. Emotional Cleansing

The various elements of cleansing will be discussed in detail in later chapters. For now, let's take a brief look at each one.

1. *The Ultimate Cleanse:* Cleansing begins with a fast, for this is the easiest and quickest way to eliminate toxins, parasites, and intestinal plaque from the body. Fasting cleanses the body of not only physical pollutants, but many of the emotional ones as well.

Combining elements from three "tried-and-true" fasting approaches—(1) the 50-year old Master Cleanser Fast, (2) the classic Dr. Irons Fast, and (3) the Nature's Pure Body Program, used synergistically with the TheraClear anti-parasite formula—the Ultimate Cleanse cleanses the entire body, not just the colon or other single organs. Lasting eight days, the fast is based on a "lemonade" made of fresh lemon or lime juice, maple syrup, cayenne pepper, and pure water.

The *Ultimate Cleanse* allows the digestive system to rest, and lets the body use the tremendous amounts of energy it normally allocates to digestion to heal and to pull toxins out of the entire body instead. Normally, 35% (or more) of the body's energy is used to digest food. While you're fasting, all that energy is available for cleansing and healing.

Ten to twelve glasses a day of this lemonade will supply all the nutrients and vitamins needed by the body for an extended period of time. (Stanley Burroughs cites 40-day fasts.) Psyllium and bentonite added to the lemonade four to five times a day clear plaque and other debris off the intestine and colon walls. In addition to the lemonade, take TheraClear and Colon Cleanse in the morning, and additional Colon Cleanse in the evening (described in Chapter 5), plus as much pure water and herbal tea as you like.

The final, and *most essential* element of the *Ultimate Cleanse* is a quart of lukewarm salt water first thing every morning, taken on an empty stomach. This is a powerful enema, cleansing the entire digestive track, top to bottom, in 20 to 40 minutes. (The salt doesn't elevate blood pressure or cause other problems, for it washes right through the body without entering the bloodstream. As Burroughs explains in *The Master Cleanser:* "The salt water has the same specific gravity as the blood, hence the kidneys cannot pick up the water and the blood cannot pick up the salt."[1])

After eight days on the *Ultimate Cleanse,* most of the harmful toxins and parasites will have been mostly cleared from your body. Years of accumulated debris will have been flushed off the walls of your colon, allowing this vital organ to begin functioning fully. You'll feel more energetic and your immune system will be stronger, as more nutrients are absorbed through the small intestine and colon, and more toxins and parasites are eliminated. Although

---

[1] Burroughs, Stanley. 1976. *The Master Cleanser.* Auburn, CA: Burroughs Books. p. 21.

you're eating less on the fast you'll feel more energetic than ever, carrying out your usual work, travel, play, athletic, and sexual activities with surprising vigor. And your prostate will be healthier, for it will no longer be assaulted by toxins leaking from the colon, and the lymph system will have begun to drain wastes out of this important gland.

Many people worry about headaches and other aspects of cleansing too fast, often called a *healing crisis.* Try the fast for at least three days, which are the "getting-used-to-it" days of the fast. You will be amazed at how good you feel. You can always quit if you have a problem. You will have made a start, and can do it again when you are ready. Fifty years of experience by Stanley Burroughs—and several years of my own personal experience coaching others—have shown no problems so long as the salt water enema is done daily. This is a high-energy fast, and you will feel highly energized while carrying out your normal activities—from business to workouts—while your body cleanses.

Because your body is functioning better and the intestines are absorbing more nutrients and energy from your food, you'll require less food. Some people eat only 30 to 40% of what they did before the fast, yet they feel healthier and stronger than ever. Most likely, your body will no longer crave junk and fatty foods, asking you for health-giving foods instead (especially if that is a declared intent of your fast). Addictions, such as smoking, and diseases, such as diabetes, may also be cleared up during the fast if that is your declared intent. (Be sure to see the special instructions for diabetics in Stanley Burroughs' *The Master Cleanser,* page 19.)

Like other fasts, the *Ultimate Cleanse* begins the process of emotional cleansing as well. Emotional issues will

Just as dangerous as physical toxins are the negative emotions we store in our bodies.

come up for recognition and release during the fast. They may appear rapidly or slowly; they may be profound or relatively minor. Whatever their nature or cause, the fast will encourage them to arise, allowing them to be consciously re-felt and then released.

If the idea of fasting for eight days sounds a little intimidating to you, don't worry. It's fine to start with two or three days if that makes you more comfortable. Many people who have thought they could only fast for two or three days felt so good on the second and third days that they decided to go on for the full eight days. That's important, because the greatest "pay dirt" usually occurs on the seventh or eighth day, when—if you use a colander and a popsicle or throat stick—you can actually see in your stool the large amounts of debris that have been cleared out of your system.

2. *Lymph drainage:* The lymph system acts as the body's "sewer system," carrying waste products from every single cell to the liver and kidneys, where they are filtered out for safe disposal via the urine. There are lymph nodes all over the body, including the better known areas near the underarms, the groin, and legs. But the lymph system has a definite limit: It can handle only so many toxins and other wastes at a time. When it gets overloaded, wastes pile up in the lymph glands, then they back up into the body like garbage piled on the streets, encouraging disease. You can feel when a lymph gland is clogged, because it's painful to the touch. The problem is often exacerbated for men by tight muscles in the groin area. These tight

muscles squeeze down on the groin's lymph nodes, preventing them from functioning smoothly. Squeezed lymph glands can't work well, so wastes begin to pile up. But the unreleased waste products cause the muscles to tighten up even more, setting in motion a vicious, potentially deadly, cycle. And the prostate depends upon the lymph system to dispose of its wastes.

The solution for clogged lymph glands is two-pronged: (1) fasting to clear excess toxins from the body, and (2) massage to stimulate and drain the glands. Lymph massage is absolutely vital if the lymph system is to be cleaned and restored to full functioning. The massage works especially well during fasting. Lymph massage also helps to cleanse the body in general by improving circulation and speeding the removal of toxins through the skin. Lymph massage given by a professional or a loved one can be very effective. You can even benefit from doing it yourself, especially if you have observed a professional in order to learn the technique.

3. *Homeopathic remedies:* Developed by Dr. Samuel Hahnemann in the 18th century, homeopathy is a system of healing which is based on the idea that "like cures like." Instead of using powerful drugs to suppress symptoms of disease (as most medical doctors do), the homeopathic physician strengthens the body's ability to heal itself by giving patients very small doses of substances that *cause* specific symptoms in healthy people. In a sense, homeopathic remedies ("medicines") are like vaccines, which are designed to strengthen the body's built-in healing mechanisms. Although not as popular here in the United States, homeopathy is very popular in Europe. In fact, the British royal family is cared for by homeopathic physicians.

There are several homeopathic remedies that may be used to help to cleanse and strengthen the prostate. Still other remedies can help indirectly by healing the pancreas (which has a major influence on and is said to control the prostate gland), by strengthening the liver and kidneys, or by otherwise improving the body's ability to heal itself. Guided by scientific feedback mechanisms such as the BTA test, homeopathy is probably the most important tool we have for flushing out the organs and restoring them to full strength.

4. *Dental purification:* Most of us floss and brush our teeth regularly, and visit the dentist once or a twice a year. Doing so prevents cavities, but it does not prevent little-known imbalances in dental health from doing serious harm to the body. There are direct energetic connections running between each tooth and the various organs and other parts of the body. (These energetic connections follow the Chinese meridian system.) For example, the four front teeth on the bottom jaw are energetically related to the entire genitourinary area, the kidneys, and adrenal glands; the eye teeth are on the gall bladder meridian. Ill health in or around specific teeth may cause problems in the prostate or other parts of the genitourinary tract.

Improperly performed or infected root canals can indirectly harm the prostate by taxing the immune system and affecting the flow of energy from the teeth through the body. Dental fillings, commonly made of 50% mercury, can cause direct harm by leaking from the fillings into the bloodstream, and indirect harm by setting up a "battery" in the mouth which disturbs the normal flow of energy through the body's meridians. As you'll see in later chapters, there are proven protocols to restore the flow of energy through the body and help restore the body to health through a simple process of dental purification.

5. *Prostate massage:* Dependent on tiny blood vessels for cleansing and nourishment, surrounded by muscles that are often tight and restrictive, and adjacent to the colon from which so many toxins often leak, the prostate gland is an easy target for blockage and disease. And once the prostate has been stricken, men tend to become less sexually active, primarily for psychological reasons. Unfortunately the prostate (like other muscular tissue) atrophies when it's not used and the problem becomes worse.

Fortunately, the prostate responds quickly to treatment. Direct prostate massage, accompanied by massage of the muscles surrounding the prostate, frees blockages while encouraging the free flow of blood and energy. The massage can be performed by a professional or a loved one. (You can do the external massage yourself, but the internal massage, described in Chapter 10, must be done by someone else.) Regular, loving sex is also important to exercise and cleanse the prostate. As they say, you must "use it or lose it." *Note: Some respected authorities feel that prostate massage can cause existing prostate cancer to spread. If you have prostate cancer, check with your health advisor before having prostate massage.*

6. *Chelation:* Like other body tissue and organs, the prostate needs a steady flow of blood, both to nourish the gland and carry away waste products. Unfortunately, the tiny blood vessels in the prostate are easily clogged by cholesterol and other debris, causing the gland to become swollen and diseased. The *Ultimate Cleanse* helps to keep the prostate's blood vessels "clean" and the blood flowing, but sometimes additional help from chelation is necessary.

Although not very well known, chelation has been used for more than 40 years by physicians in this country and abroad to "roto-rooter" the blood vessels throughout the body, including those in the prostate, heart, legs, brain, and penis. Most men experience harder, longer-lasting erections after chelation.

The procedure is quite simple. After tests, a treatment plan is drawn up. An IV needle is inserted into your arm or hand, allowing a drug called *EDTA* to drip into your bloodstream over a period of 1½ to 3 hours. The medication restores circulation by stripping plaque, heavy metals, and other harmful materials away from the walls of the blood vessels, avoiding bypass surgery or angioplasty. You can sleep, read, watch TV, or make phone calls while having a chelation treatment. Depending on the degree of "clogging" and restriction, one to thirty treatments may be required. I had eight treatments to improve my circulation.

7. *Microwater:* Microwater has been developed in Japan, when researchers studying people who drank water from certain fast-moving, rocky mountain streams noticed that they enjoyed extraordinarily good health. Microwater emulates this naturally occurring water with a higher pH level, a different structure, and different electrical properties than regular water. Drinking Microwater raises your cellular pH and fights off the free radicals which would otherwise damage the prostate as well as general health. (As you'll learn in Chapter 6, free radicals are like cellular "buzz saws" that rip through healthy tissue, destroying everything in their wake. Keeping free radicals under control is vital.) Using a small device attached to your faucet, you can make Microwater at home. (See the appendix for information on how to order this product.)

8. *Emotional Cleansing:* There is always an emotional aspect of any illness, and prostate is no exception. Many respected practitioners believe that emotions cause 90% of most illnesses. Chapter 12 outlines many tried-and-true, old and new methods of accessing and releasing the emotions that are an aspect of any illness. Work with them to see what feels right and works for you. Most people do better by working with a professional for one or more sessions before continuing on their own, and going back to work with the professional as needed. Your personal healing plan (Chapter 15) should include this emotional cleansing.

When you have finished the eight steps of Phase One appropriate for you, you've cleansed your body and made significant strides toward restoring your cellular pH levels. Now it's time to begin the strengthening process.

PHASE TWO: STRENGTHENING THE BODY'S NATURAL DEFENSES

Although most toxins have been cleared out of your body, your colon has been cleansed, your pH has reached a healthier level, and other improvements have been made, much remains to be done. It's as if you swept all the dust out of your home after a big dust storm, and now you need to repair the cracks in the wall and weatherstrip the windows and doors to prevent more dirt from blowing in during the next storm.

Phase Two of the *Nine-Point Cleansing Program* helps you prevent physical and emotional toxins from reestablishing themselves. During this phase you'll use nutrition, homeopathy, exercise, emotional release, and rebuilding of the colon to strengthen your body.

1. *Nutrition:* When the first *Ultimate Cleanse* is completed, most of the toxins and parasites have been cleared out of your body, along with much of the debris that had accumulated in your colon. Now it's time to give your body all the nutrients it needs for energy and good health. The nutrition regimen for strengthening the body depends a lot on you and your needs. You must listen carefully to your body, learning to sense which foods make you feel good (i.e., strong), and which weaken you. In general, you should eat as many fresh, raw vegetables and fruits as possible: 50 to 80% of your diet should be made up of fresh, raw food. Keep fat intake to a minimum, limit yourself to moderate amounts of protein (no more than 50 to 60 grams a day), and eat only small amounts of dairy foods. Chapter 6 shows you how to figure out which foods are best for you, within these guidelines, and how to eat to keep your cellular pH in balance.

2. *Homeopathy:* Homeopathic remedies were used in Phase One to assist with cleansing and strengthening the kidneys, pancreas, and liver. Now, other remedies will be employed to help strengthen the body. Your homeopathic practitioner can guide you, using frequent Vega, blood, urine, saliva, stool, and Biological Terrain Assessment testing to monitor the results and adjust the program as you progress.

3. *Exercise:* We all know that regular aerobic exercise is important for keeping the heart and circulation strong. Strength-building exercises are also very important. As you will see in Chapter 10, every organ in the body is en-

ergetically linked to a muscle. Therefore, an organ can be no stronger than its corresponding muscle. During the strengthening portion of the plan you'll begin building your muscles, especially those related to the prostate. You will also begin to improve your aerobic capacity and increase your flexibility.

4. *Emotional release:* The emotions that rise to the surface for recognition and release during the first part of the program usually represent the tip of the iceberg. There are often many more emotions, deeply buried, that must be dealt with before all the emotional constrictions can be relaxed and the body restored to full health. As with nutrition and exercise, there is no set path to emotional clarity and peace. Instead, there are many paths, including spiritual guidance, meditation, and traditional psychiatry and counseling (if they have a spiritual component). Chapter 11 introduces you to various methods, showing you how to get started and how to move from one approach to the next, as you move to higher and higher stages of emotional awareness.

You don't have to be perfect to follow this cleansing regimen. You can start small and build up.

5. *Rebuilding the colon*: After it has been cleaned, the colon is typically misshapen and may be riddled with holes created by parasites working their way out of the colon and into the rest of the body. That's why it's necessary to use the Ultra Cleanse products (described in Chapter 5) for a total of at least 90 days. The stool can be regularly tested, especially at first, to make sure that the tenacious parasites are gone and don't reappear. However, a simpler approach is to

use a maintenance level of TheraClear anti-parasite formula and repeat the cleanse two or three times a year. It can take several months to become free of parasites. Art Bartunek, at BCN, is very experienced with the Ultra Cleanse process, is using it effectively, and has a nationwide referral network of practitioners experienced in parasite and whole body cleansing. Contact Art at (888) 803-5333.

In addition to nutrition, homeopathy, exercise, emotional release, and rebuilding the colon, you'll continue to use the Microwater, bodywork, and other items you chose to begin using in Phase One, as necessary.

By the time you've completed Phase Two, which takes anywhere between three to twelve months, depending on you, your body should be cleansed and your cellular pH balanced. The physical and emotional toxins that have been inviting disease and distress will be gone. Your cancer is probably gone, or at least significant progress has been made.

PHASE THREE: MAINTENANCE

Phase Three is about fine-tuning and keeping the gains you've made. With the good habits you developed during Phases One and Two, and the positive results you experienced, you'll find it easy to stick to this health-giving regimen for life. The third (maintenance) phase includes good nutrition, continued emotional release, ongoing lymph and prostate massage, a semi-annual *Ultimate Cleanse,* regular exercise and loving sex, and more. (The importance of massage and sex is brought out by studies showing that loving touch creates essential growth hormones that keep us healthy and young.) Ongoing BTA testing provides the feedback to monitor your continued good health.

A FINAL NOTE

You don't have to be perfect to follow this cleansing regimen. If you can do it all at once, fine. If you can only begin with small pieces, then start small and build up. The program is about healing. It's also about having as much fun and happiness in your life as possible. Fear, obsession, addiction, and rigidity invite disease, while love, laughter, fun, openness, and flexibility promote healing and radiant good health. You can greatly multiply this plan's healing effects by making it playful and fun, even if you are faced with serious disease.

Studies show that loving touch creates essential growth hormones to keep us healthy and young.

In the chapters that follow, we'll take a detailed look at the various elements of the program. Chapter 15 contains detailed instructions to help you put the plan into action. Let's begin with the *Ultimate Fast.*

CHAPTER 5

CLEANSING THE COLON AND BODY WITH THE "ULTIMATE FAST"

Fasting is a time-honored approach to physical health and spiritual enlightenment. Although it has been utilized for ages (primarily by spiritual seekers), many people are afraid to even *think* of going hours—let alone days—without food because they get a headache if they skip just one meal. Their fears may also be based on stories of people who felt generally lousy while fasting, and because most Western physicians discourage the practice.

Other fasts may be draining, but the *Ultimate Fast* is invigorating, giving you increased mental and physical energy as it cleanses your body of the physical and emotional toxins as well as the parasites that have made or will make you sick. Many alternative medicine practitioners and healers, more open to new ideas, have seen positive results from fasting. Dr. Bernard Jensen and others have shown that almost all illnesses can be cured by fasting and colon cleansing, and I have found that my eight-day *Ultimate Fast* is a very quick, comfortable way to "jump-start" any healing regimen.

Fasting is the first step in the *Prostate Cancer Cure* because it clears out toxins and parasites while cleansing the colon, the unwitting source of many diseases. A long tube running between the small intestine and the rectum, the colon acts as a kind of processor and "extractor" in the body. About 90% of digestion has already occurred before food, now called *chyme,* enters the colon, but important steps remain. For example, bacteria break down certain types of fiber into sugar (glucose) in the colon, while other bacteria release critically needed vitamin K, which is absorbed into the body.

Food moves from the stomach into a long, coiled tube called the *small intestine,* then into the colon. Also known as the *large intestine,* the colon is a tube about five feet long, roughly 2½ inches in diameter, sitting below your stomach like an upside-down "U." The partially digested food passes from the small intestine into the first part of the colon, called the *cecum,* then up the ascending colon, across the body through the transverse colon, down the descending colon, through the curves of the sigmoid colon, and out the rectum. Food, called *chyme* as it enters the colon and *feces* as it exits, is propelled forward by rhythmic contractions of the colon. (For excellent pictures of clear and blocked colons, and material that comes out of blocked colons, see Bernard Jensen's *Tissue Cleansing Through Bowel Management.*)

While the food we have eaten moves through the colon, any remaining nutrients are digested. Then the residue is moved along for elimination via the rectum, ideally leaving nothing behind and damaging nothing along the way. Unfortunately, in all too many of us the colon acts more like an open sewer than a sanitary "disassembly line," becoming a holding place for garbage and an ideal breeding ground for disease and parasites.

When we eat processed foods that have been stripped of fiber (and many nutrients), the colon has difficulty moving the chyme along. Processed foods tend to make for a dry, sticky chyme that does not move well through the colon. (The muscles wrapped around the colon can easily squeeze down to push fibrous, bulky chyme along, but have a great deal of difficulty with fiberless, gooey, sticky chyme.) When chyme sits too long in the colon, it becomes harder and dryer. If that was all that happened—chyme turning into hard and dry feces—we would only have to worry about constipation (from which millions of Americans suffer). But there's much, much more. After the chyme/feces plasters itself onto the walls of the colon, it begins to ferment and:

- Rots and hardens, becoming a breeding ground for parasites and a storehouse for toxic chemicals that can eventually poison the body.
- Forms a barrier that prevents the colon from interacting with and absorbing nutrients from chyme.
- Restricts movement of the colon walls, making it impossible for the colon to rhythmically contract in order to speed the chyme along its way. (How well could you do your job if you were covered with thick sludge?)

Now, with rotting bits of chyme/feces "gunking up" the works, the colon becomes much less efficient. Even if it's only slightly gunked up, the colon's ability to absorb the necessary nutrients from the chyme is hampered. An unfortunate cycle is set in motion: Small amounts of stale, hardening, and rotting chyme make the colon less efficient. The less-efficient colon cannot prevent still more chyme/feces from sticking to its walls, and further damaging the colon. The muscles that normally propel chyme through the colon and out of the body are less and less able to do their job, increasing the risk of constipation and a host of other ills. The specialized cells lining the interior of the colon cannot absorb nutrients from the chyme. Without these nutrients, the immune system and other parts of the body weaken, leaving us open to numerous diseases.

Meanwhile, the toxins, parasites, and bacteria that have been growing in this sludge that lines the colon wall begin to eat into the tissue that makes up that wall, and eventually they eat their way right through the colon. Now the bloodstream and tissues surrounding the colon are flooded with toxic substances, harmful bacteria, and parasites. The body swings into action, activating the immune system to battle with the bacteria and parasites, signaling the liver and kidneys to cleanse the toxins, and instructing the lymph system to clear away both toxins and debris from the immune system's battle with the poisonous substances.

But the body's defense and cleansing mechanisms are often overwhelmed. They simply can't keep up with routine cleansing *plus* the onslaught of poisonous substances. And the prostate, which lies right next to and touches the colon, is especially vulnerable. Assaulted by parasites and toxins, it swells in size and is increasingly vulnerable to disease. This is particularly true if the surrounding tissues and the lymph system are tight or blocked, preventing the prostate from flushing out the toxins. At the same time, the onslaught of toxins upsets the body's pH balance and turns it more acidic, which is dangerous in and of itself. (See Chapter 3 for more on pH.)

Our colons would be fairly clean—and few of us would suffer from diseases that spring from a "dirty" colon—if we ate absolutely healthful diets. But few of us eat well enough, and few of us are strong enough, to weather the storm caused by a dirty, parasite-ridden colon. That's why a special cleansing fast and parasite cleanse are necessary.

PARASITES: THE ENEMY WITHIN

It's estimated that 85 to 95% of adults living in the United States are unwitting and unwilling hosts to one or more of the 1,000+ species of parasites. These parasites are physically *in us,* living off our food and energy, draining our strength and energy, excreting their own toxins, weakening our organs and immune systems, and setting the stage for disease.

Parasites that can live in the human body range from 30-foot-long tapeworms down to microscopic organisms that burrow into body tissue or attach themselves to individual cells. Some parasites *literally* eat us, sucking their nutrition out of our cells or cutting into our body tissue in search of food. Others satisfy themselves by snatching nutrients away from the food we've eaten before we have had a chance to use the nutrients ourselves. (Indeed, some people who crave sugar may be driven to gobble up all the sugary foods they can because parasites are robbing them of their sugar.)

And it's not just that the parasites take their nutrition from us, forcing us to eat for them. The *way* they get their nutrition can also be quite damaging. Certain calcium-loving microscopic parasites, for example, burrow into our joints in order to eat the calcium that lines joints and bones, causing or setting the stage for arthritis. Other parasites love to eat proteins in the myelin sheaths that cover and protect our nerves. If these sheaths are damaged our nerves may not function properly, leading to various nervous system and other diseases. Whipworms spew out a fluid that digests colon tissue, turning it into a fluid they can "drink." Hookworms nibble away at the intestinal walls, sometimes causing the tissue to bleed or die.

90% of us are unwitting hosts to parasites that drain our energy, weaken our immune systems, and set the stage for disease.

Though they all start out there, only about 30% of the parasites remain in the gastrointestinal tract. The rest of these internal "squatters" take up residence all over the body, including the liver, blood, joints, brain, and lungs. Wherever the parasites go, they secrete harmful toxins. To the parasites, these secretions are protective fluids, waste materials, or lubricants. To us, they are poisons. Some parasites release toxins that hit us hard and fast: Think about food poisoning or dysentery. Other parasites leave us battling relatively low but chronic levels of poisons, tying up the immune system, and wasting vast amounts of body energy in doing so—energy that could better be spent living a creative, healthy life and shoring up the immune system to fight off disease.

Almost all of us have parasites because they're so easy to get. They can enter our bodies when we share food or utensils, have sex, or simply kiss someone on the cheek, drink polluted water, eat polluted food, shake hands, touch or allow pets to lick us—even when we inhale dried parasites in the dust or the air.

And once we have them, they're hard to get rid of. To begin with, we usually don't know we have them at first—some parasites can remain quiet for years before causing trouble. Then, when they begin to harm us, we often don't realize that our ailments are being caused by unwanted visitors. Relatively few of them cause obvious symptoms that say, "Here I am. I'm a parasite in your gut." Instead, our guests produce vague symptoms: lack of energy, intestinal gas, bloating, irritable bowel syndrome, constipation, loose stools, aches and pains, itching, sexual difficulties, rapid heartbeat, lack of appetite, blurred vision, numbness or tingling in the body, fatigue, allergies, kidney and heart ailments, weight problems, menstrual difficulties, impotence and other sexual problems in men, yeast infections, a burning feeling in the stomach or muscles, slow reflexes, increased appetite, pain in and around the navel, burning sensations in the stomach, headaches, memory deficits and forgetfulness, slow thinking, and other common problems. Millions of Americans who go to their doctors looking for relief from these problems wind up taking drugs that don't get at the cause—the parasites—but create new problems of their own.

Giardia lamblia, Entamoeba coli, Endolimax nana, Blastocystis hominis, and *Entamoeba histolytica* are common parasites afflicting us today. As more and more immigrants from poorer countries where parasites are common come to this country, they bring their "guests" with them. Passing through pets, children in schools, workers in the food industry, and household employees, parasites can travel rapidly, finding new homes in unlikely places. In one case, three orthodox Jewish men, whose religious dietary rules prohibit eating pork, wound up with pork tapeworms. The Centers for Disease Control discovered that all three men were infected by a housekeeper from Central America, where many are infected with the pork worm.

Giardia lamblia is an increasing problem for Americans, partly because we travel more to infected areas. The parasite can cause fever, chills, diarrhea, intestinal bloating, and muscle pain. It can also interfere with appetite and nutrient absorption, further weakening its victims. A tiny organism called *Cryptosporidium* got into the water supply in Milwaukee, Wisconsin, in 1993, causing hundreds of thousands of people to suffer from diarrhea and other stomach problems. More ominously, *Cryptosporidium* can be very dangerous to people whose immune systems are already weakened by toxins, poor diet, chemotherapy, or other factors. *Giardia lamblia* and *Cryptosporidium*, the two most common waterborne parasites in the United States, are not destroyed by chlorination.

Finding parasites is difficult for physicians because the very best laboratory tests are capable of detecting only 50 or so of the 1,000+ species of parasites. This means there's a good chance that whatever we have will avoid detection. (I know of a woman who actually saw worms in her feces, yet was told by her doctor that the tests proved she had no parasites.)

And even when we know that there are parasites within us, our doctors can't do much about them. Our standard medicines are not very effective, and they often have unpleasant side effects. They'll kill some parasites, but many times the internal invaders will simply move to another part of the body. Given that parasites are so difficult to find and dispose of, it's no wonder they can remain the body for years, even decades.

Fortunately, the Ultimate Fast works rapidly and effectively, beginning to clear most parasites from the body in the eight days of the fast. However, it is necessary to continue the whole body cleansing regime for a full 90 days to ensure that all parasites and their eggs/larvae have been cleared out of the body, and the body is healthy, no longer able to host parasites. With cancer and other serious disease, heavier doses for longer periods may be required. Seek an experienced practitioner by calling (888) 803-5333.

HOW THE ULTIMATE FAST WORKS

A clean-walled, parasite-less colon functioning at peak efficiency is the cornerstone of good health—especially prostate health. (The colon is adjacent to the prostate, touching one-third of the prostate's surface area. It's very easy for leaking toxins and parasites to "move" from the colon to the prostate.) You'll know your colon is healthy if you produce a regular stool, two to three times a day, that's soft but well-formed, two inches in diameter, and eighteen inches long. Does yours measure up? If not, it may be time for action! Fortunately, it's fairly easy to cleanse even the most "clogged" and parasite-infested colon and set yourself on the road to optimal health.

The Ultimate Fast begins to clear most parasites out of the body during the 8-day fast, with total clearance, including larva, usually within 90 days.

Good colon health can begin with the *Ultimate Fast,* which is a combination of the Master cleanser Fast, the Dr. Irons Fast, and a parasite elimination regime.

The Master Cleanser Fast was developed by Stanley Burroughs and has been used internationally since 1940. It is based on the principle that toxic foods are responsible for most diseases. Burroughs points out, "Disease, old age, and death are the result of accumulated poisons and congestions through the entire body . . . Lumps and growths are formed all over the body as storage spots for unusable and accumulated waste products, especially in the lymphatic glands. These accumulations depress and deteriorate in varied degrees, causing degeneration and decay. The liver, spleen, colon, stomach, heart, and our other organs, glands, and cells come in for their share of accumulations, thus impairing their natural action."[1]

Also known as *the lemonade diet,* the Master Cleanser Fast has been used for more than 50 years to easily and elegantly cleanse and rest the colon and digestive system. It clears out toxins and the resulting congestion that has built up in the colon and other parts of the body. It purifies the bloodstream and frees up tremendous amounts of energy within the body (since the body normally uses 35% or more of its energy to digest food, which can now be used to release toxins and rejuvenate the body.)

All told, the Master Cleanser Fast allows the digestive system to rest and repair itself while helping the body to better assimilate nutrients, fight off disease, and control weight.

---

[1] Burroughs, Stanley. 1976. *The Master Cleanser*. Auburn, CA: Burroughs Books. pp. 6–7.

The Dr. Irons Fast, the classic colon cleanse and fast utilized by colonic professionals for more than 50 years, employs a combination of fasting, colonics, and special supplements to cleanse the colon.[2] In its purest form, the Dr. Irons Fast calls for a seven-day fast complemented by daily, hour-long home colonic irrigation using a five-gallon bucket and colema board. Specially selected herbs, bentonite, psyllium, and juices are taken during the cleansing program.

Although Dr. Irons' program is quite effective, it is simply too harsh, time-consuming, and difficult for most people. Most people can't carry out their normal activities while on the fast because they're suffering from headaches and other unpleasant physical sensations. Many are forced to confine themselves to bed for several days. Not only are these side effects a strong deterrent to fasting, they're also counterproductive, for they weaken the body just when it really needs to be strengthened. That's why I feel that the Dr. Irons Fast is necessary only in extreme cases. (For more on the Dr. Irons Fast, see Dr. Bernard Jensen's classic work, *Tissue Cleansing Through Bowel Management.*[3])

Bentonite is the only product known to remove plaque from the walls of the intestine and colon. The plaque in your stool will look like egg shells on the outside of the bentonite "gel." Bentonite works most effectively when the colon is empty of food. It grabs the plaque which has been loosened by the lemon juice and the resting/fasting

---

[2] The Dr. Irons Fast is sold in kit form by many colonics professionals for about $90.

[3] Published by Bernard Jensen, D.C. 1981. Escondido, CA.

process. The salt water enema pushes out the bentonite gel and the plaque and debris that is stuck to it and in it. The salt water further cleanses the walls as it passes through, resulting in shiny clean walls.

I have found that the two Dr. Irons products—bentonite and colon cleanse, or their equivalents—combined with the lemonade and salt water enema, do a very thorough colon cleanse over eight days, but do not specifically address parasites. For parasites, additional supplementation is required. In order to best serve you, the Prostate90 Foundation endeavors to stay abreast of advancing technologies in cleansing and fasting. As we have tested new products, we have revised each printing of this book to recommend slightly different parasite protocols. While this printing outlines the fast using the PC-1-2-3 product, you may visit our website at www.prostate90.com for both past protocols and those we currently deem most effective.

The *Ultimate Fast* cleanses the colon and begins to rid the body of parasites in eight days, while allowing you to comfortably continue your ordinary activities. Even the most skeptical people have been pleasantly surprised to find that two to three days on the *Ultimate Fast* is easily extended to eight, without the loss of energy or headaches usually associated with fasting. That's not to say that you won't miss eating food, especially in the evening. (After all, our pleasure centers are designed to reward us for eating, and many of our social and business activities center around food. It may be best to avoid unsupportive friends and family during this time.) But you'll be surprised at how easy it is to quell your hunger simply by drinking more lemonade.

THE EIGHT-DAY ULTIMATE FAST

The following recommendations are for a general parasite cleanse for an individual without serious or terminal health problems. The cleanse lasts 90 days. If you are very toxic and have severe health challenges, you may need to continue the cleanse for longer than 90 days, and perhaps use some different dosages. I suggest you find a health practitioner familiar with the products to assist you in this very important component of your healing program; you can get a referral by calling (310) 577-1102.

You will not only feel great while on the Ultimate Fast, you will enjoy your usual work, play, and even long-distance travel routine.

Designed to rest and cleanse your colon, eliminate parasites, flush many of the accumulated toxins from your body, and begin the process of returning your cellular pH to normal, the *Ultimate Fast* is easy to follow. It's based on a lemonade you can easily make at home or on the road.

When preparing the lemonade, be sure to use only bottled spring or purified water.[4] (Tap water is loaded with toxins and parasites, while distilled water is "dead"

---

[4] Purified water should be made with reverse osmosis or equivalent process, not just an inexpensive home filter. Read the label on the water bottle and/or ask for the required test report prepared by an independent laboratory and filed periodically with most states.

and may also contain many oil-based toxins that vaporize in the steam.) Here's the recipe:

In a 10-ounce glass (to allow for 8 ounces and mixing room):

- 2 tablespoons *fresh* (and organic, if possible) lemon or lime juice (absolutely no canned or frozen juice).
- 2 tablespoons *real* (and organic, if possible) grade B or C maple syrup. (Don't use Grade A maple syrup or maple-flavored syrup. They are over-refined, which means that they are mostly refined sugars and lack essential minerals.)
- A small pinch of cayenne pepper (to taste).
- Spring or purified water, between room temperature and medium hot (but not cold)—fill to 8 ounces.

Mix all the ingredients by thoroughly stirring or shaking, and drink.

Or, in two 1-quart bottles (*32*-oz. juice bottles work well):

- Juice of 3 lemons, divided equally between the two bottles (about 3 ounces per bottle)
- An equal quantity of grade B or C maple syrup in each bottle (about 3 ounces per bottle)
- A pinch of cayenne in each bottle
- Spring or purified water (fill bottles to the top)

Mix all the ingredients by thoroughly shaking; then drink throughout the day.

I like to mix up four quarts in the morning and take them with me wherever I go during the day to ensure that I always have juice whenever I am hungry—whether I'm at a business lunch, on an airplane, or whatever. If well-meaning but non-supportive people ask, I simply tell them "It's an energy booster, like Gatorade."

The Ultimate Fast Shopping List

7 to 8 organic lemons (or 12 to 15 organic limes) per day
8 oz. grade B or C maple syrup per day (may be substituted with grade A)
1 bottle cayenne pepper
4 to 6 one-quart juice bottles
White colander
1 dozen throat or popsicle sticks
Electric Citrus Juicer (recommended)
2 bottles PC-1-2-3 or other parasite protocol
Nature's Whole Body Program
1 bottle Bentonite Minerals or Dr. Irons Bentonite
Dr. Irons Vit-ra-tox, Sonne #7, or equivalent
4 to 5 tsp. of Psyllium Powder/Day or Dr. Irons Colon Cleanse
1 set measuring spoons (plastic, not aluminum)
1 box uniodized sea salt
2 gallons spring water per day
Herbal teas — especially mint (optional)
Skin brush (optional)
Tongue scraper (optional)

On day 1 of your fast: Drink as much of this lemonade as you want, but make sure that you drink at least twelve 8-ounce glasses. The lemonade contains all the vitamins and minerals you need. Eat no food, and take no supplements, except for 10 drops PC-1-2-3 and one Colon Cleanse tablet in the morning, 10 drops PC-1-2-3 alone in the early afternoon, and 10 drops PC-1-2-3 with a Colon Cleanse tablet again near bedtime. (You don't have to start your fast on the morning of the first day. You can begin later in the day, even if you've already eaten. Once you begin, however, eat nothing more while you're on the fast.) It's also a good idea to read Stanley Burrough's book, *The Master Cleanser.* (See Recommended Reading.) Note: Diabetics, refer to the special instructions on page 19 of *The Master Cleanser.*

On days 2–8 of your fast: Continue drinking as much of the lemonade as you like, all day long. Make sure you drink at least twelve 8-ounce glasses each day. In addition to the lemonade:

- Drink an oral salt water enema upon arising. To do this, add 2 level teaspoons of *uniodized sea salt* to a quart of lukewarm water (the one-quart juice bottles in which most organic juices come work very well). Shake well, then drink the entire quart. Make sure you use uniodized sea salt; regular or iodized salt will not have the same beneficial effect.

  This oral enema will flush out your entire digestive tract and colon from top to bottom, usually within an hour, prompting you to eliminate several times, clearing out the plaque and debris from the walls, and the parasites that have been living there.

- Take 10 drops of PC-1-2-3 three times a day, first after drinking the salt water upon arising, again in the early afternoon, and again before bedtime.

- When you begin to feel hungry, drink your first glass of lemonade.

- Four times during the day (five if you weigh more than 150 pounds), at three-hour intervals, add 1 tablespoon of bentonite (Dr. Irons Vit-ra-tox Bentonite, Bentonite Minerals, or equivalent) and 1 rounded teaspoon of psyllium (Dr. Irons Vit-ra-tox Colon Cleanse or equivalent) to about 6 ounces of lemonade. It doesn't matter what time you start adding them, as long as you begin early enough to work in all your doses. These two substances will cleanse your colon. Indeed, most colonics professionals consider bentonite the only proven method of stripping plaque from colon walls. Shake the mixture thoroughly, then drink it immediately, before it gels. (See the appendix for information on purchasing Vit-ra-tox; for Bentonite Minerals, call BCN at (888) 803-5333.)

- Start with one Colon Program tablet in the morning and one near bedtime, working up to 3 twice a day, by the fourth day. (You should have two healthy bowel movements a day, and can adjust the Colon Program as needed.) Herbal teas, especially mint, are recommended during the day.

You can follow this program for as long as 40 days, but most people get the essential benefits in just eight days.

Though it may sound strange, the daily salt water enema is easy and powerfully effective. It keeps you feeling good by helping your body eliminate toxins as quickly as they are released.

After day 8: Although the fast is over, continue your parasite cleansing. Continue taking 10 drops of PC-1-2-3 three times a day until both bottles are taken. This should take approximately 70 days.

On the ninth day, add three Whole Body Program tablets a half an hour before the morning and evening meals.

The entire eight-day fast, including the Whole Body and PC-1-2-3 parasite cleanse, should be repeated two or three times a year.

ELIMINATING PARASITES WITH PC-1-2-3 AND NATURE'S WHOLE BODY PROGRAM

Nature's Whole Body Program, used synergistically with PC-1-2-3, is perhaps the most thorough herbal cleanse and anti-parasite program available. Based on time-tested formulas, this professional grade program has a long history of use by clinicians for clearing the body of toxins and parasites, and reestablishing your body's ability to ward off dangerous parasitic invaders. These cleansing herbs afford many other health-giving effects. Alone or in combination, they are used for indigestion, arthritis, allergies, asthma, bursitis, high cholesterol and blood pressure, diabetes, ulcers, cancer, bacteria, fungi, circulatory problems, constipation, liver, spleen, kidney and gall bladder problems, and other ailments. They are also used to stimulate the glands, strengthen the immune system, cleanse the blood, relieve "female problems," and much more.

A complete description of the ingredients in these parasite cleanse substances, and the benefits of each, is available by calling (888) 803-5333 or (323) 962-7370.

see p. 80

WHAT TO EXPECT WHILE ON THE ULTIMATE FAST

Some people are wary of fasts, fearing that they'll starve and barely be able to drag themselves through the day. That may be true with some other fasts, but not this one. You will feel great and have higher energy than normal. You might, however, feel uncomfortable during the first three days of the *Ultimate Fast* as the toxins and parasites inside your body are loosened up and washed away. It is highly unlikely—and I have never seen it occur during my extensive experience with the fast—but is it possible to experience weakness, dizziness, vomiting, and increased joint pain.

If you do feel uncomfortable or ill, remember that the toxins, not the lemonade, are to blame. Know that any uncomfortable feelings are very temporary and rejoice in the fact that these toxins and parasites are being eliminated from your body. If they are strong enough to cause a healing crisis, what would have happened if they were left in your body? If you do have a bit of trouble while on the fast, take it easy. Rest more than usual, if necessary. Exercise, preferably outdoors, and get daily massages when possible. Remember, it will be more than worth it in the end. Overall, you can expect to have an increased sense of energy and health while on the fast as the toxins and parasites are cleared. Many people who planned to fast for only two or three days have felt so good, they decided to continue for the full eight days, or more.

You should be having two to three bowel movements per day while on the fast, with the major bowel movement within an hour of the salt water enema in the morning. *Do not use colonics or enemas during this time, for the salt water enema does it all much more thoroughly and more gently.* (I have, however, found it useful to have one or more professional colonics during the fast in order to verify that the salt water enema has indeed cleansed my colon completely.)

By the second day of the fast you should put a white, plastic colander in the toilet when you eliminate so you can observe your feces. The fluids will wash right through the colander, leaving the solids behind for inspection. If you use a popsicle stick or tongue depressor to poke through your feces you'll see:

- Gel—that's the bentonite. It's often formed much like a healthy stool, one to two inches in diameter.
- Live or dead parasites, ranging from two- to three-foot-long worms to tiny ones that can barely be seen. (There will also be others that are too small to be seen without a microscope.)
- Whitish or beige-ish substances that look something like pieces of eggshell. This is plaque from the colon walls.

- "Ropey" stuff, perhaps an inch thick and one to two feet long. It literally looks like a woven rope rather than normal feces. This is composed of old, unevacuated, putrefied, rotting wastes which were stuck to the lining of the colon.
- Black stuff of all shapes and sizes. Some will be embedded in the ropey material, some will be elsewhere. This is old, accumulated wastes from the colon. The blacker it is, the older it is.
- White oval globules mixed into the gel and ropey material. This is excess mucus and/or dead parasites.

BREAKING THE ULTIMATE FAST

It's very important that you break the lemonade diet gently. In fact, gentle breaking of the fast is generally considered to be as important as the fast itself. Instead of jumping immediately from nothing but lemonade and herbal tea to regular eating, you must gradually reintroduce solid foods to your digestive system so it can start up slowly and gently.

On day 9 of the program, which is the first day after the Ultimate Fast, continue taking the TheraClear capsules and slowly drink pure, fresh-squeezed orange juice during the morning, or all day, as desired. For lunch, I recommend fresh, homemade vegetable soup, brown rice, and perhaps a salad with little or no dressing. For a light, early dinner, I suggest fresh, lightly cooked vegetables, with a little fish or chicken. Continue the Colon Program tablets and add three Whole Body Program tablets, also a half hour prior to breakfast and dinner.

On the 10th day of the program, begin your ongoing new food regime (described in Chapter 6), lightly and slowly working up to a full, healthful diet. Take great care to chew your food thoroughly, because complete chewing is the first step in the digestive process and essential for a healthy colon. Pay careful attention to the basics of food-combining, which are also essential for complete digestion and a healthy colon. Continue the cleansing program for 90 days to ensure complete elimination. Work up to five Whole Body tablets, twice a day, perhaps over three or four days

Twice annually, repeat the TheraClear and Pure Body anti-parasite cleansing program to make sure you stay parasite-free.

OTHER APPROACHES TO CLEANSING

The Gerson Institute in Bonita, California, and other clinics have very successful residential cleansing programs you may want to consider. Lee Cowden, M.D., oversees a seven-day residential cleansing program in Dallas, Texas. His program includes ozone added to the colonic waters, designed to greatly facilitate removal of wastes, parasites, and fungus through super-oxygenation of the intestines and body. In my experience, Dr. Cowden's cleanse, which includes emotional work, is the most powerful cleanse offered. You can reach him via fax at (972) 480-8909.

If you are unable or unwilling to fast, you can try other approaches to cleansing. I've found these methods to be slower and less effective, while just as uncomfortable (or more so) than fasting. Still, they can be beneficial. "Rise and Shine" and other similar herbal preparations cleanse without fasting. (However, I had headaches while on "Rise and Shine," and the cleansing was less effective than using the *Ultimate Fast.*) Homeopathics can also be used to cleanse the colon and body. They're effective, but they do not cleanse the colon walls or eliminate the parasites we all have. I strongly urge you to try my eight-day fast for a day at a time, to see how easy and effective it is.

You've begun the process of cleansing the colon, eliminating parasites, restoring the pH to proper levels, and clearing away physical and emotional toxins. All nine areas of concern—the colon/intestine, lymph system, parasites, toxins, acidity, emotions, dental, energy/aura/chakras, and organs (including the prostate)—are being cleansed. You're on your way to strengthening your immune system by sweeping away a lot of the useless work it had been forced to perform. Let's continue strengthening the body and immune system by learning about food-combining and other principles of healthful eating.

CHAPTER 6

NUTRITION: A MAJOR FACTOR IN PROSTATE HEALTH

Like every other part of the body, the prostate needs a steady supply of vitamins, minerals, amino acids, carbohydrates, and essential fatty acids, as well as enzymes, phytochemicals, and other substances found in food. A lack of any one of these vital substances could lead to disaster, especially since the prostate is exposed to toxins leaking from the colon, to which it is adjacent. Equally important and dangerous are the "negative" nutrients, such as excess dairy fats which quickly plug up the tiny blood vessels in the prostate, leaving it without a proper supply of nutrients and blood.

Hundreds of books have been written about nutrition, often suggesting a certain food regimen or diet that applies to everybody. This is a fallacy, because we each have very different needs. I believe we don't need to master complex systems. Instead, we must learn which foods work for us individually (make us feel strong), and use these foods in a diet based on five simple principles of healthful eating:

1. Give your body a large, continuous supply of all the nutrients it needs to keep itself clean and healthy, and the prostate strong.

2. Enjoy a diet based upon fresh, raw fruits and vegetables.

3. Use the scientific principles of food-combining to ensure that the nutrients you eat will be properly digested, and cellular pH and body cleanliness are maintained.

4. Drink eight or more glasses of purc water each day—but don't drink water with meals. Liquids should not be taken with meals, or for 30 minutes before or after, because they dilute the digestive enzymes, thereby stressing the digestive system.

5. Listen carefully to your body. Pay attention to how you feel physically, mentally, and emotionally, to determine whether specific foods make you feel strong or weak. Remember, foods that balance you may unbalance me. Many people change the general guidelines in order to tailor their diet to their body's special needs.

Remember, foods that balance you may unbalance me.

Ultimately, each of us needs to develop an individualized food regimen and allow it to evolve as we grow, change, and learn more about our bodies. These general guidelines are suggestions to help you devise your own regimen. With that in mind, let's take a more detailed look at each of the five points.

THE BUILDING BLOCKS OF GOOD HEALTH – AND A HEALTHY PROSTATE

The body needs a generous supply of vitamins, minerals, and all the other nutrients, including phytochemicals, a class just coming into prominence. Neither vitamin nor mineral, phytochemical nutritional values are not yet known, nor is how much, or even which ones we need every day. However, we know the adenosine found in garlic, onions, and black mushrooms helps protect against heart disease and cancer; capsaicin found in hot chili peppers can help relieve respiratory problems; some bioflavonoids found in fruits and vegetables can help prevent cancer; and soy's genistein works against tumors by interfering with their ability to get the blood they need to survive.

Ideally, we would get all the nutrients and phytochemicals we need from food. Unfortunately, many of us start with a nutrient deficit because our agriculture system is designed to produce good-looking items that don't spoil on the way to the market, instead of nutrient-packed, healthful foods. Plus, we need even more nutrients when we become ill, pick up parasites, or are exposed to toxins. That's why we must turn to supplements, but not just any supplements will do.

The typical vitamin and mineral pills so many of us swallow may not serve us well: They can place added stress on the liver, which processes these substances. Before taking them, we need to ask, "Does the benefit I get from this supplement outweigh the added stress placed on my system by the effort to digest and process it?" In many cases, the answer is no. Use feedback from regular BTAs and from muscle testing to help answer this vital question.

Liquid and homeopathic supplements are much easier on our bodies, and are more readily absorbed, such as the Bio-Oligo liquid supplements distributed by Molecular Biologics of Benicia, California.

Additionally, it is important to take supplements that specifically benefit the prostate. These include:

■ *Green tea:* When Asian men move to the U.S. and stop drinking their typically large amounts of green tea, their risk of developing prostate cancer increases twenty-fold. The catechins found in green tea are the likely "medicines" for the prostate, although it is not known exactly how they prevent or combat existing prostate cancer.

■ *Kelp:* A seaweed rich in iodine, it contains minerals that help prevent and treat prostate cancer. Also known as *bladderwrack,* kelp is valued for its ability to "rev up" underactive thyroid glands, as well as "remineralize" and revitalize the body.

■ *neoProstate ß-300:* A food supplement providing 300 mg. of standardized beta-sitosterol, the key component in herbs used for prostate health. Obtained from sugar cane or soy, it works naturally with the body to prevent the conversion of testosterone to DHT, a growth factor for the prostate. Once the male hormones are rebalanced, symptoms abate and the prostate can begin to heal, and return to normal size. It can also help normalize cholesterol and triglyceride levels. Available from BCN, (888) 803-5333.

■ *Nettles:* An herb with many uses, nettle contains vitamin C, iron, and other nutrients that strengthen the prostate. It has also been used to treat gout, arthritis, high blood sugar, excessive bleeding, and other ailments.

- *PC Spes:* PC Spes is a proprietary Chinese herbal formula, by Botanic Lab, that is reducing PSA to >1, in 2 to 3 months, for 99% of men. It also works to heal bone metastasis, even after the tumors are no longer responsive to hormonal therapy, i.e., refractory. How long it can work is not yet known, but several men are leading very normal lives after five years; some have been able to slowly wean off or cut down the dosage and still have a PSA >1. PC Spes can be most powerful when combined with the cleansing program in this book. For more information, see www.prostate90.com or call BCN at (888) 803-5333.

- *Pygeum:* Derived from an African evergreen, this herb has been used to treat prostate and urinary tract diseases for many years. Pygeum has been shown, in double-blind studies, to shrink enlarged prostates.

- *Saw palmetto:* Properly known as *serenoa repens,* it is known to shrink enlarged prostates and to lower PSA. Studies have found that this herb is far more effective than Proscar (a much-prescribed BPH drug) without the side effects or expense. Extract from the berries of this palm tree, grown mostly in Florida, has historically been used for relieving prostate problems and increasing libido. Its effectiveness comes primarily from its ability to block the conversion of testosterone into its unwanted form, dehyeroltestosterone, DHT, which can cause the prostate to swell, leading to urinary, sexual, and other difficulties.

- *Zinc:* Marginal zinc deficiency is common in older men. Since it is a major component of semen and the most abundant mineral in the prostate, supplementation can be important, especially for vegetarians.

There are a lot of prostate formulas on the market that contain all or some of these ingredients. You can experiment and/or seek advice as to which one would be best for you.

How can you tell if the herb(s) or herbal formulas are working? By feedback provided by regular BTAs and PSAs, and you can ask your doctor or prostate massager to perform a DRE (digital rectal examination) to see if your prostate is shrinking, and if its size and texture are improving. Since these supplements are known to balance male hormones, a heightened sexual desire and capacity are another clue that they are working.

The study and balancing of hormones by natural means (without drugs) is a rapidly emerging area. We're learning that a proper balance of hormones is needed for good health, with total testosterone in the mid-range of 500 to 600 pg/ml (picograms per milliliter) and about 1% of that as free testosterone. Like cholesterol, testosterone comes in "good" and "bad" forms." *Free testosterone,* the "good" testosterone, strengthens the prostate, while an increase in *dyhyerol,* the "bad" testosterone, appears to put the prostate at risk.

A simple blood test hormone panel can accurately measure your hormone levels. Unfortunately, a single test is not a solid basis for action, for it's only a "snapshot": a look at one moment in the normal daily hormone cycles. (For example, testosterone tends to be highest in the early morning and lower in the afternoon.) A series of tests, performed at different times and on different days, gives a more accurate picture. (For information on finding experts in the field of hormone balancing, see the appendix.)

GENERAL GUIDELINES FOR HEALTHFUL EATING

Should you follow the new government guidelines for eating well, the ones based on a pyramid? How about the four food groups approach? Some people have their own four food groups: fried food, fast food, frozen food, and fun food (candy).

More and more Americans are overweight, and we're falling prey to arthritis, diabetes, cancer, heart disease, and other chronic diseases. All of these problems have been linked to our unhealthy diets. Adopting these general guidelines for healthy eating will go a long way toward boosting your immune system, improving your general health, and increasing your energy.

Luckily, foods that benefit general health also keep the prostate flowing and pulsating with blood and energy. The prostate is among the first organs in the male to be affected by erosion of bodily health, for its tiny blood vessels and location (touching the colon) make it susceptible to a reduction of blood flow and an assault by toxins. A healthy body equals a healthy prostate, and vice versa. That's why good nutrition emphasizes general health first, then foods and nutrients to support the prostate.

When to eat: There's a great deal of wisdom in the old advice: "Breakfast like a king, lunch like a prince, and dine like a pauper." Although the ancient sage who formulated this advice didn't know it, the pancreas, which makes digestive enzymes to dissolve the food we eat into its component parts, is pumping out those enzymes at a rapid pace in the morning hours. Production slows during the day, reaching a low point in the evening and nighttime. It's clearly best to eat when your body is most prepared to receive your food,

Eating after 8 P.M. stresses the pancreas, especially if it's a large, rich meal.

and take only small amounts when your body is not. If you do eat a large dinner, especially one heavy in meat or dairy products, the food will sit, undigested, in your stomach for too long, rotting, releasing harmful toxins, and increasing cellular acidity. That's why optimum health comes from eating a hearty breakfast, a smaller lunch, and a light dinner. The European practice of the main meal midday is more in keeping with our bodies' rhythms than the American practice of the main meal in the evening. This could be one reason there is far less cancer, including prostate cancer, in Europe. Dr. Barry Sears, author of *The Zone* and The Zone Manager software program, believes that this is also due to a diet that correctly balances protein, carbohydrates, and fats.

The well-proportioned diet: As a general rule of thumb, the healthful diet gets 60 to 65% of its calories from complex carbohydrates, 20% from fat, and 10 to 15% from protein. The total protein intake should be tied to lean body mass (weight less percent body fat), as spelled out in *The Zone* and in The Zone Manager, by Dr. Sears. Sedentary people should have only half a gram of protein for every pound of their lean body mass. There are many books that give detailed listings of the nutrients in food. I recommend *The U.S. Department of Agriculture Nutrient Data Base*, a paperback available from the U.S. Printing Office. There are also software programs available in various formats, such as The Zone Manager and Comp-U-Diet for the Psion palmtop computer/organizer, which has the advantages of pocket availability, search functions, and recipe/percentage calculations.

Dietary do's and don'ts: Here are some additional tips to help you round out your healthful diet.

✓ *DO* eat lots of *fresh* vegetables and fruits. These are excellent sources of vitamins, minerals, phytochemicals, fiber, complex carbohydrates, and other nutrients essential for vibrant health. These foods are low in fat and contain no cholesterol, and they have valuable enzymes which are destroyed by cooking and/or freezing (but not by light steaming).

✓ *DO* eat legumes (peas, beans, and lentils). Legumes are low in sugar, fat, and sodium, and they contain absolutely no cholesterol. They have vitamins B_1 and B_6, iron, calcium, complex carbohydrates, fiber, protein, and other nutrition essentials.

✓ *DO* eat fresh fish. It contains essential fatty acids the body uses to produce prostaglandins, which are hormone-like substances that help to regulate pain and keep the immune system strong. Fish from cold ocean waters (such as salmon, sardines, mackerel, and cod) have large amounts of key fatty acids. Fish from warm waters (such as trout, perch, and snapper) have lesser amounts. And freshwater fish (such as trout and catfish) have the least.

✓ *DO* eat whole grain in moderation, rather than refined (white) breads, pasta, crackers, rice, and other grains. Whole grains such as barley, buckwheat, oats, rye, and wheat contain fiber, complex carbohydrates, various B vitamins and minerals, plus protein. Make sure the label says "whole grain," for bread or pasta that looks brown may simply be dark-colored or have a little bit of whole wheat added.

✓ *DO* eat foods that have been shown to strengthen the prostate, such as unsalted pumpkin seeds, kelp, flax seed oil, and green tea.

✓ *DO* choose organically grown foods whenever it's possible.

✗ *Do NOT* eat fatty meats. Excessively high-fat diets have been linked to prostate cancer, other cancers, heart disease, and numerous other ailments. Fat, especially dairy fat, has also been shown to cause the non-cancerous but potentially dangerous swelling of BPH.

✗ *Do NOT* eat refined sugars (cakes, pastries, candy, Jell-O, white bread, sugary sauces). And avoid artificial sweeteners such as Nutrasweet and saccharine.

✗ *Do NOT* add salt to your food, and avoid salty foods.

✗ *Do NOT* eat hydrogenated oils, such as those found in margarine, donuts, cookies, cakes, other desserts, potato chips, and other deep-fried foods. Hydrogenated oils can interfere with the way the body manufactures and utilizes cholesterol and other vital substances. And be careful not to use excessively high temperatures when you are cooking: temperatures of 350° or higher can hydrogenate any oil.

✗ *Do NOT* eat canned, packaged, or otherwise processed foods. Many important nutrients are destroyed or removed during processing, while sugars, colorings, preservatives, and fat are added in. What you're left with may taste good, but it stresses your body and harms your health.

Ample, pure water is the essential foundation of health – and even more important than food.

× *Do NOT* drink sodas, alcohol, black teas (which includes most iced teas), or coffee. Sodas contain refined sugar (and sugar substitutes, which are worse). They are heavily carbonated with CO_2, and place a heavy strain on the often already overloaded liver and kidneys which must eliminate the carbon dioxide from the body. Caffeine, which is acidifying, is equally damaging. The caffeine "high" stresses the adrenal glands, eventually weakening their ability to balance and regulate our energy for everyday life and healing.

× *Do NOT* eat or drink dairy foods, especially if they have been pasteurized. Consumption of dairy products is closely linked in America to prostate cancer. Pasteurization is primarily used in America. In many parts of Europe, where the people consume a lot of mostly unpasteurized dairy products, there is far less prostate cancer. If you do eat dairy foods, get the best quality, organic, raw, low-fat varieties available in most health food stores—and eat them sparingly.

× *Do NOT* drink liquids with meals, or just before or after meals. Liquids dilute the digestive enzymes, resulting in poor digestion, fewer nutrients being made available to the body, and more strain on the system. At the very least, reduce liquids during meals to a minimum, just sipping small amounts.

× *Avoid* using ice in your drinks. It may interfere with the stomach's digestive activity and force the body to heat the cold liquid, wasting considerable energy.

It's best to eat in the company of a friend or loved one, enjoying pleasant conversation. Chew your food at least 40 times per mouthful, and stop eating when you feel satisfied (*before* you're stuffed).

CONTROLLING ACID AND ALKALINE

Remember the BTA test from Chapter 3? Along with other factors, the BTA measures the body's pH—the acid-alkaline balance. You can use your dietary choices to help your body maintain a healthy pH balance. If your body tends to be acidic, you may want to avoid acid-forming foods such as bacon, wheat and rye bread, chicken, corn, crab, eggs, haddock, herring, lamb, lentils, liver, nuts, oatmeal, perch, pork, sardines, spaghetti, and veal.

If your body tends to be alkaline (basic), you may want to avoid alkaline-producing foods such as apricots, baked beans, beets, buckwheat, cantaloupe, carrots, cauliflower, celery, dates, figs, grapes, lemon, lettuce, lima beans, milk, molasses, olives, onions, pineapple, white and sweet potatoes, raisins, soy beans, and watercress.

FOOD-COMBINING

Although humans are capable of eating all kinds of foods, we're not designed to digest them all at once. Yes, we can do it, but forcing the body to digest incompatible foods puts a tremendous strain on the digestive system, draining the body of needed energy and forcing it to deal with aftereffects caused by rotting, fermenting, and putrefying foods.

Suppose you were using an electric saw to cut up all kinds of wood—hard wood and soft wood, dry wood and moist wood, big pieces and little pieces. Each type and size of wood requires a different setting on the saw. You'd want to be efficient, so you would begin by dividing the woods into different piles, according to type. Then you'd adjust the settings on the electric saw for the first stack, perhaps change the blade, and cut them all at once. When you had cut all the wood in the first stack you'd change the settings, and perhaps the blade, for the second stack, then cut this stack, and so on. If you put in two types of wood at once, or one right after the other without resetting the saw and changing the blade, you'd have trouble.

The same holds true for digestion, which (if you strip away the fancy biochemical terminology) is nothing more than a process of cutting (digesting) the food we eat into tiny parts. Like the wood, our foods come in different types. Some foods require one set of digestive acids and enzymes, while others require different acids and enzymes. The body digests some foods with relative ease, but must work harder on others. Just like the electric saw, the digestive system must continually "reset" itself in order to handle the different types of foods. That's easy for the body to do; it can switch back and forth with ease. Problems arise, however, when we eat different kinds of foods at once, forcing the body to deal with different types without resetting itself.

Although humans are capable of eating all kinds of foods, we're not designed to digest them all at once.

Suppose your digestive system needs to use a very acidic "blade" to cut up one type of food and an alkaline (basic) "blade" for another. What happens if you eat those foods together? The acid blade cancels out the alkaline blade and nothing gets fully digested. The two types of food sit in your stomach, rotting, until they're finally forced to travel through the intestines only partially digested, and emerge at the other end improperly processed. All the while they may be releasing toxins that poison the body, as their nutrients remain locked up inside of them. You've expended enormous energy trying to digest the foods, but instead of nutrients you've gotten toxins in return. The net result is a loss of health.

When we eat, we must be as practical as we are when we cut wood. Fortunately, the process is simple. First we divide foods into groups, and then we mix them only if they're compatible. Here are the food groups:

- *Acid fruits* such as grapefruit, lemon, lime, oranges, pineapple, strawberries, tangerines, and tomatoes.

- *Sweet fruits* such as bananas, dates, figs, prunes, raisins, and dried fruits.

- *Starches/carbohydrates* such as dried beans, bread, cereals, chestnuts, corn, grains, Jerusalem artichokes, pasta, dried peas, potatoes, pumpkin, winter squash, and yams.

- *Proteins* such as dairy products, eggs, fish, fowl, meat, nuts, seeds, soybeans and soy products, and tofu.

- *Fats/oils* such as avocado, butter, coconut, cream, margarine, olives; and oils made from avocado, corn, nuts, olive, safflower, seeds, and soy.

- *Vegetables*—all of them.

Now that the foods have been divided into separate groups, it's time to see which groups go with which. Here are the rules for food-combining:

■ *Mix and match the foods within any single group as you like.* You can have sweet fruits with sweet fruits, proteins with proteins, and so on.

■ *Enjoy vegetables at any meal.* Most vegetables, which are relatively easy to digest, mix well with other foods, so you can enjoy them with almost any meal.

■ *Eat fruit alone.* Fruit is rapidly digested in the stomach and small intestine. If it's mixed in with other foods that take longer to digest, such as meat, the fruit will be quickly broken up by digestive enzymes, but then forced to wait while the other foods are digested. While the fruit is waiting to move on through the digestive system, it ferments, releasing gas and causing other problems. Fruit should be kept moving quickly through the digestive system, which is why it's best eaten by itself (and *not* with vegetables, grains, or other foods). Enjoy fruit two hours after a meal containing other foods, or ½ hour before.

■ *Separate sweet and acid fruits.* Fruits are health-giving, nutrient-packed foods with but one disadvantage: *Sweet fruits* cannot be eaten with *acid fruits.* You can eat more than one acid or sweet fruit at a time, but do not mix the two types together, and do not eat fruits with other foods.

■ *Separate starches and proteins.* The nutrients in the foods will be better digested and absorbed into the body if starches are *not* mixed with proteins. The old American "standby," meat and potatoes, is not a healthful mixture.

■ *Separate starches from fats and oils.* Starches (such as rice, potatoes, and pasta) should not be mixed with fatty or oily foods.

The basic principles of food-combining are easy to understand, and their everyday application is simple, especially with a little experience. Whether at home or dining at a restaurant or a friend's house, you don't need to have specially prepared foods and you don't need to go hungry. Simply pick foods from groups that combine well, and dig in. It does, admittedly, take some commitment to follow these guidelines in our meat-and-potato culture, but give it an honest one-month trial and see how much better you feel. And know that the healing benefits are worth the effort of changing old habits.

Following the rules of food-combining means that you have to forgo standard combinations such as meat and potatoes, fish and rice, bread and cheese, cereal and milk, a fruit salad containing oranges and bananas, bread and peanut butter, beans and bread, and corn and rice. But you don't have to go hungry, and you don't have to give up any foods. It's simply a matter of eating the right foods together, or eating them alone, to ensure that everything is properly digested and your body is not forced to waste energy dealing with indigestible food combinations and the subsequent rotting, fermentation, and putrefaction.

Properly done, food-combining will help ensure easy digestion, fewer toxins produced by digestive difficulties, and a *tremendous increase in energy resulting in better health and joyous living.* (If you would like more information about food-combining, read, for example, *Fit for Life*, by Harvey and Marilyn Diamond.[1])

---

[1] Diamond, Harvey and Marilyn. 1985. *Fit for Life.* New York: Warner Books.

PURE WATER: OUR MOST IMPORTANT NEED

Water is the stuff of life and—solid as we may seem—our bodies are composed largely of water. Indeed, water accounts for 70 to 90% of all organic matter. Water has long been considered to have medicinal effects: Some 2,000 years ago the Greek physician Hippocrates recommended drinking plenty of water to prevent kidney stones. For centuries, all health practitioners have recommended drinking eight or more glasses of water daily as the *essential* cornerstone of any regimen. But not just *any* water will do, for some have additional healing properties.

A great deal of exciting research today is examining the health effects of water, especially the Microwater discussed on the next page. There are many books and studies on the subject, some of which are listed in the Recommended Reading section at the end of this book. For our purposes, it's enough to follow these basic principles:

1. Avoid tap water, which is loaded with chlorine, heavy metals, and human and industrial wastes. It is recommended that you don't put tap water in your car or steam iron—why put it in your body?

2. Drink spring water, purchased from a reliable company, that has been filtered by reverse osmosis. When selecting bottled water for your home or office, ask the company for a copy of their independent laboratory tests, which are performed annually and updated monthly on random samples. Reliable companies will gladly comply. If they don't, move on to a different company.

3. Purchase and install your own reverse osmosis water system. Look for certification by state and indepen-

dent laboratories. Have the water tested periodically if you do install a system. Costco currently has a five-stage system called Premier for $159. It meets California standards, and the output tests better than any other we have tested. Installation is quite simple.

4. Avoid distilled water. It is "dead" water, lacking essential energy and minerals, and often contains oil-based contaminants in high concentrations (a result of the distillation process). If in doubt about the quality of any water, ask the company for lab reports.

For best health, drink the purest water you can find. It is well worth the small investment of time and effort it may take to find the best water available in your area. You may also want to consider investing in a Microwater unit.

Microwater first came to notice in Japan, where researchers noted that people drinking water that came from certain fast-moving, rocky mountain streams enjoyed extraordinarily good health. It turned out that this naturally occurring water was alkaline (had a higher-than-normal pH) and had a different structure and electrical properties. They discovered that the water was ionized and carried an extra electron.

Water is made up of H_2O molecules, which are in turn composed of two hydrogen atoms and one oxygen atom bonded together. But the H_2O molecules are not completely stable; they will break up into smaller H and OH molecules. The positively charged H's and the negatively charged OH's can combine with calcium, potassium, or other substances in the water, creating various chemical reactions. If water has more of the positively charged H's it will become acidic, but if the scales tilt in favor of the negatively charged OH's it will be alkaline (basic). Many of the wastes that clog the body are acidic, especially those that come from our foods and soft drinks. The body's internal cleansing mechanisms depend on an abundance of water around the clock.

Unable to process and eliminate the acidic wastes, the body often stores them in the heart, liver, colon, pancreas, or other parts of the body. As the acidic wastes accumulate, the body and bloodstream become overly acidic, and the delicate pH balance in body fluids, tissues, and cells is upset, leading to heart disease, cancer, elevated blood pressure, obesity, arthritis, diabetes, and many other ailments. Drinking the alkaline Microwater helps the body clear out the acidic wastes and restore the cellular pH balance to normal. Microwater also fights off the free radicals that would otherwise damage the prostate and general health. You can make Microwater at home, using a small device attached to your faucet. (See the appendix for information on purchasing a Microwater filter.)

There are numerous other water purification systems, enhancement devices, and additives available on the market. Beware of claims that simply add to the impurities and toxins without first removing them by sophisticated filtration. You can be guided by your BTA results, and some BTA practitioners will test your water for you. Commercial testing is also available in most communities (see your local yellow pages).

However you achieve it, the need for 1½ to 2 gallons of pure water every day, away from meals, is essential to maintain a clean and pH-balanced body. Remember: cancer cannot live in a pH-balanced cellular environment.

LISTENING TO YOUR BODY

We can all learn which foods make us feel stronger and better by experimenting with our diet, looking for the combination of foods that make us feel strongest and most healthy. We're all unique—what's right for me may unbalance you. I've given you general guidelines, but now you must find the diet that is best for you.

The truth is that one diet does *not* fit all. We certainly don't want to load up on excess fat, but some people are meant to eat more fat, specifically animal fat, than others. A strictly vegetarian diet may not be right for you. And raw foods are not always best, for some people need hot, cooked foods, especially during winter. How do you know? Here are one general and two specific, reliable guides to help you fine-tune your diet to your specific needs: *self-testing, blood group specificity,*[2] and the *Nu Health* tests.

Self-testing is just what it sounds like: trying individual foods, one at a time, and seeing how you feel. This is a subjective test, but you'll find that if you "listen" carefully to your body, monitoring your physical, emotional, and spiritual responses to food, you will learn which foods strengthen and which weaken you.

We can learn which foods make us feel stronger and better by experimenting, looking for the combination of foods that make us feel strongest and most healthy.

[2] For more information, see, for example, Peter D'Adamu and Catherine Whitney. 1996. *Eat Right for Your Type.* New York: G.P. Putnam's Sons.

Blood group specificity is based on the standard A, B, and O blood grouping. Also known as *dietary serotype testing,* it recognizes that people with different blood types have a genetic affinity for certain foods. (You can find out your blood type with a simple test. If your doctor has done any blood tests on you, your blood type may already be marked in your chart. Call your physician and ask.) The dietary serotype test goes further than these well-known blood groups, however, and takes into consideration your Rh, MN, Lewis A/B group, and secretor status factors.

Blood group O, the first to evolve, represents the hunter/gatherer type. If you have O blood, you most likely produce large amounts of hydrochloric acid in your stomach, helping you to digest proteins. A diet high in meat, poultry, and fish protein would be ideal for you. Large amounts of fruits and vegetables are also healthful, for they help to balance your acid/alkaline levels. Corn, grains, and dairy products are likely to cause hives, hayfever, gas, bloating, and food allergies. People with blood group O are more likely to suffer typhoid fever, smallpox, malaria, breast cancer, viruses, autoimmune disease (such as multiple sclerosis, Hodgkin's disease, and rheumatoid arthritis), nasopharyngeal cancer, bleeding peptic ulcers, and stroke.

Blood group A represents the agrarian vegetarian societies that formed early in human history. Evolving later than the O's, the A's produce less hydrochloric acid, which means that protein from animal sources gives them more trouble. Instead, they do best on a diet of vegetables, fruits, grains, and nuts, with very small amounts of meat. Milk and cheese should be avoided altogether. Fruits and vegetables should be eaten raw, since cooking destroys the natural enzymes that help the body digest, absorb, and assimilate nutrients from food. Beans and grains, which contain lectins, can be troublesome and should be eaten in limited amounts. (Lectins are substances that can cause the glycoproteins found on red blood cells, cells of the gastrointestinal tract, and others to agglutinate, or clump together. This triggers an inflammatory response and can lead to symptoms of food allergies, including nausea, diarrhea, constipation, skin rashes, and eruptions, lack of energy, and swelling of the tonsils and sinuses.) People with blood group A are more likely to suffer from syphilis, tuberculosis, whooping cough, meningococcal meningitis, polio, giardiasis, tapeworm, blood problems associated with parasites, cirrhosis of the liver, allergic dermatosis, gastritis, pernicious anemia, heart attack; and cancers of the breast, lung, pancreas, ovary, liver, uterus, stomach, and salivary glands. They are less likely to develop influenza, plague, pneumococcal pneumonia, and urinary tract infections.

Blood group B, which evolved after O and A, reflects ancient herding and nomadic societies. People with blood group B, who tend to produce smaller amounts of hydrochloric acid, often need to take hydrochloric acid supplements and enzymes to handle the large amounts of animal protein typical of the standard American diet. Thanks to their genetic inheritance, people with B blood do best as ovo-lacto vegetarians, combining large amounts of fruits and vegetables with eggs, milk, and milk products. They do well to eat limited amounts of sunflower seeds and oil, sesame seeds and oil, chicken, buckwheat, and other foods containing larger amounts of agglutinins. People with blood group B are more likely to suffer from certain urinary tract infections, polio, malaria, diphtheria, sterility, and miscarriages. They are less likely, however, to suffer from cirrhosis of the liver.

People with blood group AB, the last to evolve, produce smaller amounts of hydrochloric acid than do the O's, and may need hydrochloric acid and enzyme supplements if they eat large amounts of protein. Overall, they do well eating vegetables, fruits, grains, and seafood, with small amounts of milk and milk products included for flavor and variety. Those in the AB group should refrain from eating large amounts of red meat, chicken, tomatoes, potatoes, and foods high in lectins. People with blood group AB are more likely to develop pyelonephritis.

> **People with different blood types have a genetic affinity for certain foods.**

(Information on how to contact Rockwood Naturopathic Associates regarding the testing is provided in the appendix.)

THE NU HEALTH TEST

The third aid to fine-tuning your diet to your specific needs is the *Nu Health* test, performed by many practitioners. Based on samples of your saliva and urine, this test serves as a snapshot of your health status at any given moment, indicating what foods and supplements tend to balance and unbalance you right now. This test is invaluable for monitoring changes as your health improves. I recommend having it performed biannually. Nu Health results are based on computer databases built during 22 years of experience balancing thousands of patients, and can thus be very specific.

The blood group specificity and Nu Health tests are very informative, and often contain several surprises. The Nu Health test, which is loaded with lots of fun, often unexpected recommendations on foods (such as bay leaves, agrimony, horsetail herbs, pumpkin pie, oysters, beer, and whiskey), can be especially startling. It's very useful in conjunction with the BTA for monitoring results objectively. For a referral to a practitioner in your area, call Nu Health in Salem, Oregon, at (503) 362-5229; fax (503) 316-9840.

Based on more than 20 years of research into balancing the human body, these two tests help us better tune into our own bodies, and learn which foods serve us best, and make us strongest. *The Zone* and The Zone Manager software program by Dr. Barry Sears also contain detailed tools for tuning into your body's needs.

CHAPTER 7

CLEANSING AND STRENGTHENING KEY ORGANS WITH HOMEOPATHY

Western medicine is a full-fledged military operation, complete with high-tech surveillance, "smart bombs," and massive assaults designed to destroy the enemy. Like a marauding army, Western medicine destroys the battlefield as it attempts to slay the enemy. Unfortunately we, the patients, are the battlefields, and it's our physical and mental health that suffers as the tests, medicines, and surgeries that serve as the soldiers of modern medicine slug it out with the germs. Ironically, many people who go to their doctor with a relatively simple problem wind up taking several medicines, most of which are designed to undo the ill effects of one or more of the others!

Modern medicine performs miracles, especially in the area of diagnosis, but:

- It doesn't recognize the deeper problem, focusing on "germs" instead of the biological terrain.

- It treats disease as the enemy, rather than as a messenger telling us that something is wrong. (That's like killing the messenger because you don't like the message.)
- It attacks only what it can see, pretending that any problems it cannot neatly measure and categorize do not exist.
- It always goes for all-out destruction, preferring to shoot first and sort everything out later.
- It harms the terrain in the process, leaving us to scrape by with weakened immune systems, added toxins, impotence, incontinence, scarred bodies, and other serious side effects—some that last for the rest of our lives.

Western medicine is *allopathic* medicine, an attempt to cure disease by trying to create conditions opposite to those of the disease. If the disease increases your temperature, allopathic medicine tries to make you colder. If the disease causes a cancer to grow in your body, allopathic medicine surgically removes it or burns it out with radiation. If the disease causes pain, allopathic medicine gives you a pill to block it. Western medicine does a lot of good, but it's a blind and blunt approach. Whenever even the slightest problem rears its head it starts smacking away with a heavy hammer, even if the problem is a little fly.

Homeopathy is an ancient, powerful healing modality without side effects.

There is a time and a place for this "opposite" approach, but we're usually better off with the "same" approach practiced by homeopathic medicine.

CURING LIKE WITH LIKE

Developed in the 18th century by Dr. Samuel Hahnemann, homeopathy's premise is that instead of applying the opposite of a patient's symptom in the form of drugs or surgery, you apply more of the same in the form of a homeopathic remedy. In practical terms this means that instead of trying to suppress the symptoms, you help the body heal itself in a manner very similar to a vaccine. Vaccines are small doses of a disease given to a healthy person in order to stimulate the immune system and increase the body's natural, built-in resistance to that disease. Utilizing the principle that "like cures like," homeopathy gives patients small doses of substances that produce certain symptoms in healthy people in order to cure the same symptoms in those who are ill by stimulating their natural defenses. (If, for example, you have a headache, the homeopathic physician might give you a very small dose of a substance that causes headaches in healthy people.)

The "vaccine-like" approach of homeopathy is based on the Law of Similars ("like cures like"), because homeopathic practitioners believe that the symptoms we feel are messages from the body telling us that something is happening on a physical, mental, or emotional level. Western medicine practitioners use the approach that the symptoms *are* the disease, and try to squelch them. Homeopaths know that the symptoms are messages describing areas of distress, and work to gently stimulate the body to heal that problem. When you feel headache pain, for example, it's because your body is trying to alert you to a disturbance or imbalance. Rather than focusing on suppressing the pain, as medical doctors do, homeopaths seek to help the body deal with the problem by itself.

There are other significant differences between traditional Western medicine and homeopathy:

■ Where Western medicine uses powerful drugs, homeopathy prefers medicines called *remedies* derived from plants, minerals, and occasionally animals. The medicines are heavily diluted in water, leaving only tiny but powerfully therapeutic amounts of the original substance. This ensures that the remedy *works with*, rather than overpowers, the body's defenses, with few or no side effects.

■ Where medical doctors tend to prescribe several drugs all at once, classically trained homeopaths give one remedy at a time, then carefully observe the effects before offering another (if necessary).

■ Where medical doctors give the same drugs to different types of people, homeopaths carefully assess their patients before prescribing. The goal is to discover the physical, mental, and emotional "essence" of the patient, then support that essence with a "constitutional" remedy. Indeed, discovering the patient's essence is as important as analyzing the symptoms. Homeopathy understands that the patient and remedy must be carefully matched if a cure is to be found.

■ Where Western medicine does not use the concept of healing order, homeopathy knows that, according to Hering's Law, symptoms clear up in a specific order as the body heals itself. Symptoms are relieved in the reverse order of which they appeared. The deepest problems—those afflicting the organs, emotions, and mentality—will clear up first, followed by the more superficial ones on the skin or in the extremities. And healing tends to begin in the upper parts of the body, moving down as it progresses.

Once a part of mainstream Western medicine, and more recently falsely branded a "sham" by rich and powerful pharmaceutical companies eager to profit from the drugs they manufacture, homeopathy has never lost favor in Europe—the British royal family regularly uses homeopathic physicians.

Homeopathy has been eclipsed by Western medicine, to our detriment.

Homeopathy is making a comeback in America, as alternatively minded physicians and other healers "discover" its powerful yet gentle properties.

TWO APPROACHES TO HEALING

There are two major subdivisions within homeopathy: *classical* and *clinical* homeopathy.

- Classical homeopathy seeks to match the specific signs and symptoms of a patient (physical, emotional, and mental) with the known effects of a homeopathic remedy. In classical homeopathy, the practitioner prefers to use one remedy at a time, in a high-potency dose. After taking one dose, the patient waits four to eight weeks before the effects are clear to the practitioner. A second dose or a different remedy is prescribed only after the first dose has ceased its action. Homeopathy may take years of study, research, and practice to master, so seek an experienced practitioner.

- Clinical homeopathy approaches the body and disease from a physiological perspective, seeking to stimulate the body's natural healing mechanisms. Clinical homeopathic formulas are composed of more than one ingredient, with the various components designed to have synergistic effects. Clinical homeopathy seeks to restore a patient's health through:

1. *Stimulation of drainage.* The goal is to increase blood flow to the organs of excretion (liver, lymph, kidney, lung, skin, colon) by combining synergistically acting homeopathic remedies of low potency.

2. *Stimulation of detoxification.* The clinical homeopath seeks to dislodge toxins from their binding sites in the tissue and get them into the blood, where they can then be excreted. Detoxification can be accomplished with homeopathic preparations of the toxin itself, or remedies that neutralize the toxin.

3. *Stimulation of regeneration.* Regeneration refers to the renewal of cells and tissues. The goal is to increase the life span of the cells of the specific organ that is being regenerated, and increase the ability of the organs to regenerate themselves.

Clinical homeopathy also works to balance the patient's metabolism by homeopathically stimulating the thyroid, adrenal, ovaries, and other organs involved in circulation in order to maximize their function.

HOMEOPATHIC REMEDIES

There is no homeopathic "cure" for prostate cancer. Instead, the homeopath will go after the root of the problem by selecting from among a number of homeopathic remedies designed to treat the whole person and strengthen the immune system by eliminating physical and emotional blockages in the body, improving elimination, energizing tired organs, improving the circulation, and cleansing the body.

One such homeopathic is Hansi, a multipart injectable and oral homeopathic remedy developed and used for years in Argentina. It has been reported in the Argentinan press to be a miracle healer of cancer, AIDS, and other serious diseases, and is believed by many to be the strongest rebuilder of the immune system yet developed. Hansi, and information about it, is available worldwide from Hansi International in Florida (see the appendix for contact information).

Homeopathy helps the whole body/mind to heal.

If you seek help from a clinical homeopath, he or she will undoubtedly use one or more "packaged" or "mixed" remedies. Some prefer classical homeopathy; others insist that clinical homeopathy is superior. I suggest that you research both approaches, and use the one that works best for you. But do explore homeopathy. It is extremely powerful and should be a part of every healing regime.

CHAPTER 8

THE LINK BETWEEN A HEALTHY MOUTH AND A HEALTHY PROSTATE

Car accidents, germs, earthquakes, drive-by shootings —we usually think of major dangers as coming from outside of us. Few of us realize that we unknowingly invite deadly bio-poisons into our bodies. We don't realize that what's in or under our teeth can slowly, insidiously, erode our health. Although most traditionally minded health practitioners scoff at the idea, a great deal of research and clinical experience has proven that heavy metals (primarily mercury-amalgam fillings) and hidden dental infections are a primary cause of most disease. These substances harm us by:

- Upsetting the biological terrain.
- Flooding the body with toxins.
- Weakening the immune system.
- Contaminating nerve junctions (ganglia) in the head and groin, causing the nerves to reduce or shut down blood supply to areas such as the prostate, creating places where fungus, bacteria, and parasites can spawn cancer.

- Disrupting the flow of energy through the body and otherwise setting the stage for disease.

One cannot be healthy unless the mouth is free of hidden infections, primarily caused by root canals and toxic metals (especially mercury, which constitutes 50% of amalgam fillings). Although this is still controversial and completely denied by the American Dental Association, the scientific and clinical evidence linking heavy metals to disease is overwhelming[1]—as is personal experience. If present, these substances must be removed from the teeth. That's the easy part. The more difficult chore is cleansing the body to restore the proper flow of blood and energy through the organs, teeth, and body.

HIDDEN INFECTIONS CAN LEAD TO MAJOR DISTRESS

Even if your fillings are in good shape, or you have no fillings at all, your teeth may still be the very hidden source of ill health.

The human mouth is filled with bacteria, viruses, and other germs. This is not surprising, for the mouth is open to the environment. We put food and utensils into our mouths, we chew on fingernails and pencil tips, we lick stamps and envelopes, we kiss each other, we put our hands to our mouths. The numerous germs that fill the

[1] Check the Internet, searching for *amalgam*. Most published studies are in German, but see (in English) *Biological therapy* 1966 XIV(3):249. Dr. Rudolf Gerschwend's and Dr. Thomas Rau's *Amalgam elimination therapy: Homeopathic, isopathic dental reference material* is available from Enderlein Enterprises at (306) 424-6025. In German, see Juenther Enderlein's *The Akmon* I, II & III on Biological Medicine. (Dentistry is not separated from medicine in Germany.)

typical mouth are not normally dangerous, because the immune system holds them at bay, preventing them from moving into the body. But sometimes—too many times—something goes wrong.

The immune system is designed to handle the germs that routinely appear in the mouth, by either holding them back or destroying them. Battles between germs that attempt to "break out" of the mouth and into the body are usually short and decisive, with the germs on the losing side. Unfortunately, our internal defenses are not nearly as effective against long-term, low-grade infections that fester in our mouths, hidden under or behind our teeth or in our jawbones. Improperly performed root canals are a major source of hidden infections. Indeed, those who practice the purest form of biological dentistry believe there is no such thing as a "safe" root canal, and begin treatment by extracting all such teeth.

There's a lot of evidence that wherever there is a serious disease, there is a problem in the mouth.

Fortunately, this extreme treatment is not usually necessary, and can be viewed as a last resort should there be no success with procaine, homeopathics, and especially Sanum remedies from Germany. (Procaine is part of the family of anesthetics used for local procedures, and is widely recognized in Germany for its regenerative properties. It has been found to have only positive side effects, including unexplained regenerative and cleansing effects.)

Treatment by a biological dentist varies according to the part of the mouth afflicted, the patient's age and general health, and the strength of the patient's immune system. You will need to find an advanced biological practitioner, physician, or dentist—or one of each, working together. It's important to have both a physician and a dentist, for mercury is stored in various sites in the body, not just the mouth. Lee Cowden, M.D., of Dallas, Texas, works with several biological dentists including Harold Ravins, D.D.S., of West Los Angeles, California. This team, and others like it, has produced excellent results in clearing cancers, multiple sclerosis, chronic fatigue, and other symptoms of toxic metals and hidden infections.

Dental infections can also be caused by the use of different metals in dental caps and crowns. The metals are often mixed (to save money) and called "gold." The mixing of metals can cause corrosion, decay, and infection in the underlying tooth, even when there is no leakage of metal into the body. This is a particularly difficult problem to discover, for few of us want to pull off our caps and crowns, at our own expense, for what we fear will be a wild goose chase. But plumbers and others who work with metals know that they can't be mixed without causing electrolysis, galvanization, and corrosion, which plumbers know eat up the pipes. The electrolysis between metals eats away at our teeth and gums. And even when only one metal is used, the person may react to it in such a way as to cause trouble. (That's why biological dentists conduct compatibility tests *before* putting any cement, metal, or porcelain into a patient's mouth.)

Whatever their cause(s), these simmering infections are breeding grounds for germs that may ultimately overpower or outwit our immune system. Then the germs spread far and wide, either loudly proclaiming their presence in the body by wreaking havoc, or quietly taking up residence in an organ or tissue, subtly and cumulatively weakening us with vague and undiagnosable pains, fevers, neurologic disturbances, and immune system disorders, or perhaps vision or hearing difficulties.

These hidden dental infections tend to be relatively low-grade. They have to be, for if they were major infections producing terrible pain or obvious disease they would be noticed and taken care of right away. However, the fact that their presence is nearly or completely invisible does not make them any less serious. On the contrary: They sap our immune systems of energy by tying them up in ongoing battles, leaving us without strong reserves, and thus more vulnerable to day-to-day toxins and germs.

Even more dangerous is the fact that infection in the mouth often spreads, eventually, to the rest of the body along numerous pathways. It can travel along the cranial nerves, migrate through the venous pathways in the brain and spinal cord, or drift down the throat to the rest of the body. Germs fanning out from the teeth needn't go far to do damage. Only a couple of centimeters separate the upper teeth from the brain. But the brain is not the only organ or body system at risk. Hidden dental infections can cause a great deal of trouble, including:

■ *Elevated blood pressure:* Certain bacteria that take up residence in the mouth can increase the amount of serotonin in the body. Serotonin in turn causes tiny blood vessels called *capillaries* to constrict (clamp down). Imagine that you are driving through a tunnel that suddenly gets smaller. You had no trouble driving when the tunnel was wide, but now that it's narrowed you keep brushing against the side. When the tunnel becomes too narrow your car gets stuck, and you can't back up because there are too many cars behind you, all pushing to move ahead.

Mercury must be removed from the mouth before it can be eliminated from the body.

Something similar happens in your blood vessels. When the bacteria-induced increase in serotonin narrows the capillaries that serve as "tunnels" for the blood traveling through the body, blood pressure rises. As blood pressure goes up, so does the risk of headaches, as well as stroke, heart disease, and other serious ailments. Millions of Americans are taking medicines to relieve their headaches, reduce blood pressure, and handle other ailments. How many would be better off if the hidden infections in their mouths were simply cleared away? (All the medications we take as a result of hidden infections, including simple aspirin, tend to acidify and weaken us.)

■ *Cancer:* Cancers develop in areas of reduced blood flow—places where there is less blood and oxygen to flush out the bacteria, fungus, and parasites that are busy multiplying. (Mercury is a major cause of reduced blood flow, which allows potential cancer-causing organisms to flourish.) It's well known that certain brain tumors are associated with fungus, and that viruses have been implicated in other types of cancer. *E. coli* and other common germs can produce or cause the production of certain cyclic hydrocarbons and other potentially carcinogenic substances.

■ *Multiple sclerosis:* Also known as *MS,* this debilitating disorder of the nervous system can leave its victims suffering from headaches, blurred or double vision, weakness, poor coordination, numbness, tingling sensations in the limbs, difficulty in speaking, extreme mood swings, incontinence, and loss of bowel control. It can also make men impotent. There is no known cause of MS, although it is generally felt that a virus or immune system disorder is to blame. Holistically minded dentists have helped many patients suffering from symptoms suggestive of MS by cleaning up their dental infections, problems that traditional physicians and dentists had been unwilling to even consider.

- *Immune system distress:* Although the immune system is a powerful fighting force, it does have limitations. Only certain numbers of fighter T-cells, suppressor cells, macrophages, and other immune-system soldiers can be manufactured at a given time, even when the body is on full-battle alert. Every infection the immune system must battle in the mouth is another drain on its resources. The majority of infections may be insignificant by themselves, but their cumulative effect over time can wear down your immune system, weakening it just enough to allow germs from hidden infections in the mouth to spread, and a vicious cycle begins.

Traditionally minded practitioners brush aside concerns about hidden infections, saying that they don't show up on x-rays or other tests, and therefore they don't exist. (It's not surprising that these infections don't show up on x-rays, which are, after all, flat, one-dimensional pictures.) Because most practitioners don't believe that infections hidden in the teeth or jawbones exist or are important, they don't look for them. Their belief that infections are unimportant and not worth looking for serves as "proof" to them that the infections don't exist. *The fact that a doctor can't find an infection means little, for you won't find what you're* NOT *looking for.*

Dental infections often remain hidden because they are under the teeth, in the pockets around the wisdom teeth, down by and under the root canals, or in cysts and abscesses in the jaw. The problem may be structural, electrical, or chemical, or it may be caused by a combination of factors. Even chronic sinus infections or inflammation of the tonsils can be to blame. Whatever the cause, the problem can be elusive. Infections may be "hidden" in the most impeccable dental work, and they may produce no obvious symptoms or immediate pain.

And, since infections often don't show up on x-rays of the mouth, many people don't realize anything is wrong in their mouths. All they know is that they've been to every different kind of practitioner possible, none of whom can explain or cure their symptoms. Electrical readings help, but are not always definitive. The most definitive way to identify the problem is often through electrical and/or energetic readings. Most of this work is outside the realm of that which is normally considered "conventional" and is not taught in American universities. Thousands of practitioners have been getting good results for 40 years, but the approach is still considered experimental—perhaps because the studies backing it are all in German.

X-rays of my own highly impeccable dental work "proved" there were no infections in my mouth. Yet electrical and energetic readings indicated that major problems affecting my pancreas and prostate were stemming from these infections. These readings improved as the infections were treated homeopathically, and all my other indicators (such as albumin, AMAS test, pH, BTA) improved.

In summary, continual low-grade infections in the mouth can alter the biological terrain, weaken the immune system, release a steady stream of toxins, and cumulatively weaken a particular organ or body system over time. Hidden dental infections are often not very dramatic (indeed, they tend to be insidious), yet the damage they produce over time is devastating. Hidden dental infections *must* be removed if we are to be healthy. (This does not always mean that the teeth involved in the infection must be extracted. The problem can sometimes be handled by conventional homeopathy, or by the Swiss practice, not practiced in the United States, of injecting homeopathic substances directly into the jaw.)

THE ENERGIZING TEETH

The energy that feeds, surrounds, and *is* the body cannot flow through the body if the teeth are unhealthy. Teeth are more than chunks of physical matter in the mouth responsible for chewing food. Teeth are living, pulsating, integral parts of the body, and of the energy that *is* the body, as well as pathways for the flow of energy.

Just as the physical germs found in hidden dental infections can harm a distant part of the body, so too can they block the movement of energy in the body. Since each tooth is energetically bound to specific organs, systems, and tissues, as well as to the body as a whole, any physical or energetic distress in a tooth will inevitably harm its corresponding organ, system, or tissue (as well as the body as a whole). An infection or any other problem with a tooth can drain energy away from its "partner" tissue elsewhere in the body. Figure 8-1 illustrates the relationship between the teeth and their associated acupuncture meridians and organs.

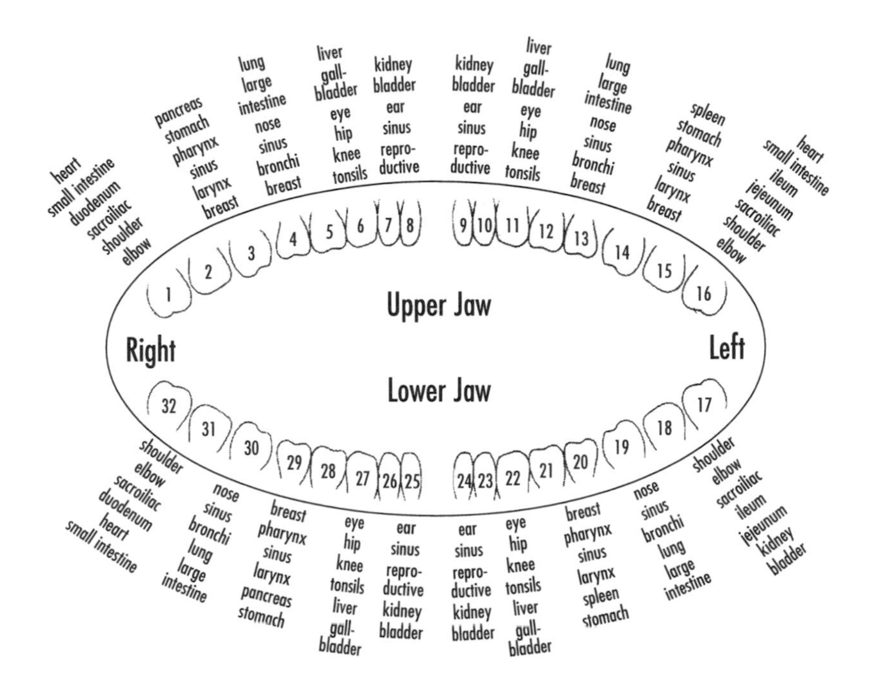

Figure 8-1. The teeth, associated acupuncture meridians, and affected organs.

Here are some of the things that are found when the energy flow through the teeth is disrupted:

- Poor digestion, bloating, diarrhea, and other gastrointestinal problems can be caused by low-grade infections from old fillings.
- An upper bicuspid infection can harm the liver.
- Infections lingering from removal of the wisdom teeth can cause heart disease years later.
- Problems with the front teeth can cause the kidneys to malfunction.

- Improperly performed root canals can indirectly harm the prostate by affecting the flow of energy through the teeth and body.

These problem are so insidious that many biological dentists strongly recommend, with good reason, that electrical readings be taken annually after initial problems have been cleared up, and that anyone with root canals, caps, bridges, or crowns have the electrical readings.

TOXIC FACTORIES HIDDEN IN THE MOUTH

As if hidden infections and disruptions to the flow of energy were not enough, we are also faced with a potentially deadly problem that is almost entirely overlooked by the medical establishment: mercury-amalgam fillings. The American Dental Association (ADA) talks out of both sides of its mouth when discussing amalgam. On the one hand, it cautions dental personnel to use extreme caution in handling amalgam, and promotes detailed rules for its handling and storage, because it is so dangerous to our health. On the other hand, the ADA maintains that amalgam is perfectly safe to put in your mouth!

Workers in other industries may be exposed to mercury on the job, where strict precautions are mandated by law, but for most of us the primary exposure is from mercury-amalgam fillings. These fillings—which contain 50% mercury, 25% silver, and the remaining 25% comprised of tin, copper, zinc, and other substances—have been used for some 170 years. Today, an estimated 85% of those of us living in the U.S. have one or more silver-amalgam fillings. Of these metals, mercury is the most harmful—more toxic than arsenic, cadmium, and lead. Mercury is said to be *the most toxic substance on the planet.* According to the World Health Organization and other leading health bodies, there is no known level of mercury in the body that can be considered safe. In other words, *any amount of mercury leaking out of our fillings must be considered dangerous.* We should assume that mercury-amalgam fillings are toxic factories spewing dangerous wastes into our mouths and bodies.

Most of us think of that silver fluid that goes up and down in thermometers when someone mentions mercury. It's harmless, we think. So what if small amounts are embedded in fillings? It turns out that mercury has many harmful effects. Mercury:

- Upsets body chemistry.
- Can interfere with cellular DNA and reproduction.
- Creates an inviting environment for parasites by killing off the "good" bacteria in the intestines.
- Increases the risk of malnutrition by interfering with the absorption of protein.
- Deposits itself in the brain, central nervous system, liver, kidneys, and other parts of the body.
- "Chews up" our nerves, leading to a variety of nervous system diseases.
- Interferes with the body's production and utilization of thyroid and pituitary hormones, insulin, and estrogen.
- Weakens the immune system, leaving us vulnerable to a host of diseases.

- Confuses the immune system, causing it to "turn" on the body and creating autoimmune diseases such as lupus.

Mercury often aggregates in the ganglia or major nerve junctions in the groin, TMJ area, or temples, causing the affected nerves to reduce or shut down the flow of blood to areas such as the prostate, testes, ovaries, uterus, brain, neck, and sinuses. The reduced blood flow in these areas allows bacteria, fungus, and parasites to take over, creating isolated, protected "pockets" where disease can develop. It's difficult to detoxify these pockets, for there is not enough blood flow to carry the detoxifying agents to the afflicted areas. Doctors in some countries inject procaine into the affected ganglia in order to soothe the nerves and "relax" them into allowing blood to flow into the distressed areas once again, flushing out the mercury and other problems. Supplements such as vitamin C, DMPS, yarrow, and chlorella are used to help the body eliminate mercury in the urine, which may be monitored to fine-tune the process.

Mercury is the most toxic substance on the planet. There is NO safe level.

Mercury has been linked to diseases and degeneration of the brain. It appears to destroy neurons (brain cells), possibly leading to headaches and a host of other problems with memory, coordination, speech, and vision. And we're not the only ones who can be harmed by mercury residing in our teeth. It crosses the placental membrane, which means it can be passed on to the fetus. Even if a baby escapes exposure in the womb, he or she may be harmed later if the mother's milk has become contaminated by the metal.

Because mercury can damage so many different parts of the body, its effects are wide-ranging. The possible symptoms of mercury poisoning include numbness and tingling, abdominal cramps, anemia, poor appetite, anxiety, bleeding gums, bloating, elevated blood fats, cervical spine syndrome, chest pain, difficulty concentrating, constipation, poor coordination, diverticulitis, dizziness, fatigue, fearfulness, food sensitivities/allergies, glaucoma, hearing problems, irregular heartbeat, hypoglycemia, insomnia, kidney infections, manic depression, memory difficulties, multiple sclerosis, muscle weakness, numbness of the arms and legs, parasites, restlessness, ringing in the ears, speech impairment, depression, thoughts of suicide, tremors, and vision disturbances.

We rarely connect our symptoms to mercury because the harm it does is insidious, gradually weakening or attacking one part of the body after another in no apparent order. And so we go to the internist complaining of aches or dizziness, to the eye doctor with vision problems, or to the allergist with a rash. The well-meaning physicians load us up with medicines that don't solve anything. The drugs do, however, have side effects. Soon we need a second set of medicines to counteract the side effects of the first set, then a third set of drugs to counteract the effects of the second set, and on and on. Now we're firmly in the grip of the drug-happy medical system. Or perhaps our doctor decided that our problems are psychosomatic and referred us to a psychiatrist. Now we're "crazy" in addition to being physically ill. All the while, mercury continues to leak from our teeth into our bodies. But we hardly notice that old problem anymore because we're so sick from the supposed "cure."

The mercury need not be intact, in chunks, or in slivers, to do damage. Mercury vapor can be just as harmful. Mercury is a volatile mineral that gives off a vapor when it's rubbed, scratched, or compressed, or when the temperature rises (think of the mercury in thermometers). That means when you chew food, brush your teeth, eat hot foods, or smoke—even when you simply grind your teeth—you are unwittingly turning the mercury in your fillings into vapor. You can't taste, smell, or see the mercury vapor rising from your teeth, but it's very real. It plunges down into your lungs when you inhale. From there it quickly and easily passes into your bloodstream and moves to every part of your body. Because mercury vapor is so toxic, even minuscule amounts can be very dangerous.

How *much* mercury becomes vaporous poison in the body depends on how sensitive your nervous system is, how many mercury-amalgam fillings you have, when and how well they were put in, how vigorously and often you brush your teeth, what kinds of foods you eat, and other factors. But unless you are exposed to mercury at work—and relatively few of us work in factories with mercury—your teeth are your number-one source of mercury poisoning. (If you want more information on this subject, see the appendix for how to contact DAMS.)

Of course, mercury isn't the only substance in amalgam fillings, crowns, or other dental work. Many metals find their way into our mouths. Here are some of the other symptoms that may be caused by just a few of these substances:

- *Copper:* Cramps, nausea, convulsions, epileptic attacks.

- *Gold:* Depression, bone pain, high blood pressure, photophobia, damage to the arteries.
- *Nickel:* Nervousness, poor digestion, constipation, headaches.
- *Silver:* Emaciation, buildup of jelly-like mucus in the throat, backache, swelling of the ankles.
- *Tin:* Nervous and respiratory system distress, various pains, colic, twitching of the lower arm and hand.

It's not enough to take mercury-amalgam fillings or other metal works out of your mouth. Improper removal can flood your body with toxic shavings and fumes. The sudden onslaught of these substances is *more* dangerous than their slow release from your fillings, so find a dentist experienced in amalgam removal who works with a practitioner experienced in removing mercury from the body.

"BATTERIES" IN THE MOUTH

If leaking mercury were the only problem with dental fillings, it would be bad enough. But there's more. The mercury and other metals in these fillings can disrupt the normal flow of energy through the body's meridians by setting up a "battery" in the mouth.

Oral galvanism, or battery-like action in the mouth, is caused by the potential differences between the poles of electrical sources in the mouth. This means that putting metal and saliva together in a closed space can produce battery-like action. The "battery" may form between the fillings of two teeth via the saliva; or between the filling of a single tooth, the bone, and the saliva.

It is a felony to bury ONE drop of mercury in the ground. Yet it's legal to use SEVERAL drops in a single filling.

If there's a "battery" in your mouth, you may notice increased or foamy saliva, a salty or metallic taste, occasional shocks or pain when touching a metal utensil to your teeth, tingling or burning along the edges of your tongue, vague discomfort in your mouth, indigestion, or weight loss. You may also find yourself becoming angry or irritable for no obvious reason. Your doctor may noticc alarming changes in your blood work and other tests, while your dentist may see discoloration of the teeth or other signs of trouble. The only way to solve the problem is to take the battery out of your mouth.

THE SOLUTION: DENTAL PURIFICATION

Simply flossing, brushing, and visiting the dentist regularly won't stop the serious health problems emanating from the mouth—because most dentists are not trained to detect hidden infections, understand the role that teeth play in the body's energy system, or handle the problems caused by mercury-amalgam fillings. They don't realize there is an energetic connection between the four front teeth on the bottom jaw and the entire genitourinary area, kidneys, and adrenal glands, or between the eyeteeth and the gallbladder. They have absolutely no idea that ill health in or around these teeth can cause disease anywhere in the genitourinary tract, including prostate cancer.

If you have a traditional dentist, it will be wise for you to seek a second opinion from a biological dentist. It's up to you to watch for the signs of trouble, including:

- Unusual or unpleasant smells in your mouth.
- Bleeding gums.
- Movement of the teeth.
- Staining on the teeth.
- Old fillings. (All fillings should be checked annually to make sure they're not leaking.)
- Tooth or jaw pain, which may be caused by a hard filling surface striking against another tooth when you chew.
- Pain caused by improperly fitted fillings or dental appliances.
- Unexplained symptoms of physical or mental disease.

Any of these symptoms can signal hidden dental infections, a disruption of energy flow through the teeth to the body, or toxic poisoning. And of course, simply having mercury-amalgam fillings is a potential source of trouble.

Unfortunately, even if we notice these symptoms, most of us are not likely to understand their importance or know what to do about them. Neither is the typical dentist. That's why it's vital that you get yourself checked out by a *biologic dentist* as soon as possible. The biologic dentist:

- Understands the toxic effects of mercury-amalgam fillings, and can carefully replace mercury-amalgam fillings with composites that harmonize with the body.
- Knows that the teeth and brain are connected, and that a problem in the mouth invariably

affects the brain. And since the brain controls the entire body, that problem is always "passed on" to an organ or body system.

- Knows that the immune system cannot be strong unless the mouth is healthy.
- Is concerned about root canals, TMJ, bite, and other aspects of dental health.
- Pays careful attention to the effects of dental problems on the body's electrical system, including jaw posture. (Poor jaw posture can dramatically harm the central nervous system, causing headaches and general stress in the body. This, in turn, weakens the immune system.)
- Knows that standard x-rays are useful only to a point and often miss infections and other problems.
- Utilizes electro-acupuncture, thermograms, electrodermal testing, dark-field blood testing, DMPS challenge tests, bioresonance, sonography, electromyography, magnetic jaw imaging, and other means to detect hidden problems that harm the body.
- Knows the importance of proper nutrition.

The biologic dentist purifies the mouth, thus removing a major source of distress, strengthening the body's natural defenses, and raising patients to a higher level of health. (See the appendix for some suggestions on how to find a biologic dentist.)

TESTING FOR MERCURY TOXICITY

Although it's probably best to assume that any mercury-amalgam fillings in your teeth should be removed, several different tests can tell you if mercury from your fillings has leaked into your body.

The best of these tests utilizes kinesiology, or "muscle-testing." When performed by an experienced practitioner, kinesiology can be used to determine whether any tooth is *weakening* your health and, if so, why. The patient simply puts the pad of his index finger on the biting surface of each tooth, one after another. While the patient is doing so, the practitioner tests the strength of the other arm. For example, as the patient touches a tooth with his right index finger, the practitioner tests the strength of the patient's left arm. Then the patient touches another tooth, and the practitioner again tests the strength of the left arm. This is done for each tooth.

The presence of mercury in a particular tooth can be very reliably determined by the strength of the opposite arm. This can be verified by having the patient hold a vial of homeopathic mercury in the hand that is touching the tooth. If the arm that was weak when the tooth was touched is now strong when homeopathic mercury is held near the tooth, there is mercury present in that tooth. This has been confirmed clinically time after time, without exception. For an excellent video that explains kinesiology, call (972) 480-8909.

A problem in the mouth is a double whammy: physically and energetically making us ill.

Hair analysis is another test. A small sample of hair cut from your head and tested in a laboratory can reveal whether any of a number of harmful substances have gotten into body and been incorporated into your hair. The hair analysis also provides a "snapshot" of your nutritional status. A typical analysis checks for nutrient minerals such as calcium, magnesium, sodium, potassium, copper, zinc, phosphorus, iron, manganese, chromium, selenium, boron, cobalt, germanium, molybdenum, silicon, sulfur, and vanadium. It also looks for additional minerals such as antimony, barium, bismuth, gold, lithium, nickel, platinum, ruthenium, scandium, silver, strontium, tin, titanium, tungsten, and zirconium, and for toxic minerals such as arsenic, beryllium, mercury, cadmium, lead, and aluminum. A great many studies in this country and abroad have shown there is a close correlation between the minerals in the hair and in the body's organs. The Environmental Protection Agency uses hair analysis to detect exposure to toxic metals. If you have your hair analyzed, be aware that sometimes mercury won't show up in the first sample, and may not show up until the body is stimulated into excreting it.

Mercury gets into the bloodstream from the teeth, causing the nervous system to decrease blood flow, resulting in illness.

Bioenergetic testing is another way to help determine if the body is suffering from mercury poisoning or from other heavy metal reactions. Also known as *EAV* (electro-acupuncture), bioenergetic testing combines modern technology with acupuncture techniques to measure the resistance at selected meridian points on the body.

The DMPS Challenge is a more complex tool. DMPS (Sodium 2, 3, Dimercaptopropane-1-sulfonate) is a sulfur-containing amino acid that combines with heavy metals such as mercury. First developed more than 40 years ago in China and later used in Germany and Russia, it has been very safely used as a chelating agent by dentists and doctors in the United States, Europe, Australia, and Japan. A chelating agent "grabs" onto target substances, binding with them to prevent them from doing damage and making it easier for the body to dispose of them. DMPS binds with mercury, arsenic, cadmium, chromium, cobalt, copper, gold, magnesium, nickel, silver, and zinc.

The DMPS is injected intravenously into patients who have been carefully screened for any allergic reaction and for any kidney weakness. Their urine is then collected and tested for the presence of mercury and other toxic metals. The test serves as both a diagnostic and a treatment tool, monitoring the levels of harmful metals as it carries them away. The substance works by drawing mercury out of the body's cells, binding with the metal, then carrying it to the kidncys for excretion.

Hair analysis, bioenergetic testing, and/or DMPS can corroborate the muscle testing. The DMPS stimulates the removal, which is monitored by 24-hour urinalysis.

IN ADDITION . . .

Removing mercury-amalgam fillings is the only way to begin purifying your body of mercury and other heavy metals. But you can do more, including rebounding on a mini-trampoline, cleansing your colon, sweating, and using homeopathic remedies.

Rebounding on a mini-trampoline to stimulate your lymph system: Like the circulatory system, the lymph system transports fluids and other substances throughout the body. But while the circulatory system's main job is to bring nutrients to the body's cells and carry "trash" away, the lymph system is primarily a drainage and defense system. A great deal of the body's "trash" is handled by the lymph system, which also plays host to many immune system "soldiers." Huge numbers of immune system cells congregate in the lymph glands that are spread through the body, quietly awaiting the call to defend the body against germs. Rebounding on a mini-trampoline is an excellent way to stimulate the lymph system, keeping the toxins and other "refuse" moving through the system and out of the body.

Colon cleansing: Cleaning out the large bowel assists by clearing out mercury deposited in the intestines. The body naturally stores some of the mercury and other substances it wants to dispose of in the intestines. But unless the metals are quickly moved through the gastrointestinal tract and out the body, they may be reabsorbed. That's why enemas, colonics, the *Ultimate Fast*, herbal cleanses such as *Experience*, and anything else that cleans out the colon can be very helpful.

Sweating: This is a simple but effective way to speed detoxification. The body's largest organ of elimination, the skin is the "port of exit" for numerous toxins. Sitting in a sauna or performing exercises that cause you to sweat pushes toxins out of the body via the sweat. Be sure to carefully rinse off after sweating, or else the toxins will be reabsorbed, and drink plenty of water to avoid dehydration.

Homeopathic remedies: These can be used to help rid the body of mercury and other toxic metals while strengthening the body. Discuss these with an experienced health advisor.

CLEANING THE MOUTH CLEANSES THE BODY

In summary, teeth are much more than simply "food-rippers." They serve as energy conduits, and can also be the unwitting source of poisonous substances leaking from fillings. Teeth, and the entire mouth, can harbor or hide infections that weaken the immune system and attack specific organs, causing a wide range of symptoms that traditional physicians and dentists cannot cure. Like the colon and rest of the body, the mouth must be cleansed if we are to be healthy. A "clean" mouth is necessary if we are to have a clean bill of health. Fortunately, a biologic dentist can cleanse your mouth and set you back on the road to good health.

Despite widespread skepticism, the relationship between a healthy mouth and good overall health is becoming more widely recognized in the United States[2] and in England. (The Germans and Swiss have years of experience and success in biologic dentistry, fostered by government support.) Accumulating evidence shows that *wherever there is serious disease,* there are also problems in the mouth stemming from hidden infections, poor jaw posture, and metals—especially mercury in amalgam fillings. The infections may be from natural causes, but are more likely due to metals or root canals. Getting the mercury out of the mouth is the essential start, but it is only the start because the metal gets into many parts of the body, continuing to cause disease until it is eliminated. Fortunately, homeopathy, DMPS chelation, and other means of clearing mercury out of the body are becoming more widely known and

---

[2] See, for example, Meinig, George. 1996. *Root canal cover-up.* Ojai, California: Bion Publishing.

practiced, although with little official sanction. (The FDA has approved DMPS for some practitioners on a temporary, data-gathering basis. One of these practitioners is Hans Gruenn, M.D., of Culver City, California, presumably because of his years of training and experience with mercury elimination in Germany.)

Time and time again, ill health in the prostate and elsewhere in the body has been traced back to the mouth. Cancer, elevated blood pressure, immune system disorders, devastating fatigue, and other problems often have their genesis in the mouth. That's why it's absolutely vital that you clean up your mouth immediately. Do your own research and act accordingly, but get started now!

CHAPTER 9

RAISING ALBUMIN LEVELS

Which germ carrier is responsible for more diseases: flies, tainted meat, polluted water, or dirty needles? The answer may surprise you. None of the above. The germ carrier responsible for more diseases is the human hand, especially the undersides of the fingernails. Even "clean" hands are filled with thousands of microscopic germs that sap the immune system's energy and can make us sick.

When we think of diseases being transferred from person to person, we conjure up images of people sneezing or coughing on each other. We picture germs hurtling out of people's mouths and noses and rocketing through the air right into our own noses or mouths to infect us. A frightening picture, but one that we need not worry about, because relatively few germs become airborne, and fewer still actually bother us. Many studies have proven that we're much more likely to be "touched" by disease than to be "blown over" by it. For example:

- When ten people were housed for three days and nights with infected subjects, but separated by a wire fence to make sure they could not touch each other, none of the healthy people became sick. They breathed the same air for three days and nights—air into which the ill people had been coughing and sneezing—but did not become ill.

- In a second study, volunteers were deliberately seated next to people with colds who sneezed and coughed. Only 1 in 12 became ill.
- In a third study, viruses were passed by simple handshakes 20 out of 28 times.

Germs aren't hurtled at us by coughs and sneezes. They're handed to us during routine—and intimate—physical contact. Every time someone shakes your hand, pats you on the back, or strokes your cheek, it's as if they're saying, "Here, have a few million germs."

Germs are handed to us because human hands—especially under the nails—are a cornucopia of germs. If you take samples from various parts of the hands you'll see that while there are tens, hundreds, thousands of germs on the backs and palms of the hands and on the fingers, there are *tens of millions, sometimes hundreds of millions of germs under the fingernails.*

The fact that the undersides of the fingernails are a breeding ground and a safe haven for germs is double-trouble. First, the fingernails are not protected by the "horny" layer of skin, making it easier for germs to enter the body via the fingernails. Once inside they can get into the many blood vessels that feed the remarkably sensitive fingertips. Second, it is with our fingertips that we commonly touch each other—and ourselves. If we greeted each other by slapping the backs of our hands together, or if we scratched our noses with our elbows, relatively few

Table 9-1. "Germ" count[1]

	Thumbnail	Index nail	Palm	Back of hand
Subject #1	50,000,000	1,100,000	4,700	400
Subject #2	820,000,000	800,000	83	1,000
Subject #3	620,000	17,000,000	470	29
Subject #4	370,000	850,000	2,100,000	170

germs would exchange hands. But we don't. Fingertips touch flesh when we shake hands, when we caress a lover, when we grab hold of someone's arm to steady them. Fingertips are involved when we hand someone a pencil or a dollar, when we touch a computer keyboard or telephone. Fingertips come into play when we scratch ourselves, floss our teeth, prepare and eat our food. Even biting our nails can be hazardous to our health. When workers in England were studied after an outbreak of staph and strep in their meat processing factory in 1980, 33% were found to be nail biters, and 50% had damaged fingernails. Of the workers with serious infections, 75% were nail biters with evidence of staph and strep in their throats. Not everyone who bites or suffers damage to their fingernails will become ill, but the link between the germs carried under the fingernails and disease is strong.

Our fingers (and opposable thumb) are a blessing, for they make it possible for us to do so much. But they are also a "blessing" to germs, who find them to be hospitable refuges, ports of entry into the body, and "shuttle buses"

---

[1] Seaton, Kenneth. 1994. *Life, health and longevity.* Huntington, WV: Kenneth E. Seaton D.Sc.

that carry them to hundreds of other people—or back to ourselves for reinfection.

AUTOINOCULATION

The average person touches their nose, mouth, and eyes many times a day. If you watch a group of adults for an hour, you'll find that 1 out of every 3 touches their nose, and 1 in every 2.7 touches their eyes.[2] Even this small amount of innocent touching is enough to carry germs from the mouth, where they were probably unable to penetrate the body's defenses, to the nose or eyes, where they have an easier time causing damage. This passing of germs from one part of your body to another, unknowingly carrying them to the places the germs like the best, is called *autoinoculation.* But whether the germs come directly from others, arrive indirectly via items we touch, or move from one part of our body to another via autoinoculation, they're bad news.

LOWERING ALBUMIN: THE "HIDDEN" PROBLEM WITH INFECTION AND DISEASE

If germs entering the body simply did their damage, that would be serious enough. But they unwittingly do far more. In order to fight off invading bacteria, viruses, fungi, and other invaders, the body sends the immune system into action. In no time at all, T-cells, B-cells, macrophages, eosinophils, and other immune system soldiers are engaged in battle with the enemy. Here's how poor hygiene can lead to health disasters:

---

[2] Seaton, Kenneth. 1994. *Life, health and longevity.* Huntington, WV: Kenneth E. Seaton D.Sc., p. 12.

- The battle against germs is a protein-based battle, because the immune system utilizes many protein-based substances to fight off the invasion.
- The immune system rapidly produces more protein-based substances to defend the body.
- There can only be a certain concentration of all proteins in the body.
- When the concentration of immune system proteins goes up, the concentration of other proteins must fall.

One of the proteins that decreases when the immune system is engaged in battle is *albumin*, and that's where the trouble lies.

Albumin is an important protein that is found in most animal tissues. Medical doctors know about albumin, and often measure the amounts found in the blood with a simple blood test. Standard blood work-ups include albumin, depicting anything between 3.0 and 5.2 as "normal." Unfortunately, physicians tend to ignore albumin, perhaps because they don't know how to raise it when it falls (the "we-can't-fix-it-so-just-ignore-it" mentality). In any case, albumin has not been a focus of traditional medicine despite the fact that *albumin levels are the single most important indicator of health status.* If the level of albumin in your blood drops, your risk of contracting a serious—possibly deadly—disease shoots way up. Statistical reports demonstrate that albumin levels correlate closely with age, but are not truly age-related. That is, albumin levels tend to drop as we grow older, but don't necessarily have to.

Albumin is assembled in the liver from more than 500 amino acids. The most abundant protein in the bloodstream, albumin has many important duties. It:

- Protects easily damaged tissues from the free radicals that can destroy cells and cause cancer by altering cellular DNA.
- Guards against heart disease by transporting the antioxidant vitamins that help keep the coronary arteries clean, binding up fatty acids that tend to clog arteries and stabilizing the ratio between HDL ("good" cholesterol) and LDL ("bad" cholesterol).
- Binds up waste products, toxins, and dangerous drugs that would otherwise damage the body and encourage disease. It also detoxifies the fluids surrounding cells.
- Protects the biological terrain by buffering the blood against pH changes.
- Helps to keep the blood flowing smoothly by preventing red blood cells and other substances from clumping together.
- Is essential for transporting vitamins, magnesium, copper, zinc, bilirubin, uric acid, sex hormones, thyroid hormone, other hormones, and fatty acids throughout the body. It regulates the movement of nutrients between the blood and the body's cells.
- Stabilizes red blood cells and growth hormones.

- Plays a major role in controlling the precise amount of water in various bodily tissues.
- Plays an important role in transporting and circulating reservoirs of thyroid hormones.
- Purifies the cerebrospinal fluid, nourishes brain cells, and maintains the blood-brain barrier.
- Helps to ensure that there are adequate amounts of certain key minerals in the bones.
- Binds and transports the "stress hormone" known as *cortisol*, reducing stress-induced damage to the thymus gland, brain, and connective tissue.

Albumin has been described as a "portable liver" because the liver is the body's chief mechanism for disarming toxins and other dangerous substances, and because albumin, which is made in the liver, does the same throughout the body. It's as if the liver has sent millions of tiny pieces of itself to every single little cell, to round up and destroy harmful substances and organisms.

Albumin plays an indispensable role in maintaining the delicate chemical balance of the nourishing fluids (interstitial fluids) that surround and support the trillions of cells in the human body. If these fluids are healthy, the cells will flourish. But if the fluids become polluted, or depleted of certain substances, the cells cannot help but fall ill, and disease will sweep through the body. Albumin is like a filter that removes toxins from water,

Although overlooked by conventional medicine, blood serum albumin levels are the single most important indicator of health.

like the net that scoops debris out of a swimming pool, like the dispenser that squirts extra vitamin D into milk—albumin ensures that bodily fluids are clean, filled with nutrients, and properly balanced. And when you're filled with health-giving fluid, you cannot help but be healthy.

WHEN ALBUMIN LEVELS FALL

Ideally, there should be 5.0 g/dl (grams per deciliter) of albumin in the blood. (Some doctors and laboratories state this figure as 50 grams per liter, which is the same thing.)

Lower levels, around 3.5 or so, are commonly seen in long-time vegetarians and people suffering from malnutrition, kidney disease, cancer, severe infections, Crohn's disease, pancreatitis, and other diseases. However, levels don't have to fall as low as 3.5 before trouble appears.

Low levels of albumin have been linked to all cancers, with the risk of developing cancer rising as albumin falls.[3] *Albumin is low in all people suffering from cancer.* You can track the progress of the disease by looking at the patient's albumin level—the lower the albumin, the more rampant the cancer.[4] In fact, a low albumin level may actually *cause* cancer. Albumin normally neutralizes aflatoxin, nitrosamines, and other powerful carcinogens (cancer-causing substances).[5] Without sufficient albumin to keep these and other carcinogens under control, cancer can flourish.

---

[3] Stevens, R. 1990. Iron, risk of cancer. *Med. Oncol* Tumor Pharm 7(177).

[4] Blade, J. et al. 1989. Prognostic system multiple myeloma. *Br J Haematol* 72(507).

[5] Peters, T. 1986. *All about albumin.* New York: Academic Press, p. 238.

Back in 1775 we learned that at least one form of cancer could be caused by "dirt." Chimney sweeps exposed to soot were more likely to develop scrotal cancer than other people. Simply washing themselves carefully every day reduced their risk to normal. Few of us are anywhere near chimney soot these days, but we *are* exposed to many airborne chemicals, especially if we live in polluted cities or near certain kinds of factories and plants. We also know that some forms of cancer are caused by viral infections. That's why it's vital that we regularly and carefully wash away any germs or chemicals that can cause cancer, as well as those that can indirectly cause the disease by overwhelming our immune systems and reducing our albumin, allowing cancer to sneak in the "back door."

Declining albumin also indicates an increased risk of heart disease. A long-term British heart study found that a low albumin level was a good predictor of heart disease.[6] Another study stated that the odds of suffering from coronary artery disease *doubled* when the albumin level fell to 4.4 (that's only about 10% below the ideal level of 5).[7]

Low levels of albumin are associated with several other diseases, including Hodgkin's disease and HIV, the precursor to AIDS. Indeed, you can use low albumin levels as a "predictor" of mortality. People with albumin levels below 3.5 g/dl are approximately *twenty times more likely to die* from all causes than those with albumin levels of 5.0 g/dl. Many studies have confirmed this fact. Nursing

---

[6] Philips, R. et al, 1989. Albumin, mortality, cardiovascular disease, cancer. *Lancet* 2:1434.

[7] Gillum, R., Makuc, D. 1992. Serum albumin, heart disease and death. *Am Heart J* 123:507.

home residents with albumin levels of 3.5 g/dl had a death rate of about 50%, compared with an 11% rate found in those with higher levels (around 4.0 g/dl).[8] Among men and women over the age of 70, death rates were 40% lower in those with albumin levels of 4.4 g/dl, compared to those with levels of 4.2 g/dl.[9] Hip fractures are a serious problem for the elderly, who often weaken and die after the break. Among hip-fracture patients whose albumin levels were low (3.0), the death rate was 70%. *But among those with albumin levels of* 4.0, *the death rate was only* 11%.[10]

People with cancer and other diseases have albumin levels below 4.0. People with levels above 4.4 do not have cancer.

I've looked back over my medical records to track my own albumin through the years, beginning long before I knew about hygiene—indeed, before I had any idea what albumin was or how it vital it is to good health. Unfortunately, I didn't take regular albumin tests, but there are enough to track the progress of this important indicator in a general way.

In Table 9-2, notice how my albumin, which wasn't very high to begin with, dropped steadily from 1984 to 1989, when I was diagnosed with prostate cancer. It began moving back up, then came crashing down again in 1995,

[8] Redman, D. et al. 1987. Death rate at nursing home. *J Pardner Enthral Nut* 11:360.

[9] Corti, M. et al. 1994. Serum albumin, disability, predictors of mortality. JAMA 272:1036.

[10] Foster M., et al. 1990. Assessment complications fractures of the hip. *J Orthop Trauma* 449.

Table 9-2.

Date	Albumin level	
1984	4.4	Outstanding health. Running 30 miles per week, 6 minutes per mile
1985	4.3	
1987	4.2	
1990	4.0	Prostate cancer diagnosed 12/28/90
1991	4.1	Prostate cancer healed 3/1/91
2/14/95	4.1	Major mineral imbalance, began hygiene program
3/30/95	4.4	
6/6/95	4.2	
9/5/95	4.1	Close to optimal mineral balance
12/4/95	3.8	Kidney stone diagnosed 11/27, removed 12/8
12/30/95	3.9	Fasting/colon cleanse 11/12/95–1/8/96
5/7/96	4.5	pH in balance. AMAS test shows that I'm cancer-free!
8/23/96	4.5	Continuing in healthy range

just before my kidney stone and second bout with prostate cancer in late 1995 and early 1996. Finally, in May of 1996, my albumin reached a high of 4.5 as my BTA and cellular pH showed dramatic improvement and the AMAS test showed that I was free of cancer. I still have a way to go to reach 5.0, but the overall trend is clearly up. I am thrilled to have reached 4.5 by following the program detailed in this book, and using Ken Seaton's *High-Tech Hygiene*. All during the years I battled cancer my albumin remained low. It was only when I reversed the trend and began to push it up that the cancer was finally cleared.

WHY DOES ALBUMIN FALL?

Albumin levels drop when the immune system engages in a battle with invading bacteria, viruses, fungi, and other germs. It also falls when the body is forced to deal with an onslaught of toxins and other dangerous substances that we inhale, drink, or eat, or that get into the body through the skin, respiratory system, or other ports of entry. The fact that the body mounts a powerful offensive is good, for otherwise we would die. But the unintended consequence, the shortfall in albumin, is harmful in the long run.

Temporary drops in albumin levels are necessary, and not a problem. It's as if we miss a credit card payment one month because of unexpected medical expenses, then make the missed payment, with interest, the next month. Our credit takes a small "hit," then quickly recovers before any permanent damage is done. The problem comes when we're *continually* battling infections, parasites, and toxins. Then our albumin runs low for months on end and, like a person who doesn't make a credit card payment for several months, our "credit" is eventually ruined. Now we're facing serious illness, and we never seem to have enough resources to beat the disease and "get ahead."

INCREASING YOUR ALBUMIN LEVEL

It's important to monitor your albumin level and make sure it stays high, since low albumin has been linked to an increased risk of death from all causes in both sexes and among all races and age groups.[11] The ideal

---

[11] *Lancet* 2:1435 (1989). *JAMA* 272:1036 (1994).

albumin level is 5.0, but the average level in the United States is only about 4.2—too low for optimal health and low enough to encourage disease. Albumin is produced in the liver, but there's no way to encourage the liver to make more—no drugs, no diet, and no form of exercise that will spur production.

Prostate cancer is directly linked to low levels of albumin.

Doctors can infuse albumin into the body, and may do so for patients suffering from cancer and other serious diseases associated with low albumin. Unfortunately, "albumin shots" don't work. When albumin is infused into the body, it upsets the carefully calibrated concentration of proteins (osmotic pressure). The liver attempts to get the concentration back to normal levels by halting its own production of albumin. And if that doesn't work quickly enough, it starts destroying albumin in a frantic attempt to get things back to normal in the body. The liver doesn't understand that the extra albumin may be helpful; it only knows that something is out of balance, and balance must be restored.

The only way to keep albumin levels high is to stay healthy. I know that sounds like circular reasoning—low albumin causes you to be sick, and the only way to increase albumin is to not get sick—but it's not. When we have an infection or have been injured, the total number of antibodies and certain other proteins rise. Since there can only be so many proteins in bodily fluids at one time, if the antibodies and other proteins associated with infection or injury rise, *then the albumin must fall.* Remaining healthy is the only way to keep the antibodies and other proteins at normal levels, leaving "room" for plenty of albumin.

Fortunately, we *can* lower the risk of infection by paying scrupulous attention to personal hygiene. Infection is often caused by the foreign bodies (germs) that enter our body through the mouth, nose, eyes, and fingernails, as well as through cuts in our skin. Good hygiene won't prevent cuts, but it can eliminate many of the germs that are lurking around our eyes, mouth, nose, and fingernails. By preventing the germs from getting into our bodies and causing infections, we keep our antibodies at a normal level, allowing our albumin level to rise.

OTHER PROBLEMS THAT MAY BE PREVENTED WITH GOOD HYGIENE

Prostate problems, including cancer, are known to be linked to high testosterone, which is kept in balance by albumin. But it's not just men with prostate cancer who can be helped by proper hygiene. A great many ailments are caused or worsened by poor hygiene and the inevitable drop in albumin, including:

- *Acne.* Bacteria can grow in the sebum that abounds in glands just underneath the skin. Scratching, rubbing, or pinching acne can introduce even more germs to the infected areas.

- *Allergies and asthma.* Many of the substances carried in the fingernails, including *staph aureus* and worm eggs, can trigger allergic reactions or asthma when we autoinfect ourselves.

- *Athlete's foot.* Our fingernails can pick up from our feet the fungi that cause athlete's foot, and then deposit it to other areas of skin, spreading the infection.

■ *Arthritis.* Infectious and rheumatoid arthritis can both be caused by invading organisms that can be kept out of the body with proper hygiene.

■ *Candida.* A common problem, especially for women, the fungi and yeast that cause candida can produce annoying to serious infections in the vagina, gastrointestinal tract, and elsewhere. There are women who had suffered with chronic vaginal yeast infections (for as long as 20 years) who had their problems disappear in one week on the hygiene program, especially from the baths.

■ *Colds and flus.* Although we instinctively flinch when someone with a cold coughs or sneezes on us (or anywhere near us), most of the moisture expelled from the mouth during a cough or sneeze *does not* contain many germs. That's because cold viruses do not routinely "hang out" in the saliva pools that comprise most of the droplets shot from the mouth by coughing and sneezing. Instead, the viruses congregate in the nose, which has the temperature and other conditions they prefer. Not only do cold viruses favor the nasal environment (the nasal passages are more hospitable for cold viruses), they also have a better chance of getting into the body and its cells via the nose. Since we touch our noses many times during the day, the chance of carrying germs to and from the nose is great.

■ *Diabetes.* Recurrent infections are a problem that plagues diabetics. Stopping the infection/autoinfection cycle will help many diabetics avoid needless infection and allow their bodies to concentrate on healing.

■ *Measles.* Although generally harmless when it strikes in childhood, measles can be a very serious disease for adults. It's very difficult to get people, especially children, not to scratch or touch themselves when infected, raising the likelihood of contagion. Excellent hygiene of the hands, especially the fingernails, may help to keep the disease contained.

■ *Pneumonia.* Often called the senior citizen's "best friend" because it leads to a relatively quick and painless death, pneumonia often strikes after or in conjunction with other respiratory ailments. This means that a cold or flu can prepare the way for pneumonia—the same cold and flu that can be prevented with impeccable hygiene.

■ *Worms.* Almost everyone plays host to these tiny invaders at some point in their life—and perhaps many times. Worm eggs are easily picked up by our fingernails when we touch various surfaces or other people, and then enter our body via the mouth, nose, or eyes when we touch ourselves. Worms can be draining and debilitating, damaging body tissue and robbing of us nutrients and energy. It's best to wash away worm eggs before they get inside and force us to employ stronger measures to get rid of them.

And that's not all. AIDS, chicken pox, circulatory problems, cystic fibrosis, dandruff, ear and eye infections, fat metabolism disturbances, herpes, multiple sclerosis, sex hormone imbalances, skin diseases of various kinds, and thyroid disorders can also be helped or avoided by good hygiene, which helps prevent germs from entering the body and keeps albumin levels up.

The 20% of immune system effort that's normally tied up battling the germs under our fingernails can be redirected toward better health when those germs are eliminated.

TOO SIMPLE TO BE TRUE?

I know this sounds like a simple idea, perhaps too simple to be worthwhile. However, it is no more than an extension of the work of the great Austrian doctor, Ignaz Semmelweis, who created an incredible uproar in the medical community in the 1840s when he insisted that doctors wash their hands before examining women in the maternity ward. (The doctors often came right to the maternity ward from the morgue, where they had been dissecting cadavers, without stopping to wash their hands.) Pregnant women used to plead to be cared for by the midwives rather than doctors, because those who were cared for by the midwives (who did not cut up dead bodies) had a much higher survival rate. But the doctors refused to heed Dr. Semmelweis' plea. They were insulted by the very idea that they might be carrying germs to their patients and killing them. So they drove Dr. Semmelweis out of the hospital and into the insane asylum, where he died.

Yes, washing your hands sounds like a very simple solution to an incredibly complex set of problems, but the simplest ideas are often the best. Sometimes changing just one thing produces dramatic results. Scurvy used to decimate the crews of ships sailing the high seas in the 15th, 16th, and 17th centuries. The problem was solved when sailors began eating citrus fruits or drinking lemon or lime juice. Pellagra was a terrible scourge for many centuries in various countries. It attacked many in the United States, leading to the "Four D's": diarrhea, dermatitis, dementia, and death. This mysterious and impossibly complex disease was eradicated by adding niacin, one of the B vitamins, to the diet. A solution doesn't have to be complex. It simply has to work. And good hygiene works!

AN EXCELLENT CLEANSING SYSTEM

Throughout history, people living in cleaner societies have had higher albumin levels and longer lives. Dirty fingernails, which are indicative of overall cleanliness, have long been associated with lower albumin levels.[12] Cleanliness may or may not be next to godliness, but it's certainly a path to better health and longer life!

Germs and viruses are transferred primarily by the human hand.

Regular washing of the hands and face—at least five times a day—is an excellent start, but it's only a beginning. Careful scrubbing for a full minute, which few of us do, can remove up to 90% of the germs from most of the body, but not the fingernails. Neither will regular hand and face washing eliminate the germs hiding in the nose and eyes. And scrubbing with regular soap is not enough. In fact, washing with some soaps can actually *increase* the numbers of germs. Something more is needed.

It's not possible to be completely germ-free. Neither is it desirable, for we need certain germs (for example, in our gastrointestinal tract, to manufacture vitamin K). But we do want to rid ourselves of the harmful germs. A great way to start is to regularly and thoroughly wash away germs hiding in the fingernails, nose, and eyes.

The best cleansing system I've found—one that really gets rid of germs under the fingernails, in the nose, eyes, and elsewhere—is the High-Performance Hygiene line of

---

[12] Muehrcke R. 1956. Fingernails hypoalbuminemia. *Br Med J* 1:1427. Sahi and Bansal. 1988. Yellow nails hypoalbuminemia. *Br J Clin Prac*, 42:36.

products, manufactured by High-Performance Hygiene of Cleveland, Ohio. The facial dips and soap, developed by Dr. Ken Seaton, are a revolutionary approach to increasing your albumin level and energizing your health by taking the burden off your immune system. (See the appendix for information about how to contact the company.)

Here are the instructions for using the various soaps, as explained in Dr. Seaton's instruction sheet:

1. This system of hygiene replaces bar, liquid, and hair soaps, as well as skin creams. *You must follow instructions exactly to get the results.*

2. If the soap dries out, put the lid back on.

3. *Hand washing:* It is essential to prod the thumbs and fingernails (with dry hands) into the soap several times for approximately three seconds, then use the excess soap clinging to the fingertips to rub all over the rest of the hands. Then wet, create lather, and rinse. Wash hands at least five times a day.

4. *Skin cream:* These soaps contain their own unequaled moisturizer. For best results do not use any skin cream. If necessary, we recommend sunflower or corn oil.

5. *Face washing:* Massage the soap into the skin, lather, then rinse. For those with acne or other skin problems, use frequently. The facial dip is explained below.

6. *Bath/shower:* Use the sponge supplied. Wet both body and the sponge. Then turn off water and create a rich lather using the sponge and soap. Rinse.

7. *Hair:* Wet hair, use plenty of soap, massage into the scalp for 30 seconds, then rinse. Use a conditioner only if necessary.

8. *Teeth:* Use Super Teeth Soap once or twice a week, and toothpaste in between. Rinse mouth thoroughly with warm water after using the soap.

9. *Facial Dip A & C:* Use Facial Dip A (hydrogen peroxide/zinc/magnesium) most of the time, preferably first thing in the morning, because it's very soothing to the nasal passageway and eyes. Use Facial Dip C (iodine/HOI) especially at the first sign of any infection (usually if Facial Dip A isn't working). It is safe to use up to 4 half-eyedroppers of Facial Dip C during infections such as colds, sore throats, or sinus problems. Do *not* use Facial Dip C every day month after month.

With Facial Dip A, use a capful in a normal hand basin containing 5 to 8 quarts of very warm water. With Facial Dip C, use between 1 and 4 half-eyedroppers in 5 to 8 quarts of very warm water. *It is essential to add 1 to 2 tablespoons of salt (sodium chloride) at least 80% of the time, yet not all the time.* Do *not* mix Facial Dip A and C together. Use the hand basin, *not* a separate bowl. (The bacteria in the hand basin are essential to activate the process.) Mix the solution with running water, never your fingers. Do *not* draw the water to the back of the throat. Simply allow the first two inches of the nasal passageway to be cleaned.

10. *Bath:* Add half a pound of table salt, plus 5 half-eyedroppers of Facial Dip C when you are actually in the water. *Supervise young children.* This bath is good for very young children who cannot perform the facial dip and to clean the genital tract in males and females. Do not add any soap for 10 minutes because it deactivates the iodine.

11. *Mouthwash:* Add one capful of Facial Dip A plus a teaspoon of salt or baking soda to half a glass of warm water. Rinse the mouth thoroughly. Use when necessary.

12. *Foot soak:* Add 4 to 6 half-eyedroppers of Facial Dip C to one gallon of hot water, plus a tablespoon of salt. Soak feet for 10 minutes, particularly if you have problems or fungal infections.

13. *Vitamin supplement:* This system works very well with 1,000 mcg (not sublingual) of vitamin B_{12}, but not with multivitamins. It is a good idea to fast one day a week, perform sensible exercise, and go to bed early, around 8 p.m., about twice a week.

14. *Please note:* Cleaning the fingernails, nasal passageway, and eyes is very complex. Do *not* use any other chemicals. Follow these instructions exactly.

YOU CAN RAISE YOUR ALBUMIN

Studies with High-Performance Hygiene have been overwhelmingly positive, with albumin levels rising significantly in people who use the soaps. On the following page, Table 9-3 shows how albumin levels rose in people using the hygiene regimen for months at a time. In the selected cases, the average (mean) albumin level increased by 0.4 (from 4.3 to 4.7). Not everyone's albumin rose, but the overall trend is definitely up.

My own experience confirms and parallels these improvements. Good hygiene equals a high albumin level, and a high albumin level equates to good health. Therefore, excellent hygiene is an important cornerstone of your healing regimen.

Table 9-3. Albumin levels of people using High-Performance Hygiene program for months at a time.[13]

Volunteer	*Albumin Level*	
	Beginning	*Ending*
Male, age 46	4.8	5.3
Male, age 49	4.4	4.7
Male, age 50	4.4 (est.)	5.4
Male, age 50	4.0	4.7
Male, age 52	4.5 (est.)	5.0
Male, age 53	4.0	4.3
Male, age 70	3.4	5.2
Female, age 34	4.5	4.7
Female, age 34	4.5 (est.)	5.0
Female, age 41	4.0	4.4
Female, age 48	4.3	4.4
Female, age 48	4.2	4.8
Female, age 52	4.5	4.7
Female, age 62	4.5	4.5
Female, age 72	4.1	4.1

Average (mean) increase:
from 4.3 to 4.7 (by 0.4)

[13] Adapted from Seaton, K. 1994. Reproductive Health: The Prostate Gland. *Health Freedom News*, July, p. 28.

CHAPTER 10

BUILDING HEALTH WITH EXERCISE AND BODYWORK

Now it's time to get physical, and look at the health-enhancing things we can do with our bodies and have others do for it. The keys are *movement* and *freedom:* moving your body hard and fast enough to get aerobic benefits, moving your muscles against weight, moving the muscles in your groin area to "loosen up" the prostate, moving waste products through your lymph system, massaging emotional blockages out of your muscles, and even allowing energy and blood to move freely by selecting the right clothing.

Let's begin with a look at aerobic exercise, and then examine the benefits of strength training and massage for the prostate and lymph system.

AEROBIC EXERCISE

The bloom may be off the health boom of the 1970s and 1980s, but there's still good reason to exercise. Whether it is jogging, swimming, bicycling, rebounding on a mini-trampoline, aerobics classes, or any other exercise that revs up the heart for 20 to 30 minutes at a time, regular exercise benefits the body in many ways. It:

- Burns calories
- Stimulates the metabolism
- Improves circulation (including erections)
- Helps drain the lymph system
- Raises HDL (the "good" cholesterol)
- Burns off potentially dangerous "stress chemicals" such as adrenaline
- Increases endorphins (which help fight pain and depression)
- Improves energy levels
- Strengthens and tones muscles

Exercise keeps us slim, stokes the body's fires, keeps the arteries clear and the blood flowing, rids the body of wastes, dissipates the physical effects of stress, triggers the release of our "feel-good" chemicals, and gives us energy and strength. All in all, exercise strengthens and rejuvenates the body. And one specific kind of exercise—strength training—has the most powerful medicinal effects. It has been shown to reduce diabetes and colon cancer, and to slow or even reverse the aging process.

Any type of aerobic exercise is a good start. An aerobic exercise is one that gets your heart beating at 70 to 80% of its maximum rate and keeps it there for 20 to 30 minutes. Good aerobic exercises include jogging, riding a bicycle, aerobics classes, swimming, rowing, and even brisk walking. The trick is to do them fast enough to keep your heart beating in the 70 to 80% range. (To find your target range, subtract your age from 220. Your goal is 70 to 80% of that. If, for example, you are 40 years old, subtract 40 from 220 to get 180. Your goal is 70 to 80% of 180, or 126 to 144.)

Exercise is fundamental to having healthy, strong organs.

Activities such as tennis, baseball, badminton, martial arts, and ballroom dancing tone certain muscles; improve reflexes, balance, and flexibility; and are fun. But they don't offer aerobic benefits because they are not continuous. We tend to start and stop at these activities, so our heart rates goes up and down rather than staying in the aerobic range for a full 20 to 30 minutes. That's why a healthful exercise program must include at least one aerobic activity that is sustained for 20 to 30 minutes, three or more days a week. Which exercise is best? The one you enjoy doing.

STRENGTH TRAINING = BETTER HEALTH & LONGER LIFE

Aerobic exercise is a great start. It strengthens the heart, improves circulation, stimulates the metabolism, and otherwise adds to health. But it can't keep us young. For that we must turn to strength training.

Like body builders, strength trainers lift weight to build muscle mass. But instead of striving for the largest and most visually appealing muscles (as body builders do), strength trainers strive for greater overall health.

Experts such as William Evans, chief of the Tuft University Human Nutrition Research Center on Aging, believe that strength training is the single most important step one can take to slow the aging process. "Changes in muscle mass drive many of the other changes we associate with aging," he says. "If in fact [it's possible to] maintain or even increase muscle mass [as we age], many of these things we call 'biomarkers' of aging might actually be 'biomarkers' of inactivity." In other words, what we normally think of as the inevitable signs of aging may actually be caused by lack of activity. If we remain active, we won't have to see our metabolism slow down and our bones become thin. We won't watch in dismay as our youthful, tight, and strong muscles turn to mush and become buried under mounds of fat.

If shrinking muscle mass prompts the unhappy changes of aging, then keeping our muscles strong can halt or reverse them. A great deal of study has shown that strength training can:

- Keep the metabolic rate high, jamming the body into a youthful "high gear."
- Keep our bones thick, preventing the thinning that leads to osteoporosis.
- Keep our body fat low, helping us maintain a slim, youthful look and feel.
- Reduce the risk of diabetes by controlling blood sugar.
- Lower the risk of colon cancer by helping to keep the colon active.

In addition, strength training has an as-yet unmeasured psychological benefit. Maintaining a youthful, strong, and slim body as we age is bound to make us feel better about ourself and life. That good feeling will inevitably carry over into our work and personal life, improving our confidence and enthusiasm. And as we see ourselves sticking to our strength-training schedule and becoming stronger, we realize that we can set and accomplish goals. These good feelings will be translated by the brain into endorphins and other beneficial biochemicals that will strengthen our immune system and otherwise help to keep us healthy and strong.

Both physically and emotionally, the benefits of strength training and other forms of exercise are worth the time and effort.

DEVELOPING YOUR EXERCISE REGIMEN

The general principles for your exercise regimen are simple. It should include:

1. Aerobic exercise
2. Strength training
3. Stretching

Aerobics: Three to four days a week, perform whatever aerobic exercise you enjoy most for 20 to 30 minutes of sustained activity. You can perform the exercise—jogging, for example—the "traditional" way, in the park or on a track, or you can get high-tech and use a treadmill, rebounder, StairMaster, or similar device at a gym or at home. Whether you're indoors or out, exercising the "old-fashioned" way or surrounded by the latest gadgets, working out in a group or on your own, it doesn't matter—as long as you keep your heart beating at 70 to 80% of its maximum rate for 20 to 30 minutes. Choose an aerobic exercise that you can safely perform and that you enjoy.

Strength training: The goal is to lift weights two to three times a week. Each time, you should perform eight to ten different exercises that work different major muscle groups. Do at least one set of eight to twelve repetitions for each exercise. Which exercises should you do? There are many simple and excellent exercises, such as the bench press, military press, stiff arm pull-over, bent-over barbell rowing, bicep curls, dumbbell tricep curls, and upright rowing. The trainer at your gym will help you develop a strength training program using these and/or other exercises.

Strong, active muscles equal strong, active organs.

When working with the trainer, be sure to emphasize that you want to approach strength training slowly and surely, starting at lower weight levels and carefully working your way up. Remember, you're training *your* muscles, not Arnold Schwarzeneggers'. The goal is to gently and gradually challenge and strengthen your muscles, not to lift a zillion pounds. If 5 or 20 pounds is all you can safely and comfortably lift, then limit yourself to those 5 or 20 pounds. (There are also many good books that will help you develop a strength-training program, including those by Joe Weider, which are considered by many to be the basic works in this field.)

Some people will tell you free weights (barbells and dumbbells) are best, while others swear by Nautilus and other weight machines. Which is best? Both work well. Weight machines help keep the weights under control, free weights allow for more flexibility. Use whichever you feel most comfortable with. And if you can't get to a gym or afford to buy your own free weights, lift cans of food or water bottles, do push-ups and sit-ups on the floor, use a sturdy tree branch for pull-ups. With a little ingenuity, you can develop an in-home "gym" for very little money.

Stretching: Stretching keeps you flexible and reduces the risk of injury while exercising. Yoga stretches are best known: you can learn them at any of the numerous yoga studios around the country. Yoga and/or stretching classes are also offered at most gyms, as well as through many "extension" or community courses at junior and senior colleges. There are also many videos and books that demonstrate various stretching routines.

I like to work out at the gym. I begin with a 5- to 30-minute aerobic warmup: jogging, rollerblading, riding the stationary bicycle, or climbing on the StairMaster. Then I use the weight machines and free weights, and finish with yoga stretches on the floor. My entire routine takes less than an hour—a minimal investment with a giant return. I feel great, and my physical and psychological health continually benefits.

Before you begin your exercise regimen, check with your doctor to make sure you're able to exercise safely, and discuss any limitations you might have.

PROSTATE AND SURROUNDING TISSUE MASSAGE

Now that you've worked out, it's time to let others work on you: massaging your body, your prostate, and surrounding areas to increase blood flow, soften and shrink the gland, and relax the surrounding muscles.

The blood that carries oxygen to every cell of the body is vital to physical health, abundance, and spirituality. Only with an abundant supply of oxygen can each cell breathe and pulsate with energy, and process out the toxins and waste, while continually renewing itself. This is especially true of the prostate. Dependent on some of the tiniest blood passages in the body for its blood and oxygen, it relies on a steady flow of both. When the flow is crimped or interrupted, even briefly, the prostate becomes a target for infection, enlargement, or cancer.

Medical literature contains many reports of temporary and permanent softening and shrinking of enlarged prostates as a result of digital massage. There is specific mention of improved urinary stream, reduction of the hesitation associated with prostate infection, a return to a more normal prostate size and shape, and remission or reduction of tumor size. Yet the medical establishment continues to ignore the benefits of prostate massage: I have been unable to find any discussion in the literature about prostate massage as a healing or treatment modality, though it has been a tantric practice for at least 8,000 years.

That hasn't stopped practitioners such as Roy Dittman, O.M.D., of Santa Monica, California, from using and teaching prostate massage. Dr. Dittman points out that most prostates (and bladders) are choked off to some degree by surrounding tight muscles and tissues—primarily the abductors, obliques, and psoaz. The pliability and normal pulsation a healthy prostate needs can be restricted by the tightness of the surrounding muscles and tissues. If muscles are tight, the prostate doesn't expand and contract with each breath, and doesn't get the blood and oxygen it needs to remain healthy.

This tightness is quite easy to release by external and internal massage. Self-massage your prostate and surrounding areas by lying on your back with your legs extended. Now bend your knees and hips, drawing your knees up to your chest. Then spread your knees apart and press the soles of your feet together firmly. Keep your soles pressed together as you extend your legs to the floor. Repeat this up-and-down motion 6 to 12 times daily while you are massaging the prostate (the firm lump just above the anus) and perineum.

Bodywork helps us move physical and emotional blockages out of the body.

External prostate massage is a good start, but it's more effective when accompanied by internal massage. Internal prostate massage is an expansion of the digital rectal examination (DRE) that the doctor performs during a prostate examination. Pressed up against the wall of the rectum, the prostate can be felt and manipulated by a gloved, lubricated finger inserted into the rectum. An enlarged prostate can be gently massaged by a physician or healer to induce the prostate to soften and shrink. A loving partner can also perform prostate massage. (This has been a part of tantric practice for thousands of years.) The prostate and surrounding tissue soften dramatically with even occasional massage, while the process becomes more and more comfortable after an initial period of discomfort. Internal prostate massage is often applied by physicians when patients complain about urinary problems or that their bladder never feels completely empty.

It may be best to be massaged by a professional first. However, if your lover is willing, she can quickly learn to perform the massage. Here's how it's done. Insert a lubricated, gloved index finger into the anus, and then gently massage around the chestnut-sized and -shaped prostate. Gradually increase the finger pressure, until firm. Expand the massage to the surrounding muscles on both sides, changing hands and position as necessary. These muscles, which may be sore and hard at first, will release and soften dramatically with continued massage. Massage of the prostate and surrounding muscles may be uncomfortable or painful at first. Tolerate as much as you can at each session. You may yell and scream a lot; that's fine, for it helps to release stuck emotions. You will be surprised at how great you feel as you release these areas. Prostate massage feels better when you are somewhat erect and excited, and it will produce a very thrilling ejaculation if it's done during lovemaking.

The prostate responds dramatically to bodywork.

A single massage can produce dramatic progress, freeing the gland and surrounding tissues, increasing the flow of blood and energy to the prostate, and releasing the energy that has been trapped in this sensitive area. This newfound physical openness allows more blood and oxygen to the area, creating healing and general softness of the prostate. It will also enhance your lovemaking.

> *Caution: If you have a prostate infection or cancer, prostate massage, in theory, may cause the offending "germs" to spread—and the massage may be quite painful if your prostate is inflamed. Our experience, however, has been very positive, as are the literature reports of massage during examination.*

Although there are reports of men with acute prostatitis experiencing beneficial flushing and dissipation of their pain after having massage performed, medical opinion is generally opposed to prostatic massage in cases of acute prostatitis or cancer. I favor massage, seeing great benefits with little risk, but you must make your own decision. (Spinal physiotherapy in the lumbar, lumbosacral, and sacral regions will also indirectly stimulate the prostate, so care should be taken when undergoing these procedures.)

Regular sexual activity is also good for the prostate. The rush of blood and energy, as well the prostate's pulsations during ejaculation, help the gland to maintain its muscular strength and freedom, and also act to cleanse the organ. Regular but not too frequent ejaculation also helps to release the emotional blockages that cause hardness and tightening of the prostate and surrounding tissues. In general, massage, visualization, lovemaking, and stretching increase blood flow in the area, which is beneficial.

In addition to increasing blood and energy flow, bodywork also relaxes the surrounding muscles. Once these muscles are loosened up, an enlarged prostate usually returns to normal size and shape in just a few minutes. Men over the age of 40 tend to have tight muscles, especially in the groin and legs.

Working with structural integration bodyworker Deed Preston of Santa Monica, California, I learned that these muscles can be "released" through internal and external massage. With the muscles relaxed, an enlarged and lopsided prostate quickly returns to its normal size, texture, and shape in anywhere from one to a few sessions. This bodywork can be uncomfortable and painful at first, but the results are dramatic: many men whose prostates remained enlarged despite powerful drugs have experienced quick and permanent healing. Just a few minutes of massage, which costs far less than drugs or surgery, can work wonders.

An enlarged prostate can quickly return to its normal size and shape when surrounding muscle tension is released by bodywork.

MASSAGING THE LYMPH SYSTEM

Your aerobic exercise program will help keep your heart strong, your blood flowing, and your metabolism "cooking." Your weight training exercises will rejuvenate your mind and body. Massage and bodywork will loosen constricting muscles to allow blood and energy to flow freely to your prostate. The final phase of getting physical is helping drain your lymph system through massage, and through exercise such as gentle rebounder work.

Like the circulatory system which carries blood, the lymph system consists of "pipes" running everywhere in the body. But instead of ferrying fresh blood to the cells, the lymph system transports fluid and waste products away from the cells. Like any good "sewer system," the lymph system filters out dangerous substances. Located where many lymph "pipes" join together, at junctures called *lymph nodes*, these "filters" consist of macrophages, T-cells, B-cells, and other powerful immune system cells. Lying in wait in the more than 600 lymph nodes spread throughout the body, these specialized cells eagerly detect and destroy bacteria, viruses, fungi, certain pesticides and cellular waste products, and other potentially harmful substances.

But, like a filter in a swimming pool, the lymph system can handle only so much waste before it gets backed up. When that happens the germs and wastes pile up in the lymph glands and pipes, eventually backing up into the body, like water gushing out of a clogged toilet. (You can easily tell when a lymph gland is clogged with fluid and wastes; it's swollen and tender to the touch.)

With the lymphatic system blocked and backed up, the disease-fighting immune system cells can't get at the wastes and toxins; germs and poisons are left to fester and spread throughout the body. Meanwhile, the body is deprived of the good things in the lymph system. Fifty percent of lymph fluid consists of nutrient-rich plasma proteins. When the proteins are not allowed to flow through the lymph system and back to the body's cells, the cells suffer. Starved of nutrition, forced to stew in its own wastes, the body is an easy target for disease.

The prostate, which depends on the two major lymph nodes located on each side of the groin, is especially vulnerable. If wastes are not flushed out of these nodes, the prostate becomes susceptible to cancer and other problems, as the wastes remain in its tiny vessels instead of being transported into the lymph system and away for disposal.

Nearby tight muscles can squeeze down on clogged lymph glands and make the problem worse. Tight muscles make it more difficult for the lymph system to function, increasing the likelihood that it will become backed up.

The solution is twofold:

(1) Fasting/cleansing/detoxifying to reduce the amount of waste and toxins in the body, and

(2) Lymph massage and exercise to stimulate and drain the lymph glands.

Most men need lymph massage. They can either have it done professionally, or they and/or a loved one can learn how to do it. Begin the massage in the groin area, working until sore, tight areas become free. Coconut oil (available in most health food stores), used as a massage oil on the genital area, is thought to greatly benefit the prostate, and it feels wonderful.

THE IMPORTANCE OF WHAT WE WEAR

A loose, "free" groin area is so important that we need to also pay attention to what we wear. Tight clothing restricts the flow of energy and blood to the groin. It also encourages tight muscles by hindering body movement, and holds the testicles rigidly in place. The testicles need room to move to allow normal blood flow and to regulate their temperature at the optimal level for sperm and hormone production. (Fertility specialists have long prescribed loose boxer shorts and trousers for maximum fertility.) Self-observation quickly shows the constant expansion and contraction of the testicles.

Freedom to swing encourages blood and energy flow, enhancing prostate health. That's why it's best to avoid tight jeans and undergarments in favor of loose boxer shorts and loose-fitting jeans and trousers. Stay away from tight belts, for they also restrict the flow of blood and energy. Opt for looser waistbands worn with suspenders, if needed. Tight jeans may be "in" and suspenders out of fashion, but you may want to prioritize health over fashion.

According to Dr. George Schuchard, large nickel belt buckles and nickels in the pocket can also be problematic, due to their tendency to reduce the flow of blood. Lee Cowden, M.D., emphasizes the importance of wearing any belt buckle off-center so it doesn't block the vital center meridians.

CHAPTER 11

THE HEALING POWER OF ENERGY

We're all familiar with the arteries and veins that carry blood and other substances through the body—miles and miles of vessels carrying nourishment to every part of the body, connecting each part to all the others. There are also the lymph and nervous systems, the former an important part of the immune system, the latter energizing and integrating the body via the nerves (which serve as our feedback system).

Although Western medicine has never acknowledged the fact, another system permeates the body, carrying vitally needed nourishment and connecting the body to the universal flow of energy. These are the *chakras*, openings through which energy flows in, through, and out of the body. There are seven major chakras, plus many minor chakras, lesser chakras and acupuncture points, all serving as conduits for energy.

The chakras receive energy from the universe, "digest" it into smaller parts, then "feed" it to the appropriate parts of the body. Each of the chakras is linked to a major nerve plexus and endocrine gland. (The chakras also send ener-

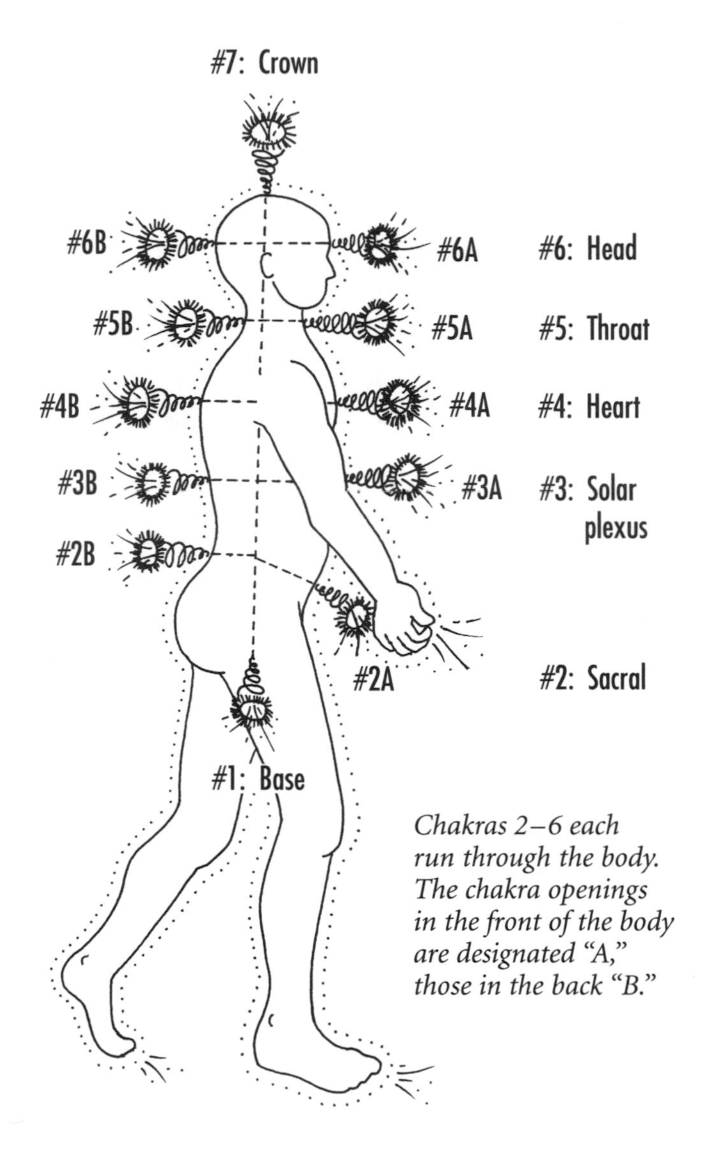

The words we use to locate and describe the chakras are inadequate to the task. At best, they give a sense of the chakras, but only real-life, hands-on experience with the chakras can give one a true sense of their location, "dimension," and status.

Figure 11-1. The seven major chakras (front and back views).

gy back out to the universe.) If, for any reason, a particular chakra is blocked, the part of the body it supplies with energy will suffer, becoming more susceptible to disease and distress. If, for example, the sacral chakra running from the lower belly through the body and to the lower back is blocked, the prostate may be starved of vital energy, setting up the conditions that allow cancer to take hold and spread.

Chakra		Parts of Body Energized
#1.	Base	Adrenal glands, kidneys, spinal column
#2.	Sacral	Sex glands, reproductive system
#3.	Solar plexus	Pancreas, nervous system, gallbladder, stomach, liver
#4.	Heart	Thymus gland, heart, blood, circulatory system
#5.	Throat	Thyroid gland, larynx, lungs, breathing and speaking apparatus, alimentary canal
#6.	Head	Pituitary gland, lower brain, nervous system, ears, nose, and left eye
#7.	Crown	Pineal gland, upper brain, right eye

Just as they energize the physical body, the chakras also nurture our psychological aspects. The major chakras energize our will, feeling, and mental centers, all three of which must be strong if we are to enjoy psychological health. The chakras also allow different aspects of self-awareness to develop during the appropriate stages of life, and connect energy to our non-physical bodies.

CHAKRAS AND THE UNIVERSAL ENERGY FLOW

This energy that the chakras channel in and through the body is generally called the *universal energy force.* The universal energy force simultaneously comes from elsewhere and springs from within you; it both penetrates and surrounds you; it is every thing in the universe and it is, at the same time, uniquely you. It penetrates and pervades all space and all objects, whether living or not, flowing from object to object as it connects one to all.

We take this energy from the universe to sustain ourselves, and we give it back to sustain everyone and everything else. Energy is freely exchanged and shared between all things in the universe, living and non-living, without being diminished. Unlike the energy we use to power our appliances and run our cars, the universal energy force is self-sustaining. It breaks the Second Law of Thermodynamics, which states that you cannot take more energy out of something or someone than you have put in; in other words, energy is constantly being "used up," and we must look for more. But the universal energy force is self-renewing, constantly giving birth to more energy.

This energy is normally described as looking like light, or an *aura* emanating to/from the body. Although it's organized into distinct layers or *bodies*, its appearance and structure varies from person to person, even from day to day and moment to moment in each person. And each layer within the energy force surrounding and springing from your body is composed of swirls, points, lines, and webs. Some of the light is pulsating and some is steady, some is moving while some is stationary. The aura creates the body, not vice versa; therefore, it has a profound effect on the health of the body.

The chakras (including the major, minor, and lesser chakras, as well as the acupuncture points) are conduits through which the universal energy force flows into and out of our aura. The chakras act as "antennas" or "valves," controlling the flow of energy. When our valves, or chakras, are open, we take in lots of health-giving energy. We are conscious of the universe and our connection to it; we feel that we are a part of the universe. But when our valves are closed, when the flow of energy is restricted, we become diseased. Just as the human heart suffers when blood cannot flow freely through the coronary arteries, so the human body and being suffer when energy cannot flow through the chakras.

WHEN ENERGY FLOWS THROUGH YOUR CHAKRAS

When energy flows freely through the chakras, the associated benefits will likely be:

#1: Base. You have a strong will to live in the physical world. You radiate power and vitality.

#2A: Pubic. You give and receive physical and sexual pleasure with ease and joy.

#2B: Sacral center. You are filled with sexual energy.

#3A: Solar plexus. You feel that you belong to the universe, that you are at home. Your emotional life is fulfilling but not overwhelming.

#3B: Diaphragmatic center. You have a strong desire to keep your physical body as healthy as possible, and you work hard to accomplish this goal.

#4A: Heart. You have a great desire to love, and you love life, people, animals, and the universe with ease.

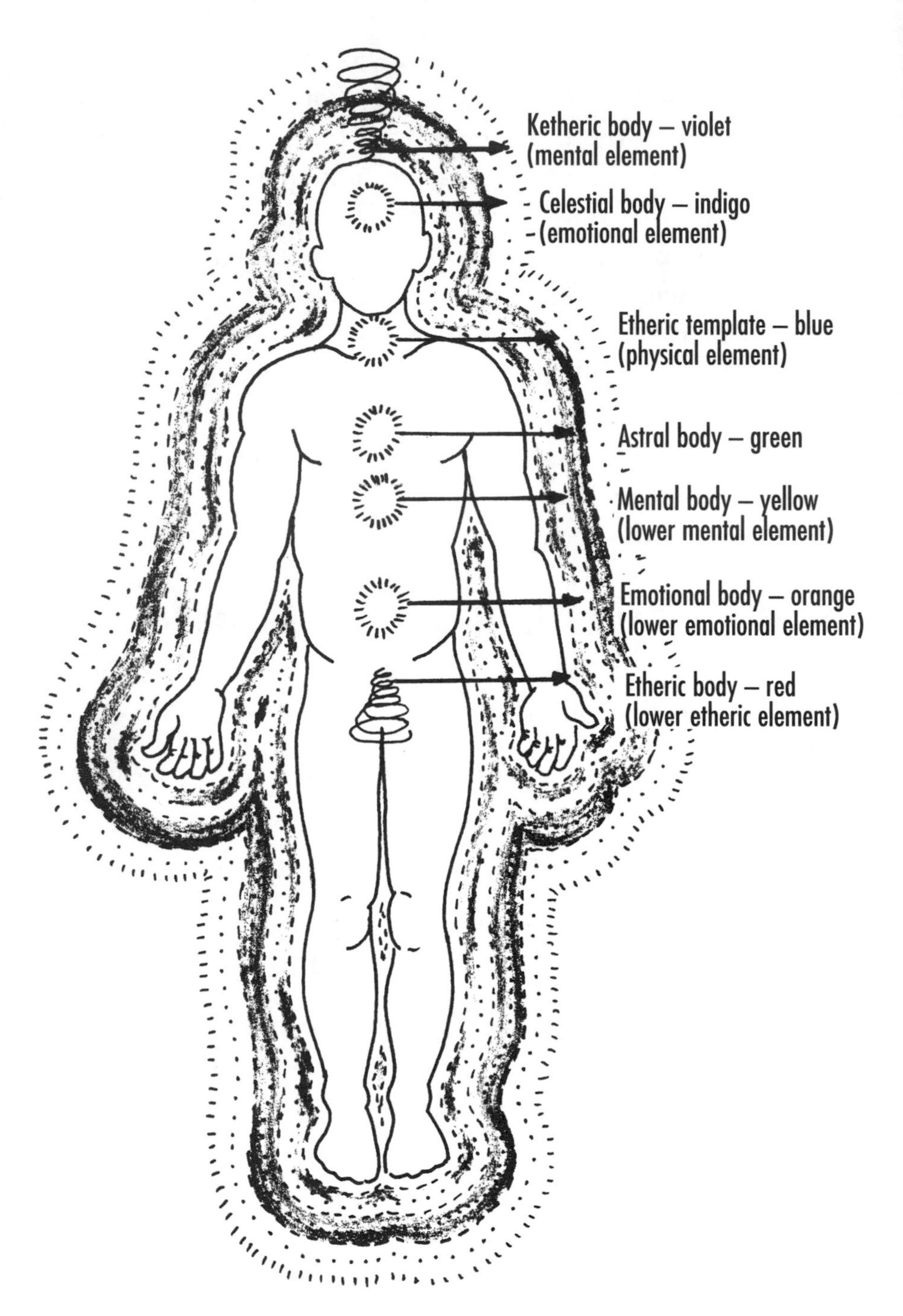

Figure 11-2. The seven aural bodies.

Each layer in the "aura" or life force emanating into our bodies is linked to a chakra.

The first layer (red), linked to the first chakra, is associated with physical sensations and physical functioning.

The second layer (orange), linked to the second chakra, is associated with feelings and emotions.

The third layer (yellow), linked to the third chakra, is associated with linear thinking.

The fourth layer (green), linked to the fourth chakra, is associated with humanity and love.

The fifth layer (blue), linked to the fifth chakra, is associated with expression of ourselves and our higher consciousness.

The sixth layer (indigo), linked to the sixth chakra, is associated with love of life and the universe.

The seventh layer (violet), linked to the seventh chakra, is associated with higher consciousness and integration of mind, body, and spirit.

Each succeeding layer springs from all the previous layers, incorporating all that has come before and adding to the body. Thus, the second layer includes all that was in the first, the third includes all that was in the second, and so on.

A blocked aura will manifest in an illness in the physical body.

#4B: Will center. You believe that you can accomplish the things you set out to do. Your positive attitude encourages others to help you achieve your goals.

#5A: Throat. You take responsibility for your life. You understand that success in any aspect of life is up to you, and do not blame others for your shortcomings. You are able to receive nourishment.

#5B: Professional center. You are well suited to your profession, and derive a lot of satisfaction from your work.

#6A: Forehead. You are able to clearly visualize and understand mental concepts, and work your way through problems.

#6B: Mental executive center. You are able to turn your thoughts into successful actions.

#7: Crown. You feel that your physical body, mind, emotions, and spirit are well integrated, and that you are connected to the universe.

WHAT HINDERS THE FLOW OF ENERGY?

Ideally, the chakras are wide open, allowing energy to flow between the universe and the body. At the end of each chakra, which is called the *chakral heart* or *root,* are "valves" that regulate the exchange of energy. If the valves are wide open the energy flows freely. Trained energy healers can see the energy moving into the chakral valves; it looks like a little tornado or whirlpool swirling right above the openings to the chakra. If the universal energy is flowing into the chakra, the "tornado" is swirling in a clockwise direction; if the energy is moving out of the body, the "tornado" rotates counterclockwise.

Unfortunately, our chakras are not always wide open; the universal energy does not always flow freely into our physical and aural bodies. In many people, one or more chakras are closed, partially blocked, or torn, and the two-way flow of energy is impeded. Things that can disrupt the chakral valves include predispositions, unhappy events in life—even surgeries and physical injuries to the body.

Predispositions: Every single cell in the human body contains DNA, the master blueprint that determines our sex, hair and eye color, body type, native intelligence, and other physical and mental characteristics. We also have "spiritual DNA," the blueprint for our life patterns, embedded in the seventh aural layer (the ketheric level). Much of the information written into our DNA is fixed. You can't, for example, change your eye color. But the instructions in our spiritual DNA only set the *patterns* of our lives; they do not fix the events or the outcome. Our will is free, our choices are our own. (In fact, what we do and what we think throughout life continually "edits" our spiritual DNA.)

Our spiritual DNA sets our life's work, or task. Before a person is conceived, he or she meets with their spirit guide to plan out the coming physical incarnation and to determine what is to be accomplished. The person-to-be may need to learn how to handle money, how to give and receive love, how to deal with loss gracefully, how to accept success, etc. Our goals are written into our spiritual DNA. So are our general patterns of thought and action, as well as our chakral predispositions.

Imagine, for example, that your task in this life is to develop a strong will to live: to be physically, mentally, and emotionally vibrant and robust. You might be born with a weak first chakra, the chakra that relates to your will to live. Your task in this lifetime is to deal with your will to live. As you do so, your first chakra will strengthen, and more energy will flow into your will.

Unhappy events in life: We have many physical defenses against unpleasant experiences: we step back, we hold up our hands to defend ourselves, we run away if necessary. We also defend ourselves against unhappy emotional events, shying away from people who hurt us, avoiding situations that have been distressing in the past, sometimes even hiding in our rooms rather than risk pain. These real-life defenses are mimicked on the energy level as our chakras close themselves to the flow of unpleasant energy.

Suppose, for example, a youngster is rebuffed time and time again when he tries to be loving to others. He may then feel a subconscious need to stop being so loving. His heart chakra closes up in response, choking off the flow of energy to his heart. That "solves" his immediate problem, for he will no longer reach out with love to others, and he will no longer be rejected. But without a steady flow of universal energy through his heart chakra, he becomes susceptible to physical diseases of the heart, blood, and circulatory system. If, on the other hand, someone feels that a hostile world filled with hostile people is determined to prevent her from succeeding in life, she may close off chakra #4B, which energizes one's will to deal confidently and lovingly with the outer world. With this chakra closed off, she feels as if she cannot succeed unless she runs right over people, trampling even loved ones underfoot.

Physical injury: Trauma to the body can upset a chakra, especially if that chakra is already weak. If a child who does not feel secure in his mother's love falls off his bicycle and damages his coccyx (tail bone), the combination of insecurity and physical injury may further damage his first chakra (which relates to the will to live and is located near the tail bone).

WHEN THE CHAKRAS ARE BLOCKED

Both the physical and aural bodies suffer when a chakra is blocked. The resulting disease can take many different forms, and the distress may be major or minor. But distress is inevitable, whether it is physical, mental, or emotional, and it will affect the physical body if not resolved and released.

When the chakra is blocked and energy flow through it is disrupted, the result will likely be:

#1: Base. You will lack physical vitality. You will avoid physical activity, may be sickly, and will not have a strong physical presence.

#2A: Pubic. You will have difficulty in your love relations with the opposite sex.

#2B: Sacral center. You will not have much interest in sex, and may find sexual relations difficult or unsatisfying.

#3A: Solar plexus. Your emotions and feelings will be weak. You will find it difficult to become passionate about anything.

#3B: Diaphragmatic center. You will find it difficult to heal yourself.

#4A: Heart. You will have difficulty loving, and will feel unloved.

#4B: Will center. You will believe that the only way to survive is to step on other people, most of whom are out to "get" you or stand in your way.

#5A: Throat. You will not develop a mature ability to take responsibility for your life, preferring instead to blame others for your problems and failings. You will be unable to recognize and accept good things offered to you.

#5B: Professional center. You will not derive satisfaction or self-esteem from your work. Instead, you may develop an excessive and false pride in your work to cover the lack of satisfaction.

#6A: Forehead. You will have difficulty generating useful, positive, creative ideas.

#6B: Mental executive center. You will have difficulty turning your ideas into reality.

#7: Crown. You will lack spirituality, feeling unconnected to the universe and others.

The front and back part (or "A" and "B") of chakras 2 through 6 work together. If one end is obstructed, the flow of energy throughout the entire chakra is hampered. Opening one end significantly wider than the other is not as helpful as opening them both, even to a lesser degree.

CLOUDING THE AURA

The flow of universal energy through the chakras can be diminished or interrupted in several different ways. When that happens, the physical body is likely to be harmed, and the aural bodies suffer, also.

The energy system that flows in and around the body controls our health.

The aural layers are more than lights emanating into your physical body; they are bodies unto themselves, each containing all the forms and elements of the physical body. The seven layers, or *bodies,* begin in the same space as your physical body, with each successive layer reaching out a little farther from the physical body than the previous ones. And it's in the aural layers that our emotions take tangible form.

The thoughts we think, the emotions we experience, and the actions we take are given form in the aural layers. (A healer skilled in the art of viewing the aural layers can literally see dark clouds of anger in the aural bodies, or brighter-colored areas of happiness and love.) There's a reversal on the aural level: Our physical body, which seems so solid and real on this plane of existence, is not tangible on the aural level. And our thoughts and emotions, which we can't see or touch on this physical plane, take "solid" form in the aural bodies.

The thought bodies remain in place, growing stronger or weaker as you put more or less emphasis on them. If you're often angry, your aural bodies will be filled with anger. Other people can sense the thought forms in your aura, and react accordingly. That's why we tend to shy away from angry people, or are drawn to friendly ones: We sense the emotions in their aura.

You created the aural thought forms with your thoughts, emotions, and actions. Now they continually re-create you—which is great because you can change those thoughts and change your life (i.e., heal). They're around you all the time; it's as if you bump into them every time you move. When you bump into an angry thought form you may lash out at your spouse, children, or a friend, without knowing why. When you bump into a thought form labeled "I'm helpless," you may suddenly find yourself unable to complete a task. And when you bump into a happy and energetic thought form, you may suddenly find yourself attacking a problem with renewed energy and joy.

Our energy fields can be cleansed to maintain optimum health by balancing the chakras.

In some people the thought forms are of a similar kind (for example, optimistic), and are well integrated with each other and the person's overall consciousness. Such individuals are mentally and emotionally steady. In other people, whose auras are distorted by closed chakras, the thought forms are not well integrated with each other or the person's general consciousness. These people can bounce rapidly from emotion to emotion, bewildering themselves and others with their lack of consistency. They can even get caught in a loop, hopelessly bouncing from one thought to another until they are emotionally—and often physically—exhausted. Ricocheting from "I'm hopeless" to "I'm going to leave her" to "Nothing ever works for me" to "It's all my fault" to "I'm a loser" to "If I don't act now I'll never settle this" to "I'm really angry" to "It's her fault" to "I can't change things" to "I don't know what to do," then back to the beginning, the individual finds it absolutely impossible to decide what to do and stick to a plan. How can they, when they're thrown from one emotional state and thought to another, never settling down long enough to take stock of the situation, prepare a plan of action, and follow through?

CHAKRA BALANCING

Fortunately, it is possible to change our thought forms, to restore the flow of energy and cleanse our auras. There are many meditations and exercises designed to balance, open, and renew the chakras. I recommend the ones by Lazaris, available on tape by calling Concept Synergy at (800) 678-2356; and the "chakra dancing" taught by Dr. Susan Lange, O.M.D., L.Ac., of the Meridian Center in Santa Monica, California, (310) 395-9525.

You can keep your aura in tip-top shape by doing regular chakra meditations to balance your energy. Since your aura in turn creates your body, this will balance your physical body energies and facilitate optimum health. Keep yourself in balance with daily or weekly meditation sessions of 15 to 20 minutes. The sessions are a fun, energizing, easy way to tune into and release the blockages that are or will eventually affect your health. You can also work with energy healers. The most advanced and effective are graduates of the four-year Barbara Ann Brennen School of Healing in New York, such as Dr. Susan Lange of Santa Monica.

CHAPTER 12

RELEASING THE EMOTIONS THAT CAUSE DISEASE

Emotions? Feelings? Forget it. They're are not manly. Only girls and sissies get "emotional" or cry. In fact, there's something "sick" about a man who cries.

From the time little boys begin to stumble and scrape their knees they're told to "Be a man"—to ignore pain and negative feelings. They're told that "Big boys don't cry." And they learn that disregarding or stuffing down feelings is the "manly" thing to do.

We've come a long way, but a lot of people still believe that only women should express their emotions, and men should "tough it out" when faced with difficult situations. These people think that if a man feels a negative emotion such as fear, anger, embarrassment, or loneliness, he should maintain a calm facade. After all, the reasoning goes, holding onto your feelings may not always be the best or easiest thing to do, but it can't hurt. The reality is quite different.

Young boys are taught to be "tough" – not to cry or feel – creating disease in later life.

Of course, men *do* have feelings—feelings that can be just as painful as those suffered by women. When these feelings are not recognized and expressed they become blockages in the body, impeding the flow of blood and energy. This is not just a theory. Numerous studies have tightly linked the mind and body, proving that poor health is *always* related to unhappy thoughts. We cannot be completely healthy until we clear away any emotional blockages, so releasing them is important "medicine."

Since men tend to stuff their negative feelings about sex and sexuality into their prostates, this gland becomes an easy target for enlargement (benign prostate hypertrophy), infection (prostatitis), and cancer. That's why clearing emotional blocks is a vital step in the process of healing from prostate cancer—or any other disease.

THE PHYSICAL DEPENDS UPON THE EMOTIONS

The human mind and body are intimately connected. What happens in the mind immediately registers in your physical being, and what goes on in the body is instantly recognized in your mind. It cannot be any other way, for mind and body are merely different aspects of the unity that is you. Think of the mind/body as a spider web: a little vibration on any part of the web shakes the entire thing.

A new branch of medical science called *PNI* (psychoneuroimmunology) is devoted to studying the mind/body links. Described below are just a few of the many PNI studies proving that there is no separation between mind and body.

Early evidence of the mind/body connection surfaced in the U.S. back in the 1960s, as our rocket scientists were successfully sending one rocket after another into outer space. But even as the space program was fulfilling one goal after another, the federal government was terribly worried. For some unknown reason, their brilliant young rocket scientists were dying off at an alarming rate. Some thought that the Russians were to blame, but Dr. Robert Elliot, sent to investigate, identified the real culprit: FUD.

The physical is governed by the emotional.

Dr. Elliot showed that the scientists were dying because they were filled with *fear, uncertainty,* and *doubt—FUD* for short. You see, after every successful launch program the government laid off a large number of scientists and technicians. (The rockets were up in the air, so many of the scientists who put them there were no longer needed.) And though they were very talented, their work skills were very specific—they knew about rockets, and that knowledge didn't translate well to civilian jobs. They couldn't find jobs that paid as well, or were as prestigious, when they were laid off. Many of them wound up bagging groceries in markets, hoping to be hired on again when—or if—a new space program started up. Feeling tremendous pressure to perform, and constant fear that they would soon be unable to pay their mortgages, an alarming number of the young scientists began to suffer from necrosis (death) of heart muscle. *Their fear, uncertainty, and doubt literally killed them.*

These unfortunate scientists served as unwitting human counterparts to laboratory rats who were deliberately subjected to FUD. As an experiment, a group of rats was locked in a cage and forced to listen to a tape recording of a cat that was chasing rats. The poor rats didn't understand that this was only a record. They thought that a real cat was going to burst into their cage and attack them any minute. They had no place to run, nowhere to hide. They were filled with fear, uncertainty, and doubt—and their FUD killed them, just as it did the rocket scientists.

Another early study of the mind/body connection had startling results. Conducted by a team of scientists at the University of Tennessee Center for Health Sciences,[1] the program involved 32 patients suffering from chronic, intractable pain that had not been relieved by the standard measures of the day. The researchers began by measuring the endorphin levels in the patients' spinal fluids. (Endorphins are natural morphine-like substances found in the human body that block certain pain signals and elevate mood. The endorphins play a crucial role in our ability to block unnecessary pain.) After measuring the endorphin levels, the scientists gave each patient a placebo, a medically worthless "sugar pill." But the patients were told that they were receiving a strong medicine, and that they would soon feel better.

Of the 32 patients, 14 reported that they did indeed feel better. That's not surprising, for the placebo effect works 30 to 40% of the time, proving that the mind does have an influence on the body. But here's the astonishing part: When the 14 people who responded to the placebo were retested, it was found that their endorphin levels *had risen!* They felt better because there were more pain-blocking endorphins in their bodies. What caused the endorphins to rise? Not the placebo—that was a worthless

[1] Fox A, Fox B. 1095. *DLPA to end chronic pain and depression.* New York: Pocket Books, p. 187.

sugar pill. The "miracle medicine" was the patients' positive thinking, their strong belief that they would feel better. *Their thoughts* were what pushed their endorphin levels up, and *their thoughts* were what quelled their pain. Here was strong scientific evidence showing that: (1) positive thinking, as represented by the placebo effect, can make us feel better, and (2) positive thinking makes us feel better by improving our body chemistry.

The Tennessee study wasn't the only one showing that thoughts can alter biochemistry. A later study at the University of California at Los Angeles showed the same thing, in a different way. In this study, actors were instructed to play out happy and sad scenes. These were method actors who tried to "become" the characters they portrayed—to experience their feelings, and to be as happy, sad, angry, puzzled, etc., as their characters were.

Before, during, and after the presentation of the happy and sad scenes, researchers took various measurements of the actors' bodies, including a small amount of saliva. The saliva sample allowed them to measure the *T-cell proliferation rate,* which is one indicator of how rapidly the immune system responds to a challenge.

When the actors acted out the happy scenes, their immune systems grew stronger (as indicated by a higher T-cell proliferation rate). But when the actors acted sad, their immune systems weakened. Here was strong, direct proof of the link between mind and body, of the powerful influence thoughts have on the immune system. And not only do our thoughts influence our biochemistry, but we can choose which thoughts we focus on. The actors were only pretending to be happy or sad, but it didn't matter.

> *The mind doesn't know if the thoughts are "real" or not. It simply revs up the immune system when it sees happy thoughts, and puts on the health brakes when it sees sad ones. This means that if we tell ourselves that we are happy, we will be healthier.*

Of course, the opposite is also true: acting sad can weaken the immune system. So, feeling sad, anxious, or fearful can have a powerfully negative effect on the body.

The harmful effects of negative thoughts were demonstrated in a study of 20 women undergoing chemotherapy for ovarian cancer. The powerful chemotherapy drugs made them nauseous, weakened their immune systems, and had other unpleasant side effects. Simply returning to the hospital for another treatment, *just walking through the door,* made some of the women feel nauseous—before they received the medicine. That was not surprising. After all, the stomach has long been considered the "barometer of one's emotions." We often feel our stomach tying into knots or feeling queasy in unpleasant situations, or in situations where we expect to soon be uncomfortable. That their stomachs became upset when the women returned to the hospital for their chemotherapy sessions was expected, but this was not: Their immune systems weakened *before they were given the drugs!* The thought forms in their minds (anticipation of what they knew was going to happen) weakened their immune systems *before any chemotherapy was given.*

Just how powerful is the mind/body link? How sick or healthy can we make ourselves with our thoughts? One of the most powerful pieces of evidence linking mind and body came from a skeptic of the mind/body connection concept. David Speigel, M.D., of Stanford University, had believed that psychological counseling and other forms of social support could improve the quality of life for victims of advanced breast cancer, but could not help them actually live longer. However, in the groundbreaking report on his ten-year study in the prestigious medical journal, *Lancet*,[2] Dr. Speigel reported that women who were placed in support groups lived twice as long as women who were not. (Both groups received the same treatment otherwise.) Here was strong evidence that the kind of supportive, positive thoughts engendered by caring friends in a support group could actually lengthen life.

Emotional blocks in the body become physical blocks, creating disease.

Findings by Dr. Philip dovetail nicely, with a fascinating study of the link between joyful anticipation and health.[3] The study involved Jewish men and Passover, the holiday that celebrates the liberation of the early Israelites from Egyptian slavery. This is an important time for older Jewish men, who lead their families in the celebration. A 1990 report in the *Journal of the American Medical Association* described how mortality among Jewish men dropped significantly shortly before Passover, then jumped way up just after Passover, before settling down to normal rates. The researchers concluded that the men's joyful anticipation, and their eager desire to lead the cele-

---

[2] Speigel, D., et al. 1989. Effect of psychosocial treatment on survival of patients with metastatic breast cancer. *Lancet* 2(8668):888–91.

[3] Philip, D. and D. Smith. Postponement of death until a symbolically meaningful occasion. *Journal of the American Medical Association*, 4/1/90, 363(14):1942–51.

bration, revved up their immune systems and other natural defenses enough to keep them alive, at least until the party was over. This phenomenon is also common with anniversaries, birthdays, children's weddings, and other happily anticipated occasions.

THOUGHTS AND SPECIFIC DISEASES

There is no doubt that the mind and body are one, and what happens in one aspect of your being always affects the other. A great many studies have shown that certain types of thoughts, feelings, or emotions are connected with health and disease. For example:

- Studies of women suffering from cancer of the breast and cervix showed that being joyful and optimistic leads to a better outcome and longer life than being full of negative emotions.[4]

- The Chicago Western Electric Study, which followed approximately 2,000 workers for 17 years, linked depression to cancer. Workers who were significantly depressed according to scores on the MMPI Depression Scale were more than twice as likely to develop cancer as those who were not.[5]

---

[4] Antoni, M.H., Goodkin K. 1988. Host moderator variables in the promotion of cervical neoplasia: I. Personality facets. *J Psychosomatic Res* 32:327–38. Goodkin, K. et al. 1986. Stress and hopelessness in the promotion of cervical intra-epithelial neoplasia to invasive squamous cell carcinoma of the cervix. *J Psychosomatic Res* 30:67–76. Levy, S.M. et al. 1988. Survival hazards analysis in first recurrent breast cancer patients: Seven-year follow-up. *Psychosomatic Med* 50:520–28.

[5] Schekelle, R.B., et al. 1981. Psychological depression and 17-year risk of death from cancer. *Psychosomatic Med* 43:117–25.

■ It's well known that after the death of a spouse, the survivor's immune system is usually weakened, remaining weak for up to six months before regaining its strength. During this time, the grieving survivor is more susceptible to a host of ailments.

■ An interesting study published in the *Journal of Psychosomatic Research* in 1975 linked anger to breast cancer. Specifically, the researchers found that the ability to express anger was important. Women with benign tumors of the breast were better able to express their anger than women with malignant breast tumors.[6] It seems that the inability to express emotions, especially anger, is a "germ" that harms cancer patients by allowing or even encouraging their cancers to grow.[7] Undiscovered anger can also be problematic. It has been suggested that some men harbor anger in their prostates from circumcisions performed on them as babies that they do not even remember.

■ The desire to live can be a powerful medicine. A study published in the *British Journal of Cancer* in 1991 reported that cancer patients with "fighting spirits" lived longer than those who felt that their situation was hopeless.[8]

The desire to live can be a very powerful medicine.

[6] Greer, S., Morris, T. 1975. Psychological attributes of women who develop breast cancer: A controlled study. *J Psychosomatic Res* 19:147–53.

[7] McKinnon, W., et al. 1989. Chronic stress, leukocyte subpopulations, and humoral response to latent viruses. *Health Psychology* 8:389–402.

[8] Greer, S., et al. 1979. Psychological response to breast cancer: Effect on outcome. *Lancet* 2(8146):785–87.

■ "Ornery-ness" is also like a medicine. Patients who were perceived by their doctors and nurses as uncooperative and troublesome tended to live longer than the more cooperative and "better" patients.[9] These "ornery" patients were often the ones who made the most demands on their doctors and nurses, who insisted on maintaining control over their lives and directing their care. In other words, they were the ones who took responsibility for their own recovery and did *not* give up.

■ Even *pretending* that you are well, in the face of all evidence to the contrary, is more healthful than throwing in the towel.[10] In fact, a 1989 study published in the *Journal of Psychosomatic Research* found that denial was like a medicine for women with operable breast cancer, and could be used to predict good results.[11] (I don't advocate denial. In fact, I argue for tackling prostate cancer and other diseases head-on. But these scientific studies showing that denial has medicinal effects—to the extent that it creates a more positive attitude—emphasize the power of the mind over the body.)

The evidence is clear: positive, hopeful, joyful, optimistic thoughts, *even when there is no objective basis for*

---

[9] Derogatis, L.R., et al. 1979. Psychological coping mechanisms and survival time in metastatic breast cancer. *JAMA* 242:1504–8.

[10] Greer, S., et al. 1991. Evaluation of adjuvant psychological therapy for clinically referred cancer patients. *Brit J Cancer* 63(2):257–601. Greer, S. et al. 1992. Adjuvant psychological therapy for patients with cancer: A prospective randomised trial. *Brit Med J* 304(6828):675–80.

[11] Dean, C., Surtees, P.G. 1989. Do psychological factors predict survival in breast cancer? *J Psychosomatic Res* 33:561–69.

these thoughts, are a powerful medicine. And being able to express these thoughts make the "medicine" even stronger. On the other hand, thoughts of anger, defeat, hopelessness, and helplessness are like "germs," growing stronger when they are unexpressed and unresolved.

I'd like to make it clear, however, that the fact that negative thoughts can cause disease does not mean that those who are ill are bad people, that they brought their diseases upon themselves or deserve to suffer. That's not true. *Those who are ailing are not to blame for their troubles.* We should assist all who are suffering in every way possible. However, we must understand that what we feel, think, say, and do has a profound influence on our mental, physical, and spiritual health. We have the power to tilt the scales toward health or illness with our thoughts and feelings, and it behooves us to use that power wisely.

REMOVING EMOTIONAL BLOCKS

Just as the body must be cleansed of toxins, parasites, and other physical items that block the flow of energy and blood throughout the body, prevent the lymph system from removing waste products, and otherwise interfere with good health, so must anger, depression, fear, resentment, and other emotional and spiritual toxins be released. We must rid ourselves of the negative feelings that act as dams in our bodies, blocking the flow of energy and blood in and out of our prostates and other body tissue, weakening our immune systems, and inviting cancer and numerous other diseases. Unhappy thoughts about sex and sexuality are especially dangerous for men, for these tend to be stored in the prostate, bringing disease to the gland.

A happy mind is a healthy body.

Fortunately, there are many ways to remove emotional blocks. These include psychotherapy, bodywork, chakra clearing, homeopathics, massage, exercise, and meditation. There are also techniques taught by Wayne Dyer, Deepak Chopra, M.D., and other leaders in the field. There are spiritual centers such as Unity Church and the Church of Religious Science. Lazaris and other spirits have worked wonders. We've already discussed chakra clearing, bodywork, exercise, and massage, and most of us are familiar with psychotherapy. Let's take a brief look at a few other approaches to emotional clearing.

Bach Flower Remedies: Edward Bach, a medical doctor and bacteriologist, developed this system of healing based upon the idea that people would heal when they were treated according to their unique personality traits. He felt that conflicts between our higher self and our personality are the source of illness, with the unhappy emotions that are suppressed leading to physical disease. For example, a man who feels resentful at being poorly treated at work and suppresses this feeling—in conflict with the open expression necessary to be in the flow with his higher self—is bound to become ill. Treating his symptoms may help for a little while, but unless his resentment is cleared away he will remain ill—and invariably become worse.

Bach felt the solution to these problems was the vibration of flower essences, which he believed would encourage release and help rebalance. Bach Flower Remedies consist of drops made from individual flowers, which are mixed with water and consumed several times a day. Elm is useful for those who feel overburdened by their responsibilities, chicory for those who are over-involved with

Fortunately there are many ways to remove emotional blocks.

family and friends, beech for those who are intolerant and ready to find fault with others, and larch for people who are sure that they will fail. Several varieties of flower essences are now found in most health food stores.

Lazaris and other spirit guides: Many spirit guides offer valuable insight and help with healing. One such guide is Lazaris. Rather than telling people what to do, Lazaris believes that deep down, people know what is best for them. The problem is that they've created hurdles and then forgotten they did so. They continually trip over the hurdles despite the fact that they, the builders of the obstacles, know best how to overcome them. Thus, Lazaris makes suggestions, pointing out helpful ways of approaching and dealing with the reality that you have constructed. Rather than telling you what to do, Lazaris explains how you can understand how you have constructed your life, and then suggests 15 or 20 different ways to change it. In a sense, Lazaris is like a mirror, allowing you to see yourself more clearly, and to see into yourself, discovering the hurdles you have created and ways of removing or getting around them. (See the appendix for information on Lazaris's tapes and books.)

Lazaris has been my principal teacher since I was introduced to him in 1987. Almost immediately, my life began to change in major, positive ways. Magic entered my life. My business and personal relationships improved dramatically. Business became much more profitable and fun. My spiritual learning accelerated dramatically. I began to release the enormous tension and rigidity stored in my body and to feel better about myself than I ever had. This has, of course, been a process, one that continues at present, becoming ever more subtle.

Meditation: An ancient healing technique, meditation has been used to treat a variety of ailments, from anxiety to cancer. There are different techniques of meditation, including listening to a recording, silently repeating a word (mantra) over and over, and counting your breaths. Whatever the specific technique, the goal is to cleanse your mind of everyday thoughts and troubles in order to relax mind and body. Biofeedback and other studies have shown that meditation favorably alters brain waves, slows respiration and heart rate, lowers blood pressure in many people, decreases oxygen consumption, and otherwise rests the body and mind. Studies show that people who meditate enjoy better sleep, relationships, attitudes toward work and life, sense of purpose and tranquility, and health in general.

Meditation is especially helpful in combating the detrimental effects of stress, especially the "fight-or-flight" response. Designed to make us instantly fight or run for survival when faced with danger, the fight-or-flight response floods our bodies with cortisone and other powerful chemicals. That's good, because it saves our lives. But the cortisone and other substances have side effects. If they are present in our bodies in large amounts for long periods of time, they can compromise the immune system and harm the body in many other ways. That wouldn't be a problem0except that most of us trigger the fight-or-flight response far too often, at inappropriate times. We trigger it when we get angry at clerks or the IRS, when someone insults or slights us, when a car cuts us off, when the utility bill goes up. None of these are life-threatening problems, but we threaten our own lives by allowing the release of massive amounts of these stress chemicals. With no one to fight and nowhere to run, the chemicals of stress simmer inside our bodies, slowly destroying our health. Meditation protects and restores our health by relieving stress and allowing the chemicals to be cleared out of our body.

In the 1970s Dr. Herbert Benson of Harvard University studied meditation and demonstrated that it effectively counteracts the effects of the fight-or-flight response. He also developed a "secular" form of meditation, not tied to any religious philosophy, which he called the *relaxation response.* The technique is simple:

- Sit in a quiet, comfortable position with your eyes closed.
- Beginning at your feet and working your way up your body to your head, relax your muscles. Silently tell yourself that your feet are completely relaxed, your ankles are relaxed, your calves are relaxed, etc.
- Pay attention to your breathing as you inhale and exhale through your nose. Say the word *one* silently to yourself with each exhalation.
- Continue breathing easily and naturally, saying "one" with each exhalation, for 10 to 20 minutes. When you're finished, sit quietly with your eyes closed for a few minutes, then sit for a few more minutes with your eyes open. (Do not get up immediately after meditating.)

Don't worry if at first you have trouble clearing your mind during the meditation, or if you are not as relaxed as you would like to be. As you keep working at it, practicing once or twice daily, you'll become better able to relax.

Meditation relieves stress, allowing harmful chemicals to be released, and gives us insights on more effective ways to live our lives.

Professional help: You can access practitioners who can assist you with clearing emotional blocks. See the appendix, under "Emotional Blocks, Clearing," for several organizations and practitioners. Notable among them is Art Schaar, who practices the "One-Brain" system that clears many years of emotions in a single session.

Unity Church and the Church of Religious Science: These and similar churches, found nationwide, combine many traditional religious values with positive thinking. Pray to God for guidance and comfort, they say, but praise yourself, and recognize the tremendous goodness that is and always will be within you. Never doubt that God always helps you. He gave you the ability to succeed, which means that you can succeed if you put your mind to the task. Unity, Religious Science, and similar churches offer many opportunities for you to face and conquer your fears as you reach for success.

Visualization: Visualization is based on a simple yet powerful notion: What we "see" in our heads, with our mind's eye, has just as powerful an influence on our health as our thoughts and words. In fact, mental pictures may be even stronger than words, for the images we conjure in our minds are often more startling and evocative than anything we could describe.

After noting that some cancer patients seemed to survive for no reason other than they had a strong desire to live, O. Carl Simonton, M.D., and his wife, Stephanie Matthews-Simonton, began using visualization to treat cancer patients. As part of their program for assisting cancer patients who are undergoing "standard" therapies such as radiation or chemotherapy, the Simontons offer the following guidelines for effective visualization (adapted from *Alternatives in Cancer Therapy*):[12]

1. Visualize the cancer cells as being weak and confused—perhaps as a pile of sand that can easily be kicked over, or a stack of beer cans that falls apart when struck by a baseball.

2. See your treatment as being very powerful. Perhaps you visualize your treatment as a foot kicking apart the pile of sand, or a baseball knocking over the stack of cans.

3. With your mind's eye, notice that healthy cells have no trouble repairing themselves if they are slightly damaged by your treatment.

4. Imagine a powerful army of white blood cells ready to attack and destroy your cancer. You might visualize an actual army, with soldiers and tanks and jet fighters. Perhaps you see a bunch of Pac Men gobbling up the cancer cells, or thousands of baseballs knocking down stacks of beer cans.

---

[12] Pelton, R., Overholser, L. 1994. *Alternatives in Cancer Therapy.* New York: Fireside, p. 234.

5. See how eager and aggressive your "army" is. It can't wait to rip the cancer to pieces.

6. Now watch, with your mind's eye, as the dead and defeated cancer cells are kicked out of your body.

7. See yourself as being healthy, and doing all the things you love to do.

Positive, joyful, optimistic thoughts, even when there is no objective basis for them, are a powerful medicine.

8. End the visualization session by seeing yourself achieving your goals and living a purposeful, happy, and meaningful life.

Perhaps today's best-known advocate of visualization is Bernie Siegel, M.D., author of *Love, Medicine and Miracles* and *Peace, Love and Healing*. Many others have written extensively about different ways to clear emotional blockages, including Deepak Chopra, M.D., Wayne Dyer, and Louise Hay. Their books are available in most bookstores.

Homeopathy, Lazaris, meditation, visualization, psychotherapy, Unity Church, the Church of Religious Science, and the popular authors listed above all offer helpful techniques for getting in touch with your feelings and clearing away emotional blockages. (See the appendix for information on finding practitioners of these approaches.) As good as they are, however, these techniques are, for most people, only a beginning. Most people need one or more sessions with a professional in order to access their deeper emotions. These deeper, "out-of-reach" emotions in the unconscious are usually the ones causing disease. It is vital to release them.

TWO LEADING MODERN METHODS OF DEEP EMOTIONAL REPROGRAMMING: NLP AND EMDR

Neuro-linguistic programming, or NLP, dates from the mid-1970s and is now a major method of psychology used worldwide. NLP practitioners are widely available to assist in reprogramming old emotions and patterns, which are often a cause of illness as well as less-than-optimum patterns of living and being. This section provides a short introduction to NLP and resources for learning more.

"Neuro" refers to the neurological processes of seeing, hearing, feeling, smelling, and tasting, which form the basic building blocks of our experience. "Linguistic" refers to the ways we use language to represent our experience and communicate with others. "Programming" refers not to computer programming, but rather to the strategies we use to organize these inner processes to produce results.

NLP is based on the belief that the world in which we each live is not the real world. Rather, it is a model of the world that we create unconsciously, and then live in as though it were real. Most human problems derive from these models in our heads, rather than from the world as it really is. As you develop your practical understanding of how these inner models work, you can learn to change unhelpful habits, thoughts, feelings, and beliefs into more useful ones.

Neuro-linguistic programming offers specific, practical ways to make desired changes in the health and behavior of yourself and others. NLP suggests that you ask yourself how you would like to redesign your life, and what you could achieve in both your personal and professional life if you knew how.

One of the leading NLP practitioner-teachers in the U.S. is Anne Linden, M.A., psychotherapist, co-author of *The Enneagram and NLP*, and founder and director of the NLP Center of New York. The Institute can refer you to practitioners worldwide. Call (800) 422-8657 or visit their web site (http://www.nlpcenter.com).

Emotions are your friends, your allies. They are not to be used as excuses to avoid thinking or taking action; rather, they are to be respected and learned from. When you allow yourself to feel something, you are "in process." That process moves you forward so that pretty soon you're feeling something else and moving on.

Sometimes people are afraid that if they "give in" to their emotions, they'll drown in them. Just the opposite is true: giving into them will move you through the tunnel to the light of learning and change at the end. Emotions don't get us into trouble—it's the emotions we have about our emotions that trap us and keep us on a treadmill of negativity and stagnation. Emotions are our teachers and opportunities to learn and change. Listen for the message, and don't kill the messenger!

Eye movement desensitization and reprocessing, or EMDR, is a complex method of psychotherapy that integrates many of the successful elements of a range of therapeutic approaches in combination with eye movements or other forms of rhythmical stimulation in ways that stimulate the brain's information processing system. With EMDR therapy it is unnecessary to delve into decades-old psychological material; rather, by activating the information-processing system of the brain, people can achieve their therapeutic goals at a rapid rate, with recognizable changes that don't disappear over time.

The major significance of EMDR is that it allows the brain to heal its psychological problems at the same rate that the rest of the body is healing its physical ailments. Because EMDR allows mind and body to heal at the same rate, it effectively makes time irrelevant in therapy.

Given its wide application, EMDR promises to be "the therapy of the future." Fourteen controlled studies support the efficacy of EMDR, making it the most thoroughly researched method ever used in the treatment of trauma. Five of the most recent studies with individuals suffering from traumatic events (such as rape, combat, loss of a loved one, accident, and natural disaster) found that after only three EMDR treatment sessions, 84 to 90% of the individuals no longer had post-traumatic stress disorder.

A recent study financed by Kaiser Permanente revealed that EMDR was twice as effective in half the length of time compared to the standard traditional care. However, clients and clinicians should note that EMDR is not a "race." While many people show dramatic response in a very short time, there are also those who progress more slowly, and that slower progression is not abnormal. As in any therapy, we progress at the rate appropriate to us as individuals and to the clinical situation.

The success of EMDR is evidenced by these statements:

> "EMDR therapy has emerged as a procedure to be reckoned with in psychology . . . Almost a million people have been treated . . . Also, further research appears to support the remarkable claims made for EMDR therapy."
>
> – *The Washington Post,* July 21, 1995

"New type of psychotherapy seen as boon to traumatic disorders."

– *The New York Times,* October 26, 1997

"EMDR is the most revolutionary, important method to emerge in psychotherapy in decades."

– Herbert Fensterheim, Ph.D., Cornell University

"EMDR is a powerful new tool for relieving human suffering; its study opens new doors to our understanding of the mind. It is one of the most significant advances since the introduction of psychopharmacologic drugs."

– Steven Lazrove, M.D., Yale University

Dr. Francine Shapiro is the founder of EMDR; director of the EMDR Institute in Palo Alto, California; and received the 1994 Distinguished Scientific Achievement Award from the California Psychological Association. Dr. Shapiro explains: "Regardless of their primary psychological orientation, clinicians generally agree that most psychological complaints stem from the impact of earlier life experiences. The EMDR protocols guide clinicians to utilize specific history-taking procedures to ascertain (a) what earlier life experiences have contributed to the symptomatology, (b) what present triggers elicit the disturbance, and (c) what behaviors and skills are necessary to prepare the client for appropriate future action.

"For instance, the clinician identifies the specific events which taught the client such negative self-assessments as

I'm not good enough, I'm not lovable, I can't succeed, I'm worthless, I can't trust, etc. The assumption is that these earlier life experiences are stored in a dysfunctional fashion, contributing to the client's inappropriate reactions in the present. Consistent with recent conjectures regarding memory (van der Kolk, 1994), it is believed that experiences which provide the underpinnings of pathology have been stored without sufficient processing. When these earlier experiences are brought to mind, they retain a significant level of disturbance, manifested by both emotions and physical sensations. Reprocessing these experiences with EMDR allows the client to gain insight, shift cognitive assessment, incorporate ecological emotions and body reactions, as well as adopt more adaptive behaviors."

Information about qualified clinicians in your area can be obtained by contacting:

EMDR Institute, Inc.
(512) 451-4777
www.emdr.com

The importance of clearing emotional blocks in the healing of cancer is well established. Many methods of accessing and clearing those old stuck emotions have been presented for your use. You will need to include some form of emotional clearing in your healing plan outlined in Chapter 15.

CHAPTER 13

ENHANCE YOUR SEX LIFE FOR A HEALTHIER PROSTATE

Good health—and a healthy prostate—depend on a regular, happy sex life. The prostate is a muscle. Like all muscles, it must be used if it is to remain strong. Regular use also helps to cleanse the gland. It's no accident that the highest incidence of prostate cancer occurs in celibate men. For some men, once a week may the right amount of sex, while for others it is once or more a day, or once a month. There is no magic number that guarantees good health. It's best just to do what feels good and doesn't cause fatigue afterwards. But simply having sex is not enough. Ideally, sex is more than a physical act—it is a loving union with your partner.

Unfortunately, many men are not having as much sex as they would like—or need—for a healthy physical and emotional life. Not from want of trying, but from lack of understanding. When a man first meets the person who will become his lover and/or spouse, he can practically feel the sexual energy in the air; it's never-ending, it's self-generating. Being near this person, simply thinking about them, increases his desire. And, like him, his partner is easily aroused. With time, however, the sexual energy

The prostate is a muscle, and must be used in order to remain strong.

seems to fade away. Once at high tide, it's now at low ebb. Where before, both were almost always interested in enjoying sex, now it seems that one or both of them are constantly tired or not interested. Sex doesn't have the attraction it once had. The energy that drew them into it, and grew from it, has dissipated. And as sexual energy fades from a relationship, so does passion, sexual activity, intimacy—and eventually love.

But it doesn't have to be that way. The sexual energy of a relationship can remain as supercharged as it was in the beginning. The physical connection that seemed so urgent in the early stages of the relationship can remain strong, driven by increasing physical and emotional intimacy. The love between two people can remain strong and grow deeper on all levels, no matter how tired or busy they are.

The key is caring: thinking about it and working at it. Passionate, exciting love may "hit" out of the blue at times, but it remains only if it's continually nurtured, invited back, and treated as an honored guest. Just as we carefully clean the house before the honored guest arrives, just as we carefully plan and cook the meal, just as we spend a great deal of time thinking about what our honored guest would like to do, so must we think, plan, prepare, and nurture passionate love.

WHAT SMOTHERS OUR PASSION?

Although physical and emotional passion can remain high throughout a lifelong relationship, it is often dimmed by neglect, poor communication, preconceptions, and differing goals.

We don't deliberately neglect our love. Rather, we get caught up in work, family obligations, mowing the lawn, and trying to get away one day a week to hang out with the guys. All of this is necessary, but it takes time away from the pursuit of passion.

Neither do we deliberately fail to communicate. But often we are too embarrassed to say what we need to say. We don't know what to say or how to say it. We may feel afraid of appearing weak, needy, argumentative, demanding, odd, or "dirty." And sometimes we don't even realize anything needs to be said, so our needs are unexpressed, our angers repressed, and our disappointment stews until we reach the boiling point. When we finally do speak, our requests or suggestions may come out sounding more like accusations or attacks. Our partner pulls back defensively or counterattacks, and the battle lines are drawn.

Our communication difficulties are exacerbated by our preconceptions. We all have notions about relationships and marriage—ideas about male and female roles based on our family, cultural, and religious background. Preconceptions are bound to cause problems unless they dovetail perfectly with your partner's, which is unlikely. At some point you'll *know* they should be doing or saying something that they are *equally* sure they shouldn't do or say.

Even if we pay careful attention to our lover, communicate expertly, and rid ourself of preconceptions, we still face a difficult hurdle: the very different expectations and needs of men and women. Men and women are equal, but they are very different physically and emotionally. Their needs are different, and they go about satisfying those needs in different ways.

Both men and women want intimacy. But to a man, intimacy means sex—and lots of it. As far as a man is concerned, more sex means more intimacy and a better relationship. To a woman, intimacy is something very different. It's a wonderful spiritual closeness to her man, a feeling that she has found her soulmate. For men, intimacy is a physical matter. For women, intimacy is a product of the feelings and heart. That's not surprising, given that men are by nature sexual beings. Our genitalia are on the outside of our bodies, our interest in a woman is made obvious by an erection, and our biologic urge is to propagate by "hunting" and "conquering."

While a man is a sexual "extrovert," a woman is generally a sexual "introvert." Her sexual organs are within her, she has trouble speaking of her deepest longings and feelings, she is closed and protective. She must feel loved and comfortable before she will open up—either figuratively or literally—to a man. For women, sexual passion is a result of intimacy. When women feel that special spiritual connection with their mate, they can become truly passionate. When they don't feel that intimacy, they may search fruitlessly inside themselves for passion, but it will not be there, and they will not be satisfied with sex. Lacking passion, and not finding satisfaction, they will naturally turn away from sex.

Passionate, exciting love must be constantly nurtured and treated like an honored guest.

With widespread neglect, poor communication, preconceptions, and differing needs and goals, it's no wonder that so many relationships wither, and sexual intercourse becomes a bone of contention or is gone entirely. And it's no wonder that so many relationships lack the passion of spiritual and physical love. But it doesn't have to be that way. You and your partner can be a passionate couple, united in passionate physical and spiritual love, until you depart this earth.

THE UNION OF TANTRA

While the poor relationship habits foisted on us by a society fearful of passionate love drive us apart, tantra brings us back together again, spiritually and physically. It is in our nature to be as one, just as the universe is one. According to ancient tantric philosophy: there is "maleness" and "femaleness" in our physical reality, but in the larger realm of spirituality there is no such duality, for all is one. A perfect union of maleness and femaleness exists in the undifferentiated One that created us and all that is.

Tantra is an ancient Eastern philosophy that, among other accomplishments, introduced the concept of chakras. As you recall from the previous chapter, there are seven major chakras, each of which receives energy from the universal energy that is all life, generates energy of its own, and acts as an energy reservoir for the body and spirit. Through meditation, visualization, and sexual exercises and practices, tantra can bring a man and woman together as one, utilizing the strengths of their opposite natures.

Generalizations are not *always* true, but they can help illustrate these opposite tendencies. Men tend to be more extroverted sexually, while women are naturally infused with more cautious energy. Men are physical, women more intuitive. Men are active, women receptive. Men and maleness are *yang* in quality, while women are *yin*. These are all equal opposites. This opposition, however, is not divisive or bad. To the contrary, it is good, for it invites us to unite our own masculine and feminine natures, to engage in role reversal, and to join as man and woman. Men and women can be as one, acting, being, and loving in concert. It's only our lack of understanding that drives us apart and makes the differences seem like insurmountable hurdles. Tantric wisdom and exercises can bring us back together, making us balanced, equal, and one, filling us with physical and spiritual satisfaction. Differences become points of pleasure, as they were meant to be.

The deeper, loving, more spiritual sexual experiences made possible through tantra deepen the spiritual relationship between a couple. This produces greater vulnerability, which increases the bond between the partners. Couples who engage in the practice of tantra usually find that everything else in their lives works much better, and they become radiantly healthy.

DEVELOPING TANTRIC UNITY

Tantra balances and harmonizes the yang and yin of masculine and feminine, within our own bodies and between a man and a woman, making them spiritually one. There are practices or exercises you can do to build harmony (such as *spooning*), and others to use when that harmony has been lost (such as *aligning the mind*). These are covered briefly here to provide you with a taste, and to interest you in learning more from the many workshops, books, and videos available. Workshops are especially recommended, for they provide experiential learning for you and your partner.

Connecting: Tantra couples learn to relate deeply by committing to the practice of at least two 10-minute connecting sessions every day. These sessions range from just holding—preferably making eye contact—to spooning, caressing, brief penetration, or outright lovemaking. Connecting is a time to share feelings while putting all else aside, including the kids (who will be thrilled with the added closeness they sense between you and your lover). Connecting is a time to be together, morning or evening, without expectations other than feeling and sharing your love in whatever form inspires you in that moment.

It is recommended that at least one connect be sexual and include penetration, even if only briefly. This may lead to extended, full-on lovemaking when that is appropriate for both, but intercourse should not be an expectation. Couples who commit to this practice experience new levels of closeness, caring, understanding, and excitement in their relationship, including lots of extended lovemaking following the practices discussed later in this chapter.

Spooning: This simple, yet powerful, form of physical communication should be practiced at least twice a day, as part or all of a connect, or any time a disagreement occurs. Although the exercise takes physical form, it is primarily designed to work on the spiritual level. Both you and your partner should lie down in the "spoon" position, both of you on either your left or right side. The partner on the outside (who is looking at the back of the other's head) envelops the one on the inside. Your groin snuggles up to your partner's rear end. (Whether you're on the outside or inside changes, depending on who needs more nurturing at that moment.)

Find a comfortable way to lie in the spoon position. If you're on the outside you might reach around and rest your hand on her breasts (fourth chakra), belly (second chakra) or groin (first chakra). Your chakras will be aligned, the fronts of yours with the backs of hers, when you're in this nurturing position.

Couples who engage in the practice of tantra usually find that their lives work much better, and they are radiantly healthy.

Lie quietly in this position with your eyes closed, relaxed. Take deep breaths as you let all thoughts leave your mind. Listen carefully to your own breathing, visualizing the breath entering your body to give you life, then leaving. When you feel comfortable, start listening to your partner's breath. Hear her breathing, hear yours, and hear them align as you begin breathing in unison. Acting together, but without either of you leading, take comfortably deep breaths, hold for a moment, exhale, and pause before breathing again. As you repeat this breathing over and over, together, begin giving or accepting energy. If you're on the outside, give your energy to your partner. If you're on the inside, accept the energy. The one who is giving the energy emphasizes the exhalations, while the one receiving pays special attention to the inhalation.

Now begin focusing your attention on your chakras, one at a time. Let the energy-giving partner lead the way, telling the other to begin focusing on the heart (fourth chakra) for three full breaths. Then focus on each of the other six chakras, for three breaths apiece, in this order: forehead (sixth chakra), base (first chakra), sacral (second chakra), solar plexus (third chakra), throat (fifth chakra), and finally the crown (seventh chakra).

Up to this point you have been working together, emphasizing unity. The only difference has been that one has been giving energy, emphasizing the exhalation, while the other focuses on inhaling and receiving energy. Now it's time to emphasize the differences between the two of you. One inhales as the other exhales (this is called *reciprocal charging breathing*). Even though there is a separation between the two of you, indicated by the alternating breathing patterns, you are still one, working together toward a common goal. With your skin touching hers, with energy flowing between your chakras, and your breathing in unison or alternating, you are as one. The focus on breathing, the chakras, and working together creates energy. This physical but non-sexual exercise will help you attune your energies and kindle the sexual fires that may have become dormant within you.

The entire spooning exercise should take about ten minutes. When you're finished, communicate nonverbally to your partner that it is time to return to doing the things of thc daily world.. When appropriate, there may also be a brief verbal exchange of whatever you and/or your partner may be feeling in the moment—not designed to "fix" anything but just to honor and share, to be vulnerable with each other.

Yab yum: This is another very sweet way to align the chakras and energies. The man sits yogi-style, legs crossed, on the floor or a thin pillow, while the woman sits on his crossed legs facing him. Their eyes and chakras are aligned in this delightful position for hugging, kissing, rocking, eye gazing, just breathing or talking, or serious lovemaking. But yab yum need not be sexual; you can simply talk to each other. Some stretching exercises may be in order to fully enjoy this position for extended periods, but it is worth the effort. In the beginning, even very short sessions can be wonderful.

Aligning the minds: The warm, light, extroverted, physically oriented male and the cool, dark, introverted, intuitive woman are bound to come into occasional conflict. Indeed, if they *didn't* it would probably be because one member of the partnership was stifling every urge in order to be "agreeable." That kind of agreeability, however, inevitably blows up, leading to conflict. When conflicts do occur they often grow worse because the man attempts to solve it with logic, while the woman looks at it emotionally. A man struggles to explain that he didn't know his wife had planned a special night for just the two of them and couldn't help being late from work, but she feels that he ruined their romantic evening together. Neither person is right or wrong; they simply have different inborn ways of looking at life and dealing with problems. Logic and emotion work well when they are in harmony, but create fire when in conflict.

When disharmony occurs, when one partner is arguing from logic and the other from emotion, the first person to realize the problem should say something like, "We're not on the same wavelength. We're not in harmony. We're not going to solve this until we're in harmony again." Then the man and woman should begin the spooning exercise, even if they are angry with each other. Performing this exercise doesn't "solve" the problem over which they were arguing, but it helps them align their mental energies and shows their commitment to the relationship. As they work through the exercise, consciously focusing on each other, their chakras will begin to align themselves on an energetic level. Within five to ten minutes, the energetic alignment will be complete. Now, although they still have issues to settle, they will be working together toward a harmonic solution rather than driving each other away. If you still have trouble talking through the problem without becoming angry, simply hold each other with love.

Use these exercises often, remembering that there are no perfect ways to do them. The key is to approach and touch each other with love and a genuine desire for harmony and unity. If that is your desire, then that will be the eventual outcome. Your lovemaking—indeed, your entire relationship—will take on an exciting new genuineness that supports each of you in becoming more of who you are. Your relationship will be infused with tremendous amounts of energy, setting in motion a positive new circle of love and abundance in all things. Remember that for a woman, the lovemaking begins hours or days before the physical event. If you are loving to her all the time, in effect making love to her all day, every day, she will be turned on most of the time—and so will you. Most men come to realize that their ultimate pleasure is pleasuring their woman. When she is happy, they are happy, especially when she is really turned on, being the passionate woman that she can be. This is the approach that an exciting, happy relationship thrives on. It is also a primary source of support for a happy and healthy prostate.

AWAKENING THE GODDESS

Western sex is a "divided" approach to lovemaking: I have my needs and you have yours, I have my orgasm and you have yours. When I'm done my interest diminishes. Maybe I'll "finish" you up, but my mind is elsewhere. Not only are we inwardly focused when it comes to sex, many of us feel guilty about wanting or having sex, or we feel ashamed of ourselves or our bodies, or we have had bad experiences and we've never learned how to delve into sex together, to work as one. This is often especially true of women, who have been made to feel that sex is only for making babies; otherwise, it is a sin. Men are often products of this same teaching, leading to feelings of guilt that end up as constrictions in the prostate.

Our negative attitudes toward sex and sexuality are obvious in our words. A penis is a nasty "prick," a mechanical "boner," or a mindless "love machine." A vagina is a "hole," a "pussy," or a "cunt." Making love is "fucking," "screwing," "doing it," or "making the beast with two backs."

Before we can fully appreciate the beauty and unity of sex we must rid ourselves of the words which carry such nasty connotations. In tantra the penis is called the *lingam,* which means "wand of light," and the vagina is known as the *yoni,* which means "sacred space," the temple of pleasure, golden doorway, or the precious gateway. Using these ancient Sanskrit words will help reshape attitudes in positive ways.

The next step toward true sexual unity is to awaken the woman, the goddess, spiritually and physically. This is often necessary because a woman is more likely to have suffered from harsh cultural and religious attitudes toward sex, and because she may be carrying emotional hurts in her sexual center, as men do in their prostates. Five orgasmic levels describe and define all women:

- *Preorgasmic,* which includes women who have never enjoyed an orgasm.
- *Occasionally orgasmic,* a frustrating stage because she has tasted this pleasure, but does not know how to make it return, or if it ever will.

- *Orgasmic,* able to enjoy one orgasm per love-making session.
- *Multiorgasmic,* filled with delight and pleasure as she experiences multiple and full-body orgasms.
- *Extended orgasm,* delighting in intense arousal that can last up to 15 or 20 minutes as she leaps from one orgasm to another.

Although many women are preorgasmic or occasionally orgasmic, every woman can enjoy extended orgasms every time she makes love. It's simply a matter awakening the goddess, with love. The first step in the awakening is stimulating the woman's two pleasure poles.

One pleasure pole is the clitoris (also called the *northern* or *forward pole*); the other is the sacred spot within her vagina (also called the *southern pole*). The sacred spot is known in modern times as the *G spot.*

Finding and stimulating the clitoris, which sits atop the yoni like a jewel on a crown, is relatively easy. Not just the clitoris, but the entire first inch of her yoni is a powerful pleasure center. With a little experimentation, a woman can discover what combination of holding, rubbing, caressing, licking, kissing, sucking, or pulling best stimulates her clitoris. She can explore by herself, or with her man, using his lingam to stimulate her.

Learning to use the sacred spot is difficult for a woman to do by herself, for it is hidden within her. Although it is the seat of great spiritual and physical pleasures, it is also the spot where psychic hurts take residence. Awakening the sacred spot can

Loving sacred spot work revitalizes a relationship.

produce an unexpected torrent of anger or tears as she remembers her past pain. This is a temporary phenomenon, however, that will quickly subside (in minutes, seconds, or milliseconds) as pleasure takes its place. She may swing back and forth, releasing more pent-up emotions, then enjoying pleasure again, moving quickly through stages of laughter, pain, ecstasy, anger, etc. It will always be different. Have no expectations. Just be there for her, no matter what. Allow her expression to be whatever it is. That is the healing. Compliment her and encourage her to express whatever she is feeling.

Before beginning the process of awakening the goddess, the woman should empty her bladder, then lie on her back on a bed, raising her legs onto her lover's shoulders as he sits by her yoni, or bending her knees so that her feet are flat on the bed, a pillow under her buttocks. After lovingly kissing or caressing the woman, or perhaps fondling her clitoris or kissing her yoni until she is lubricated, the man, after asking permission, inserts his ring finger into her precious gateway. Gently inserting his finger as far as it comfortably goes, palm facing up, he slowly pulls it back toward the underside of the clitoris, stroking the "ceiling" of the yoni as he does so. About halfway back, between the pubic bone and the clitoris, is the sacred spot. The woman will feel the energy of her sacred spot that lies not on the wall of the vagina, but is a little recessed. The man will feel a slightly "rougher" or bumpy texture, like the petals of a flower that open as she opens. (With a little practice and patience, the man can learn to locate the sacred spot quickly and elegantly.)

At first, touching the sacred spot may alarm or anger the woman, or cause her to experience a confused fearfulness. She may also feel as if she has to urinate, even though she has already emptied her bladder. Some areas may be uncomfortable or even painful. Move away from these areas but revisit them as they open and disappear, as the goddess within her—the goddess that she is—begins to awaken. Neither the man nor the woman should try to "force" pleasure from the sacred spot. And do not shy away from any negative feelings the early contact causes, for these emotions must rise to the surface before they can be discarded. They are like a splinter that must be pulled out of the body: It hurts when the needle breaks the skin and digs the splinter out, but once it has been expelled the pain vanishes and the healing is quick. Every time you stimulate her sacred spot, whether with your finger or your lingam, the goddess within her will awaken further. When the goddess is fully awakened you and your woman will be able to unite physically and spiritually. Until then, your job is to lovingly help her by charging her sacred spot with the positive male energy from your finger or lingam. Having an orgasm is not the goal at this time; that will come later.

The sexual energy of a relationship can remain as supercharged as it was in the beginning.

Initially, it is often best for the man to simply place his finger in the yoni, finger resting on the sacred spot, with his other hand resting on her breasts, pubic area, or clitoris, looking into her eyes and breathing in unison with her. When the breaths are in harmony and both partners feel at peace, he may begin gently caressing her sacred spot, perhaps for just a minute or two. Then they should quietly look into each other's eyes and breathe together again, until they feel calm and as one. Now he may again gently caress her sacred spot, and, if she can handle the joy that comes from the stimulation of both of her power poles, stimulate her clitoris as well. Alternating periods of stimulation and harmonic quiet will teach the woman how to tap into the tremendous spiritual and physical power of her sacred spot, awakening the goddess within her. And when all negative influences have been gently caressed out of her sacred spot, when she has learned how to draw from the deep well of her inborn sexuality, the woman will rise rapidly toward the fifth full-body orgasmic level. Another sign of her awakening may be the nectar/ejaculate, a light liquid that flows from the area of the sacred spot. The source of the fluid is still unclear; its sweet smell and taste attest to the fact that it is *not* urine. Historically called *the nectar of the goddess* and dispensed in ancient temples, this ejaculate is the *amrita,* a powerful fluid that energizes the one who drinks it, both physically and spiritually.

> *This healing will have a very powerful effect on the relationship as well as the prostate, which benefits from the happier, sexier relationship as well as from its own healing. The principle that "the healer is healed as he heals another" holds true in relationships. Men heal by healing their women.*

CHOOSING THE MOMENT

As the goddess awakens, it is time for the man to learn to slow down in his pursuit of that which he wants most, so that he may have more.

Western attitudes toward male sexuality stress ejaculation —the more ejaculations, the better. Indeed, young men often brag about "doing it" two or three times in one night, and older men bemoan the fact that they must wait an hour or five hours before the refractory period passes and they can engage in intercourse again. Tantric philosophy, however, emphasizes the intense, explosive pleasure of the inner orgasm even as it recognizes the physical delight of ejaculation. With practice, a man can learn to separate orgasms from ejaculation, and experience multiple orgasms apart from ejaculation. He can join his lover in multiple orgasms for hours, before or without ejaculating. He also can learn how to control and delay ejaculation, to continue making harmonious love with his goddess for long periods of time, enjoying the intense pleasure of multiple inner orgasms before ejaculating when he chooses to (if he desires to do so).

With practice, a man can learn to separate orgasms from ejaculation, and join his lover in multiple orgasms for hours.

The longer a man waits before ejaculating, the longer he can make love and the greater the buildup of his sexual energy. This makes for lengthy and delightful inner orgasms, and explosive "best-ever" ejaculations. It also allows time for the goddess to become fully aroused.

It's relatively easy for a man to learn how to delay ejaculation indefinitely. It takes only time, practice, patience, and desire. The exercises for achieving control are simple:

■ *Muscle building:* The pubococcygeal muscle, which runs from the coccyx (tail bone) down and around to the pubic bone, plays an important role in sexual control. This "love muscle" makes a man's erection strong and helps him to control ejaculation. The stronger the pubococcygeal muscle, the more control a man can exercise. But first he must strengthen the muscle with exercise. To do so, every time you urinate, contract the muscle to stop the flow once or twice. You'll notice that at first you're clenching other muscles in addition to the pubococcygeal. With practice, however, you'll learn how to squeeze only that muscle. And with regular practice, the muscle will become strong. When the "love muscle" has been built up, you can use it to delay ejaculation. Simply stop all movement and contract the muscle, breathing deeply and slowly until the urge to ejaculate has gone. Look into your partner's eyes as you wait, letting her calm wash over and into you.

- *Breathing control:* Breathing, which rises and falls with our passion, plays an important role in ejaculatory control. A man breathes harder and faster as he approaches orgasm, the increasing respiration rate being driven by his desire. But he can reverse the process, dampening the urge simply by slowing and deepening his breathing.

- *Loving from higher chakras:* The second chakra is the chakra of desire and sexual energy. This is the chakra that usually propels us forward to orgasm. When the desire becomes strong, switch focus away from the second chakra to the fourth or the sixth chakra, the chakras of the heart and emotions. With practice you'll be able to shift quickly and easily; it's all a matter of focus.

- *Squeezing the lingam:* Approximately an inch below the tip of the lingam, on the underside, is an area called the *frenulum.* Gently but firmly squeezing the extremely sensitive frenulum for up to twenty or thirty seconds reduces the momentum for ejaculation. The man must withdraw from the woman in order to do so; oftentimes, she will perform the squeeze. The lingam softens somewhat but that is only a temporary condition; it will soon become hard again.

■ *Pressing the "missing lingam":* We tend to think that the lingam ends where the penis "attaches" to the body, for that is all we see. However, the lingam continues into the body, running parallel to the area that runs between the testicles and the anus, until it ends at the anus. If you touch this area when you are aroused, you will see that it is sensitive, just as the penis is, and becomes hard in anticipation of intercourse. Pressing on the "missing lingam," approximately halfway between the testicles and the anus, will diminish the urge to ejaculate. Either the man or the woman can press gently but firmly when the man desires to prolong the pleasure by delaying ejaculation. The man need not withdraw from the woman when his "missing lingam" is pressed. Either he or she can press this spot as he remains within her, keeping still, slowing his breath, and focusing on the higher chakras.

■ *Squeezing the scrotum above the testicles:* When the urge to ejaculate becomes great, gently squeezing and pulling on the scrotum (not the testicles) where the lingam and scrotal sac meet will allow the man to delay.

Muscle building, breathing control, moving to the higher chakras, pressing the "missing lingam," and squeezing the scrotum will help you delay ejaculation as you cease activity and lie quietly inside of, or with, your woman. Look deeply into her eyes as you do so, matching slow, deep, calm breaths. Don't worry if your lingam becomes slightly less hard; that is natural. Once your urge to ejaculate has passed and you have resumed activity, your erection will quickly become as hard as it was before. If you squeeze the lingam, do not let it be a jarring and upsetting act. Make it a part of your love play, a way to work together as one as you move toward harmonious unity.

When you have learned to delay your ejaculation, you can begin developing the "explosive" orgasm that all men are capable of. Controlled breathing is particularly important. Begin to slow your inhalations as you notice your urge to ejaculate building. Concentrate on deep, sustained inhalations, breathing louder and louder. Let your breathing become like a song, vocalizing to energize your throat (fifth chakra). Let the fifth chakra act as a "magnet," pulling your focus and internal energies up away from your groin and to your higher chakras.

Don't let the orgasm remain in the groin. Inhale deeply as you climax, feeling the energy of love dancing through your body. Picture the energy springing out of your groin (second chakra), flying up toward the higher chakras, to your heart (fourth) and throat (fifth), then into the delicate pleasure centers of your brain (sixth and seventh chakras). But don't let the energy of orgasm run entirely out of your body. Instead, visualize it returning down through the chakras as you exhale powerfully. Use your breath and the power of visualization to keep the exquisite energy of the orgasm within you as long as possible.

THE DANCE OF LOVE

Many Americans refer to sexual intercourse as "doing it" or "screwing." From the perspective of tantra it is the dance of love: a sacred ritual, filled with spiritual and physical delight, that carries us closer to godliness. Rather than an opportunity to quickly "get your rocks off" or "grab a little nookie," sexual intercourse is a sacred ritual, or perhaps a prayer. Just as we prepare to pray by cleansing our minds of impure thoughts, so should we prepare for the dance of love.

Begin by cleansing the body, bathing separately or together. Wash away your problems and anger and worldly thoughts with the soap and water as you wash away the sweat and dirt. Don't apply too many lotions or mask your body's odors entirely. Use lotions and perfume that enhance your natural smells, which are natural aphrodisiacs.

Begin cleansing your mind as you wash, letting routine cares and thoughts float away as you focus on the dance that is to come. Meditate while you bathe, or visualize the delights that lie ahead.

Begin your dance of love in a special place: a room or area that has been specially decorated and has comfortable pillows and furnishings.

Look into each other's eyes as you dance the dance of love. You are not a man simply hoping to ejaculate soon. Instead, you and your partner are two halves of a whole, thinking and moving together as one through a complex dance.

The dance includes kisses that may use only the lips or the tongue as well. Gentle bites to the inside and outside of your lover's lips can be incorporated into the kissing, along with sucking the lips or other parts of the body. The man kisses his lover's yoni just as he does her lips—with the lips or the tongue, with gentle bites or sucking or blowing. He may move his lips across her clitoris, using his flickering tongue like a finger to stimulate her northern pole. He may gently suck her clitoris and the area surrounding it into his mouth. The woman kisses the man's lingam in the same way (but does not blow onto or into the opening of the urethra). The woman may also finger the lingam's shaft as she kisses it, as if she were playing a flute. She may lick his testicles, or take the entire scrotum into her moist mouth. She can lick the lingam the "long" way, simulating intercourse, or move her tongue across the "short way," or round and round the shaft to provide a different kind of pleasure.

The dance includes deliberate touching designed to exchange and enhance energy as much as to impart sensual delight. The touch can be stationary, allowing the energy to flow from one body to another; or it can be moving, and may include squeezing, gentle pinching, or light scratching. Stroking anywhere can be very erotic when the stroke is light as a feather—in fact, feathers are very erotic tools to have at your bedside. (While the yoni prefers a gentle touch, especially to the clitoris and the first inch of the gateway, the lingam likes a firmer touch.) Perhaps he touches her anus while caressing her clitoris with fingers or tongue. Perhaps he touches her yoni with his lingam—but only touches, not enters. Even a semi-erect lingam can be held in his or her hand and rubbed against her clitoris. While touching, the woman may slip her finger into her lover's anus and massage his prostate. If done gently and carefully, this can be both erotic when the man is aroused, especially during ejaculation, and health-enhancing.

The dance includes a thousand and one ways for the lingam and yoni to touch, rub, caress, rub, and delight each other. Perhaps the lingam gently "rubs the door," gently caressing the clitoris. It can also slowly and gently step through the doorway, only slightly, then come back out again, many times in a row. It may plunge deeply into the yoni, or find a position midway. The lingam can move rapidly, slowly, or not at all; the external stillness of the yoni can be complemented by internal rhythmic contractions that create a delightful sensation of movement within the woman. (The woman can also produce "movement" by contracting and relaxing her own muscles.) The dance of love can be a dance of angles and circles and sideways movements, as the lingam moves in a circular motion while inside the yoni, or from side to side or up and down, varying the angle of movement along with the speed and depth of movement.

The dance may be danced with either the man or woman on top, with the partners side by side, or with the man behind the woman. They may be lying down, sitting down, reclining, or standing. The lovers greatly enhance their dance with their own sounds of love, with "hmmms," sighs, moans, or other sounds of pleasure. Sound is a very important expression of feeling, moving one's energy and communicating what is pleasurable in the moment to one's partner.

When women feel that special spiritual connection with their mate, they can become truly passionate.

Whatever patterns the dancers choose, they build to the eventual physical and spiritual climax. When the man and woman explode into contact with the God and Goddess within themselves, they move beyond their bodies to touch the thing that is greater than us all. Depending on the chosen position, one lover may have placed a finger against the other's anus during climax. Maybe one of them caressed her clitoris as she climaxed, or she placed her hand to his scrotum. She can remain still during her climax or contract her yoni muscles, either in a few, powerful squeezes, or a series of light and rhythmic ones. It is important that she let her jaws relax and be very vocal during climax: this enhances whole-body orgasm, carrying her to higher levels.

Afterwards, the man may remain within her, basking in the energy. Now, with essence gone, he is most open to receiving her healing energy, and she his. Wrapped in the energy of their love, they remain coupled together, he within her, gazing into each other's eyes, breathing in unison, feeling each other's bodies and spirits. The moments after orgasm are as precious and powerful as all those that have preceded.

Tantra is an art form, one that takes time to master. Do not be concerned if you cannot find her sacred spot on the first try, or if you cannot attain complete mastery over your ejaculation in the first week or two—or even the first few months. Like all skills, tantra requires practice and patience. Classes are available in most areas from many teachers. I especially recommend Charles and Caroline Muir (who live in Hawaii and teach across the U.S.). The Muirs teach beginning to advanced levels, emphasizing deeper relating and the healing aspects of tantra. They relate well to singles and couples from all walks of life: from the staunchest establishment to New Age types.

HOW OFTEN SHOULD YOU "DANCE THE DANCE"?

To deepen your relationship while dramatically enhancing or reviving your sex life, it's recommended that you and your partner enjoy intimate holding and sharing of feelings twice a day, for at least 10 minutes per session, one of which includes penetration. This deeper relating and enhanced love life lifts a couple to new levels of happiness and is good for the prostate. The prostate benefits from the happiness as well as from the more regular loving and blood flow. How often one ejaculates varies greatly among men, with some young men thriving on daily or even multiple ejaculations per day, while other men being quite happy ejaculating once a week or month. (At the extreme, Taoist literature suggests one ejaculation per year, and none after the age of 40.) I'm not aware of any definitive studies linking ejaculatory *frequency* to health, except those which show that the highest incidence of prostate cancer occurs among celibate men.

The best way to determine how often you should "dance the dance" and ejaculate is how you feel afterward. If you are energized when you finish, you have probably found the right frequency for you. If, on the other hand, you immediately roll over and fall asleep, leaving your woman with the terrible feeling of "coming, coming, gone," then your sex life is exhausting you. While age and general fitness are important factors, many healthy men over the age of 70 enjoy frequent ejaculation without any loss of energy, which is the key measure. Based on the available literature and my work with many men, I believe that once a month is probably the minimum frequency for a healthy prostate, with once a week being preferable for most men—and the more loving each ejaculation is, the better. Ejaculation in anger does not benefit the prostate or general health, and is probably no better than no ejaculation at all.

The best way to determine how often you should ejaculate is how you feel afterward.

Experiment to discover the frequency that feels right for you. If you are in doubt, use the BTA to monitor your health as you approach the right level. You can also use hair analysis to look at your zinc level and zinc/copper ratio, which will be off if you are ejaculating too frequently (a 2:0 copper/zinc ratio is ideal).

After much experimentation and testing, I've found that two to three times per week is ideal for me at age 64—sometimes up to three times a day, but I always do multiple tantric "hold-backs" before ejaculating, which makes a big difference in my energy level and how I feel throughout the day. Hold-backs before ejaculating recirculate the energy through the body, leaving you feeling energized rather than depleted. BTA and hair analysis show that this works well for me.

Should choosing not to ejaculate leave you with "blue balls" or pressure in the prostate, relieve the pressure by recirculating the energy. Sit on the edge of the bed with your testicles hanging freely, and squeeze your testicles gently while using deep yoga breathing to move the energy from the groin up and down the body. If you still experience pressure, it is best to ejaculate to release it.

A FINAL NOTE: IS SEX A CURE FOR CANCER?

Not only is sex fun, it's good for your prostate—and may prevent cancer. Dr. Banrejee of the Manchester Royal Infirmary in England found a correlation between the number of ejaculations and the risk of prostate cancer.[1] The doctor divided 423 men, ranging from 60 to 80 years old, into two groups: 274 who had prostate cancer, and 149 who did not. When the men estimated their ejaculatory frequency during the years they were most sexually

[1] As described in Bechtel. S., ed. 1996. *The practical encyclopedia of sex and health.* Emmaus, PA: Rodale Press, p. 261.

active, it was found that the ones who wound up with prostate cancer ejaculated much less frequently, on average, than did men who avoided the disease. (A full 31% of the cancer-free men had ejaculated 5 to 7 times per week, compared with only 13% of those with the cancer.)

Not only is sex fun, it's good for your prostate, and may prevent cancer.

Whether you begin practicing tantric sex or remain with your current practices, I urge you to have regular, loving sex. In addition to the physical pleasures and benefits, a loving sexual relationship improves and deepens your relationship with your partner, promoting overall health and well-being.

CHAPTER 14

OTHER INTRIGUING APPROACHES

Although I'm firmly convinced that my *90-Day Prostate Cancer Cure* is the best therapy for cancer, and have seen it work, I also believe that other healing arts have interesting ideas that may be helpful. To the extent that these therapies cleanse and detoxify the body while they strengthen the immune system, they work with and corroborate my approach.

As you search for healers familiar with various aspects of my program, you will undoubtedly hear about antineoplaston therapy, Essiac tea, Gerson therapy, and other alternative approaches to treating cancer. It may help if you are familiar with these therapies so you can discuss them knowledgeably with friends and prospective healers. These brief introductions to some intriguing approaches will get you started on your research. With that in mind, let's take a look at these noted therapies.

ANTINEOPLASTON THERAPY

According to Stanislaw Burzynski, M.D., Ph.D., the immune system is not the body's only defense against disease. There is a second tier called the *biochemical defense system*. While the immune system protects against invasion by bacteria, viruses, and other external enemies, the biochemical defense system guards against defective cells. Where the immune system uses large and complex structures such as T-cells and macrophages to destroy invaders, the biochemical defense system uses smaller substances called *antineoplastons* to reprogram defective cells, making them healthy again before they become cancerous.

Dr. Burzynski developed his theory after noticing that cancer patients had low levels of antineoplastons in their blood. He theorized that the small, previously overlooked substances were part of the body's biochemical system, specifically assigned to repair damaged cells by fixing their DNA, their "instruction manuals." He felt that cancer only arose when cells became defective and grew beyond normal limits. If they could be kept under control until they died a natural death, like all healthy cells do, there would be no cancer.

As he continued studying the antineoplastons which, like proteins, are made up of amino acids, he concluded that there were several types. Although they all helped to restore scrambled DNA programming in defective cells, certain antineoplastons were effective against specific types of cancer. For example, antineoplaston-L was effective against leukemia, while antineoplaston-O seemed to be most effective against osteosarcoma. One of the substances, antineoplaston-A, was effective against several different types of cancers.

Dr. Burzynski's antineoplaston theory has not gained the support of the Food and Drug Administration (which is not necessarily indicative of how effective the therapy actually is), but it has won praise from some doctors and researchers in different countries. Burzynski feels that not only can cancer be treated with antineoplastons, but that low levels of neoplastons in the blood are indicators of cancer.

Antineoplaston therapy consists of intravenous and oral doses of antineoplastons. Treatment lasting from several months to a year is given on an outpatient basis. (Treatment lasts for this long because it must continue until the cancerous cells, now repaired, live out their normal lives. If the treatment is stopped, according to Dr. Burzynski, the cells which have been repaired by the antineoplastons will "break" and become cancerous again.) The type and strength of antineoplaston given depends on the patient's cancer. Dr. Burzynski has treated thousands of people, many who were in advanced stages of cancer and had been advised by Western physicians to go home and die. Hundreds have been given extra years of health and life, although the doctor cautions that his therapy will not help everyone. (See the appendix for the location of Dr. Burzynski's clinic.)

AYURVEDA

Part of the ancient Indian philosophy called the *Vedic system,* Ayurveda is a complete school of health and healthful living. According to Ayurvedic thinking, disease is caused by either an imbalance in body humors, karmic disturbances, or both. Deepak Chopra, M.D., Pablo Airola, and Gabriel Cousins, M.D., are among the better-known practitioners of Ayurveda.

There are three *body humors* (also known as *doshas* and *life forces*):

- *Vata*, the *air humor*, is centered in the colon and spreads throughout the body's empty spaces. In control of all physical processes, Vata is the most important to health of the three humors.
- *Pitta*, the *fire humor*, is centered in the small intestine and is responsible for perception and metabolism.
- *Kapha*, the *water humor*, is centered in the stomach and is the stuff that makes up most of the body tissues.

Cancer is considered to be a negative, parasitic force that steals energy from the person's body. It is believed to be caused by eating foods that have been stripped of their nutrients during processing, by exposure to toxic chemicals in our environment, by lack of exercise, by negative emotions, and/or by leading a life devoid of a spiritual purpose. When one or more of these factors unbalances our humors or sets up a karmic disturbance, cancer is inevitable.

Emotions play an important role in causing cancer. When negative emotions are held in, they lodge in various parts of the body, poisoning cells and inviting cancer. It's important to remember, however, that cancer is not a disease that just appears. Instead, it is a part of us, a natural outgrowth of an unhealthful physical, emotional, or spiritual lifestyle.

Symptoms of disease vary according to the humor in which they manifest. If the cancer manifests itself in the Vata (air) humor, the tumor will be dry and hard. The patient will likely be depressed, anxious, or fearful, and his skin will be gray or brown. If the cancer manifests in the Pitta (fire) humor, the tumor will be infected. The angry, irritable patient will bleed and feel as if she is burning. If the cancer manifests in the Kapha (water) humor, the tumors will be benign (non-cancerous) at first. Later, as the patient suffers from fatigue and congestion, the tumors will become cancerous. Although cancers appear in one body humor, the disease eventually involves all three as the body is flooded with toxins and its digestive fire is dimmed.

In addition to standard medical tests used to make a diagnosis of cancer, the Ayurvedic physician will also carefully examine the patient's pulses and ask many questions about his or her lifestyle and feelings. Ayurvedic therapy for cancer varies according to the humor in which the cancer manifested and the patient's physical, emotional, and spiritual make-up. Detoxifying and strengthening the body are the first steps in treating disease. A vegetarian diet, exercise, internal cleansing, massage, baths, meditation, and lifestyle changes will be prescribed. Herbs will be used to eliminate toxins from the body, cleanse the blood, strengthen the circulation and immune system, and clear out the respiratory system. Considerable attention is given to restoring the person's natural body rhythms and each humor's natural cycle during the days and seasons of the year.

Depending on the type of cancer and the patient's constitution, certain metals, crystals, and colors may also be used. Gems can be important, with diamonds used to improve longevity, yellow topaz and yellow sapphire to boost the immune system, red coral and ruby to bolster circulation, and blue sapphire to expel the parasitic negative energy that created the cancer. And since emotional blockages are considered to be an important cause of cancer, techniques of emotional cleansing will also be used.

BOVINE CARTILAGE

Cartilage taken from cows ("bovine" refers to a cow) contains powerful molecular biodirectors that can help to correct structural abnormalities in cells. Research into bovine cartilage began in the 1950s when Dr. John Prudden, a professor of surgery at Columbia-Presbyterian Medical Center, discovered that bovine cartilage helped speed wound healing in rats that had been subjected to cortisone (which slows wound healing). In the 1960s, researchers from Harvard Medical School and the Massachusetts Institute of Technology found bovine cartilage could slow the growth of tumors by inhibiting the growth of the blood vessels which "fed" them. It wasn't long before Dr. Prudden successfully used bovine cartilage to dramatically shrink the tumor of a woman with malignant ulceration of the chest due to breast cancer.

In a laboratory study at the University of Arizona Health Sciences Center, bovine cartilage killed almost all the cancer cells to which it was applied in a test tube. Equally positive results were seen when the cartilage was applied to tissue containing colon, testicular, ovarian, and pancreatic cancer. The initial studies with humans were also encouraging. Dr. Prudden conducted a long-term study of 31 cancer patients who were considered incurable after standard radiation and chemotherapy. After 11 years of bovine injections and capsules, 35% of the patients had experienced complete remission, and 19% had their tumors shrunk by 50%.

Bovine cartilage is believed to work against cancer on three levels: (1) strengthening the immune system, (2) normalizing deviant cells, and (3) preventing tumor cells from dividing to form daughter cells. Bovine cartilage has also been used to treat arthritis, allergies, ulcerative colitis, psoriasis, and herpes infections.

BURTON'S IMMUNO-AUGMENTATIVE THERAPY

A fifteen-minute cancer cure? The newspaper headlines were certainly exaggerated, but Dr. Lawrence Burton was reported to have injected something into mice that caused their tumors to shrink in less than an hour, witnessed by attendees of an American Cancer Society science writers' seminar. He later repeated the feat for oncologists at the New York Academy of Medicine.

Dr. Burton developed his therapy while serving as an oncologist at New York's St. Vincent's Hospital. The treatment, *immuno-augmentative therapy,* does not directly cure cancer. Instead, it strengthens the immune system, allowing the body to deal with the problem naturally, on its own. The active ingredients are four proteins isolated from human blood: tumor complement, tumor antibody 1, tumor antibody 2, and deblocking protein. When administered in the appropriate amounts and proportions for each patient, these proteins are purported to enhance the immune system, leading to a reduction in tumor size. The dosage is based on a daily analysis of the patient's blood. No special diet is recommended while on the therapy, although Dr. Burton suggests eating chicken, eggs, cheese, nuts, fish, and some red meat in order to supply proteins that support his four immune-enhancing proteins.

The non-toxic therapy is reputed to shrink tumors in 50 to 60% of patients. Many people, including some with metastatic cancer of the abdomen and colon, have experienced long-term remission with the therapy. One of those helped was the former chief of thoracic surgery at New York's Roosevelt Hospital, who testified before Congress that immuno-augmentative therapy controlled his prostate cancer, which had metastasized.

CHAPARRAL

The chaparral (*Larrea tridentata*) that grows over hundreds of square miles in Arizona and California contains a powerful antioxidant called *NDGA* (nordihydroguaiaretic acid). NDGA was used to prevent oxidation from spoiling foods during World War II. It appears to work against cancer cells by preventing them from "eating" the blood sugar they need to survive—in other words, it starves them to death. Chaparral also contains polysaccharides, which stimulate the immune system. Chaparral is generally taken as a tea. Although there have been several reports of chaparral shrinking tumors, chaparral therapy is toxic and has potentially serious side effects. It should be taken only under supervision.

ESSIAC TEA

Between the 1920s and 1970s, Rene Caisse, a Canadian nurse, used an herbal tea to treat thousands of cancer patients. Many of the people who had been deemed hopeless, and told to go home and die, enjoyed longer lives than anyone thought possible, thanks to a simple tea that they drank or had injected into their bodies.

The formula for this tea came to Nurse Caisse from an Indian healer by way of a patient they both treated. There is some dispute about which company has the authentic recipe for Caisse's Essiac tea today, but the primary ingredients are burdock root, Indian rhubarb, sheep sorrel, and slippery elm bark. Although both burdock root and Indian root have anti-tumor properties, most people familiar with Essiac tea feel that all the ingredients, working together, are responsible for its healing properties.

Nurse Caisse felt that some of the ingredients in Essiac slowed the growth of tumors, some fought infection associated with cancer and tumor growth, some carried away dead tissue and other debris, while still others stimulated the immune system. As she treated people with her tea, she noted that often the tumor would grow larger and harder at first, then begin to soften and shrink. The patients would slough off dead tissues and pus as the tumors disappeared. Essiac tea did not always eliminate the tumor. Sometimes the tumor shrunk down to operable size, and sometimes she used it after a patient had surgery, to eliminate any cancerous cells remaining in the body (because the cells might take root and begin to grow all over again).

Many physicians in Canada and the U.S. have used this tea on themselves or their patients, or observed its use by other patients. Dr. Charles Brusch, former physician to President John Kennedy and founder of the Brusch Medical Center in Cambridge, Massachusetts, stated that he cured his own cancer with the tea: "I endorse this therapy . . . for I have in fact cured my own cancer, the original site of which was the lower bowels, through Essiac alone."[1] Essiac teas are available in most health food stores.

[1] Walters, Richard. 1993. *Options: the alternative cancer therapy book.* Garden City Park, NY: Avery Publishing Group, p. 105.

GERSON THERAPY

Perhaps the oldest alternative therapy for cancer, Gerson therapy was devised by Germany's Dr. Max Gerson, who was looking for a cure for his own migraine headaches. After solving his problem by developing a low-salt, largely vegetarian diet, he began to use the same regimen to successfully treat people suffering from tuberculosis and other problems. One of his patients was the great humanitarian Dr. Albert Schweitzer, who, after receiving Gerson therapy for his diabetes, said: "I see in [Dr. Gerson] one of the most eminent geniuses in the history of medicine. He leaves a legacy which commands attention and which will assure him of his due place. Those whom he cured will attest to the truth of his ideas."[2]

Gerson therapy is an eclectic approach based on the idea that cancer is caused by toxins and electrolyte imbalances. It is felt that when cancer, toxins, or other mechanisms damage a cell, the cell loses potassium. As the cellular potassium drops, the concentration of sodium rises correspondingly, drawing water into the cell. Soon the soggy cell is too swollen with fluid to function properly. It can no longer produce the proper amount of energy and the body weakens. Therefore, a key element of Gerson therapy is detoxification and restoring the electrolyte balance by severely restricting sodium intake while increasing the amount of potassium consumed.

The therapy consists of a low-sodium vegetarian diet, and taking potassium supplements, thyroid extract, liver extract, digestive enzymes, and coffee enemas. Much of

---

[2] Pelton, Ross, and Overholser, Lee. 1994. *Alternatives in cancer therapy*. New York: Fireside Books, p. 42.

the diet—which consists of up to 20 pounds of fresh vegetables and fruits per day—is juice that is consumed once an hour for 13 hours every day. Many foods are to be avoided, including milk, butter, coffee (unless it's taken by enema), chocolate, alcohol, soybeans, berries (except red currants), cucumbers, and pickles; and processed, frozen, canned, bottled, smoked, salted, dehydrated, and powdered foods.

The Gerson therapy promotes healing as follows:

- The easily assimilated diet helps to purify the body by reducing the amount of toxins that enter the body via denaturalized, processed foods. This low-protein diet is believed to stimulate the immune system. The flaxseed oil in the diet is rich in the omega-3 fatty acids that are known to kill cancer cells, without harming healthy ones, in laboratory cultures.

- The potassium supplements help restore electrolyte balance.

- The thyroid extract revs up the thyroid gland, which in turn causes the individual cells to produce more energy that can be used to clear toxins and waste products from the body.

- The liver extract, given via injection for up to six months, contains vitamins, minerals, and enzymes that strengthen the liver. The liver plays an important role in Gerson therapy, for it is believed that a healthy liver can detoxify and clear most cancer-causing toxins from the body. If the liver weakens, cancer is all but inevitable.

- The digestive enzymes help ensure that as many nutrients as possible are absorbed by the body.

■ The coffee enema is designed to speed detoxification and control the pain and nausea often associated with detoxification. The coffee enema helps to eliminate this problem by drawing released toxins out of the body before they can do harm. (Rectal caffeine is felt to stimulate the liver, the great "chemical plant" and detoxifier of the body, and make it easier for waste products to be excreted via the bile ducts.)

In recent years the Gerson Institute has added new treatments including ozone, hydrogen peroxide, and live-cell therapy, and the bacteriophage virus vaccine. The entire program, including a stay at the Gerson Institute, can take up to two years, for it is believed that the liver, pancreas, immune system, and other parts of the body need that much time to fully heal after degenerating to the level that allowed cancer to develop.

Gerson therapy has not been accepted by mainstream medicine, which is not surprising. However, a team of British doctors published a positive article in the prestigious medical journal *Lancet* after visiting the Gerson Institute in 1989. Gerson therapy is regularly attacked by the medical establishment, which may be indicative of its success over many years. Dr. Gerson was also attacked personally, back in 1946, in the *Journal of the American Medical Association,* after he testified before Congress that cigarette smoking was dangerous and recommended that cancer patients be put on a strict, healthful diet.

ISCADOR

Derived from the European mistletoe (*Viscum album*), *iscador* has been used to treat people suffering from cancer of the colon, lung, stomach, breast, ovaries, and other parts of the body. It was first used by Rudolf Steiner of

Germany in the 1920s, who felt that two "forces" control body cells: "lower forces" responsible for cells' growth and division, and "higher forces" that ensure that cells differentiate properly and do not continue growing past their normal limits. The higher forces are also responsible for shaping the organs and the body. Steiner felt that when the higher forces faltered, allowing cells to proliferate beyond normal bounds, cancer followed. Mistletoe was supposed to keep the higher forces functioning.

Although the higher and lower forces theory has been discarded, mistletoe does have medicinal properties. It stimulates an important part of the immune system called the *thymus*, increases the number of immune-system cells, and spurs the cells on to fight invaders and dismantle damaged body cells.

Not considered to be a complete treatment for cancer, iscador is generally taken before surgery or radiation to help shrink tumors, and afterward to make sure that all the cancer has been destroyed. Iscador also helps the body tissues which make red blood cells recover after radiation therapy. It may be taken by mouth or via injection.

KELLEY'S NUTRITIONAL-METABOLIC THERAPY

This therapy was developed by William Kelley, a dentist who believed that cancer was caused by (1) a weakened pancreas failing to produce adequate amounts of cancer-fighting and other enzymes, (2) mineral imbalances, (3) inability to digest and utilize proteins, and (4) an electromagnetic force put out by cancer cells that weakens the immune system. Nutritional-metabolic therapy divides patients into ten categories, based on their metabolism, and then gives them special low-protein diets along with pancreatic enzymes, raw beef concentrates, and various vitamins and minerals. Coffee enemas are used for detoxification. Patients are also encouraged to explore spiritual issues.

LIVE-CELL THERAPY

Most alternative approaches to cancer are at least partially based on stimulating the immune system, which most likely would have handled the problem had it not been overwhelmed by toxins, weakened by lack of nutrients and/or energy, or otherwise prevented from doing its job. Live-cell therapy was developed by Dr. Paul Niehans of Switzerland in the 1930s. It takes a direct approach to the problem of a faltering immune system, hoping to stimulate it with injections of fetal or embryonic cells taken from humans (legal in some countries), sheep, and sometimes monkeys, calves, horses, or other animals. Injections of the live cells, which can be quite painful, are often directed right into the organ that houses the cancer.

The live-cell injections are given weekly for several weeks, then monthly for three to six months. It is felt that it takes several months for the injections to be fully effective, which is why they are usually accompanied by diet, supplements, and various detoxification regimens designed to keep the patient healthy until the injections take effect. The therapy works best for those who have not undergone radiation or chemotherapy.

LIVINGSTON THERAPY

According to the late Virginia Livingston-Wheeler, M.D., cancer is caused by a bacteria that she named *Progenitor cryptocides* ("the primordial, hidden killer"). Treatment consists of a vaccine against the bacteria, made from the patient's own blood, plus a diet based on fresh, raw fruits and vegetables, supplements, a plant hormone called *abscisic acid*, and enemas.

MACROBIOTICS

More than a treatment for cancer or any other disease, macrobiotics is a common-sense approach to life and health based on the Oriental concepts of yin and yang. The macrobiotic diet, which plays a large role in the regime, is based on one's sex, age, blood type, activity level, geographic location, and other factors, many of which change regularly.

Cancer and other diseases, which are believed to be the result of unhealthful eating, are classified by whether they are mainly yin or yang. Leukemia, cancers of the breast, skin, upper stomach, and other peripheral and upper parts of the body, as well as those in the hollow organs, are yin. Those in the deeper and lower parts of the body, and in the more compact organs, are considered to be yang. Cancers of the lung, uterus, liver, and tongue are yang cancers. Foods are also classified by their yin and yang energies. If someone has a primarily yin cancer, the macrobiotic diet designed specifically for them will emphasize yang foods. If the cancer is more yang in nature, the diet will focus on yin foods.

There is no single macrobiotic diet. Rather, there are countless variations that depend on the individual's illness, age, geographic location, and other factors. In general, however, the macrobiotic diet consists of:

- 50 to 60% whole grains such as brown rice, oats, barley, wheat, and millet.

- 25 to 30% fresh vegetables.
- 5 to 10% soups made from vegetables, beans, or grains, with the soup stock based on tamari or miso.
- 5 to 10% sea vegetables, beans, and bean products.
- Fresh water and herb teas.
- Occasional small portions of fish, fresh fruits, and unsweetened desserts.

(As you can see, the macrobiotic diet *does not* consist of nothing but brown rice and herb tea. Yukikazu Sakurazawa, who wrote under the name of George Ohsawa, outlined ten different dietary levels, one of which consisted of brown rice, other cereals, and herb tea, but that is not considered to be the "main" macrobiotic diet.")

Many of the ingredients in the macrobiotic diet, including shiitake mushrooms, seaweed, and kombu, have been shown to have anti-cancer properties. The vegetables are likely to include cabbage, broccoli, and other members of the crucifer family, which is known to contain cancer-fighting indoles.

Although diet looms large in the macrobiotic approach, it cannot guarantee better health unless its user also takes responsibility for their life and is committed to developing a well-balanced life in harmony with nature. Exercise and developing a positive mental outlook are recommended, as are wearing clothes and using cooking utensils made from natural fibers and materials. Microwave ovens, chemicals, and other non-natural items are to be avoided—along with too much television. The idea that poor lifestyle and dietary habits are responsible for disease is emphasized throughout the treatment and education period so that patients will continue their positive new lifestyle habits—including meditation, visualization, and prayer—after the health crisis has passed.

MOERMAN ANTI-CANCER DIET

Arguing that unhealthful eating weakens the body and encourages cancer, Moerman therapy is based on a diet of fresh, organically grown fruits and vegetables, whole grains, buttermilk, and natural seasonings. Fresh fruit or vegetable juice is consumed instead of water. The therapy is based on the diet of the pigeon, which does not usually suffer cancer.

OXYGEN THERAPY

Oxygen therapy is usually administered as ozone therapy or hydrogen peroxide therapy. Thanks to their unique chemical structures, these two substances release oxygen into body cells, causing the cells to literally bubble with oxygen.

Ozone, which is composed of three molecules of oxygen (O_3), has been used in Europe for half a century to treat cancer, diabetes, gangrene, asthma, and other ailments. Ozone, the stuff in the earth's atmosphere that protects us against harmful radiation, is delivered to the body therapeutically in several ways:

1. Baths.
2. Breath (from ozone air generators).
3. Rectally.

4. Via the blood. (Blood is withdrawn from the patient, mixed with ozone, and injected back into the body through a vein or muscle.)
5. Orally (via water, which the patients drink). Many major cities purify their drinking water with ozone instead of chlorine, and ozone is increasingly utilized to purify pools and spas.

Ozone is known to destroy bacteria, viruses, and fungi, but no one knows exactly how it works against cancer. One theory holds that cancer cells are simply unable to tolerate high levels of oxygen or ozone; their metabolic processes fail in the presence of O_3. Another theory suggests that ozone's primary punch comes from killing the viruses that cause a number of different types of cancer. Still another theory argues that when a patient's blood is drawn from his body and mixed with ozone, the ozone kills a few free-floating cancer cells. When that blood is reintroduced into the patient's body, their immune system recognizes the dead cancer cells as foreign and forms antibodies to the cancer, attacking the dead and live cancer cells alike. (The immune system had not attacked the living cancer cells because it was "fooled" into believing that they belonged in the body. But the dead cancer cells could not deceive the immune system.) Tens of thousands of people worldwide have been treated with ozone for cancer, with a high percentage of positive results being reported.

The other popular form of oxygen therapy utilizes hydrogen peroxide. Chemically notated as H_2O_2, hydrogen peroxide is a combination of hydrogen and oxygen best known as a cleanser for minor abrasions and cuts. When it's exposed to fluid, hydrogen peroxide breaks down into water (H_2O) and oxygen (O). The single oxygen molecule then attacks viruses and bacteria.

Hydrogen peroxide, which is naturally produced by body cells, stimulates the immune system, regulates heat, and has many other metabolic duties. Proponents of hydrogen peroxide therapy argue that while it attacks both healthy and cancerous cells, the healthy cells quickly repair themselves but the cancerous ones cannot, and die. Hydrogen peroxide also acts against cancer by prodding the natural killer (NK) cells and other parts of the immune system to fight the cancer.

PAU D'ARCO

Also known as *taheebo, ipe roxo,* and *lapacho, pau d'arco* is an herbal treatment for cancer, malaria, infections, venereal disease, colds, and other ailments. Sold in health food stores in the form of tea, powder, and capsules, pau d'arco comes from the South American tabebuia tree. Studies from around the world have shown that, taken orally, the herb can strengthen the immune system's ability to destroy tumor cells, causing at least partial regression of tumors in humans and increasing the life span of mice that have been deliberately given cancer. There are many anecdotal stories of complete cures in humans.

REVICI THERAPY

Dr. Emanuel Revici believed that good health depends on a dynamic balance between the constructive force that makes things grow, and the destructive force that dismantles things and releases their energy. When attacked, the body initiates a four-stage defense, with specific defensive substances manufactured by the body at each stage. If the defense reaction falters the body remains stuck, and continues to manufacture the substances for that stage. The body can then quickly become overloaded with these substances and fall ill. Depending on when the four-stage defense process is halted, the body will be flooded with either fatty acids or sterols, both of which can cause cancer. The solution is to counteract one offending agent with the other in order to restore balance.

SHARK CARTILAGE

The deadly shark appears to be equally dangerous to germs as it is to humans. The powerful immune systems of sharks make them impervious to many diseases—including, apparently, cancer. Indeed, despite efforts to make sharks get cancer by exposing them to powerful toxins, they remain healthy.

It appears that the explanation for the shark's invulnerability lies in its cartilage. Unlike mammals and fish, the shark has no bones. Its frame is supported entirely by cartilage. Unlike bones, muscles, and other body tissues, cartilage has no blood vessels. Instead of receiving a direct supply of fresh nutrients through arteries, it must rely on the nutrients "percolating" through and to it. That may not sound very efficient, but it probably explains why sharks do not get cancer.

Cartilage contains a substance that inhibits the growth of new blood vessels. Cancer needs the nutrients in blood in order to grow, so it secretes a substance that encourages the growth of new blood vessels from which it can feed. Without these new blood vessels, a tumor can only grow so far, then it stops. In their initial studies with rabbits, researchers proved that there is something in shark cartilage which prevents the growth of the new blood vessels cancer relies on.

Shark cartilage does not directly attack cancer—it doesn't have to. Instead, it simply cuts off its supply of food, starving or at least weakening it. Shark cartilage has been used to treat cancer patients with encouraging results. It's usually administered orally or via an enema, although capsules are widely available in health food stores and through various multi-level sources.

SUN

Limited exposure to the sun is very helpful to the body cells, which have a photoelectric element. Ten minutes of full-body sunbathing (with no clothes) each day, for five minutes on each side—making particularly sure that the sun strikes the genitals—energizes the cells, making them vibrate at a higher rate. Experiment: you'll be amazed that you can actually feel the cells vibrating after 10 minutes of exposure to the sun. These 10 minutes in the fresh air are a good time to do breathing, stretching, and eye exercises. But more is not better. After 10 minutes, it's an energy-sapping exercise, rather than an energizer.

UREA THERAPY

In the 1950s a Greek doctor reported that the urea, a substance found in urine, can kill cancer cells by disrupting their normal metabolic activities. Urine can be consumed orally, injected into the body, taken as a pill, or used as a powder to treat cancer and other diseases.

WHEATGRASS THERAPY

Developed and promoted in the U.S. by Ann Wigmore, wheatgrass therapy is based on drinking juice made from wheatgrass. Wheatgrass is considered to be a nutritional cornucopia. Ounce for ounce it has more vitamin C than oranges and more iron than spinach. It contains more than 100 minerals, vitamins, amino acids, polypeptides, and bioflavonoids. Several of these, including laetrile and abscisic acid, are felt to have anticancer properties.

Wheatgrass also contains chlorophyll, which is almost identical to the hemoglobin that carries oxygen in human blood. Like many germs, cancer cells "shun" oxygen, preferring to grow in a nearly or completely anaerobic (without oxygen) environment. It's believed that the chlorophyll in wheatgrass is converted into hemoglobin in the body, allowing the blood to carry more oxygen, thus destroying cancer cells and dangerous germs.

The therapy generally begins with the patient consuming nothing but juice for several days: wheatgrass juice, juice made from sprouts and baby green vegetables, highly nutritious vegetable juices, lemon water, and a fermented wheat berry drink called *Rejuvelac.* Wheatgrass juice baths and even retention enemas are used to assist the juices in detoxifying and rejuvenating the body. According to Wigmore, the retention enemas loosen hardened fecal matter, while the magnesium in the juice pulls toxins out of the colon, liver, and kidneys. Meanwhile, some of the chlorophyll from the juice travels from the colon to the liver, where it may stimulate liver functions and protect the organ from fat build-up.

After the juice fast, patients eat raw, organically grown foods. These foods are high in water content, making them easy to digest. They have copious amounts of fiber, which helps to carry toxins out of the body. They are filled with electrolytes to balance the body, and maintain their full complements of vitamins, minerals, and enzymes (many of which are normally destroyed by cooking, freezing, and processing). The important enzymes one gets from eating raw foods include SOD (superoxide dismutase), which guards against the effects of radiation and slows cellular aging; pepsin, which helps the body digest and deal with proteins; the antioxidant cytochrome oxidase; lipase, used to split fat; and transhydrogenase, used to keep the heart and other muscles strong. Wheatgrass therapy is considered to be complete in and of itself, so most practitioners do not recommend any additional supplements or therapies.

Although felt to be a powerful therapy, wheatgrass is not presented as a cure for cancer. Instead, it nourishes, detoxifies, and cleanses the body, allowing it to heal itself.

■ ■ ■

These intriguing therapies have helped countless people in many countries, some for many decades. Please investigate these and other alternatives carefully, letting your intuition and knowledge guide you in adding parts or all of them to your personal healing plan as *you* deem appropriate.

CHAPTER 15

DEVELOPING YOUR PERSONAL HEALING PLAN

You've discovered that you have prostate problems or cancer, and decided that the standard medical approach—surgery or radiation—is not for you. You'd like to develop your personal healing plan based on the *90-Day Prostate Cancer Cure.* Or perhaps you would like to use the *Prostate Cancer Cure* to prevent cancer, BPH, or other problems.

My *Nine-Point Healing Program,* upon which the program is based, recognizes the fact that since we are unique, there's no such thing as a "one-size-fits-all" plan. There are guidelines, but no fixed rules. You can accomplish dramatic healing within 90 days, or you can take longer. Ultimately, only *you* know what is best for you. These guidelines will help steer you through what may sometimes seem like a bewildering process. Adapt each step to your own circumstances, following your intuition as well as the messages sent to you by your body.

Step 1: Track your progress. Continue being monitored by your doctor and/or other professional(s) whom you are confident in and comfortable with. Keep a daily journal of your progress, noting everything that happens to your body, emotions, and spirit—both the pluses and minuses. Include copies of all test results in your journal.

Step 2: Get professional help with all or any part of the program. (See the appendix for suggestions on finding healers who can guide you.) Avoid any healers who want you to be fearful, no matter how many academic degrees they have. Cancer thrives on fear. Anyone who scares you is making you sicker.

Step 3: Begin *The Ultimate Fast* (or other cleansing fast) and a parasite cleanse. Do them together, for they are most effective when combined. If you can only do one at a time, opt for the 90-day Awareness parasite cleanse first. Inspect your stools in a colander and record the results. (It can be helpful for your knowledge and morale to take pictures and retain them for future reference and comparison.)

Step 4: Locate a practitioner and have a BTA performed in order to determine which of your organs need rejuvenation. Begin the rejuvenating homeopathic remedies and/or other formulas.

Step 5: Change to a low-fat diet with no processed foods. Eat a wide variety of foods, including as many fresh, uncooked fruits and vegetables as possible. Practice food-combining. Eliminate sodas and other carbonated drinks. Eliminate smoking and recreational drugs. Eliminate alcoholic beverages. If you can't give up the alcohol altogether, keep it to a bare minimum, drinking no more than a half a glass of wine on special occasions—and don't have more than four special occasions per month. Have the blood group specificity and/or Nu Health tests performed to help you fine-tune your food regimen. This regimen will change as your health improves. And different foods will serve you at different times, and at different times of the year. For example, in the winter you need more cooked and hot foods, while in the summer more fresh, raw foods, such as salads, are appropriate. My diet is continually evolving. Every few months I'm surprised by how much it has changed. As is often said, the largest variety of foods, with moderate amounts of each, is the best way to go.

Step 6: Meditate daily to reduce stress and get in touch with your higher guidance and unreleased emotions. Honestly recognize and acknowledge your fears. Thank the fear for warning you that you are headed for trouble unless you take positive action, but be clear that you are taking action and can handle your worst fear. Under the guidance of a counselor and/or spiritual (not necessarily religious) teacher, begin to get in touch with your life's purpose. Ask for help from the universe. Visualize yourself in radiant health, doing all the things you most enjoy. Reevaluate your life and associations, transforming or eliminating those that do not bring you joy. Breathe more deeply, all day long, to bring more oxygen to your blood and organs, for cancer cannot survive in an oxygen-rich environment.

Know that there is a lot of help out there. Seek out help by checking the listings in the New Age press, and on bulletin boards in bookstores and health food stores. Take classes at "New Age" churches, and at the Learning Annex and other community education centers. Go to lots of workshops. As you declare and become clear in your intent to be assisted, help will begin to appear in your life. When it does, all you need to do is be clear and open to receiving the assistance.

Develop your own plan with a definitive time goal — whether it is 90 days, 6 months, or a year.

Step 7: Happiness is a major ingredient and requisite for good health, so say "yes!" to life. (You may need to first experience your "no," however.) Live in the moment. Let go of rigidity and judgments about people and events. We often miss wonderful things that show up in our lives because we are too attached to rigid programs of our own. Make sure you don't miss anything by being open to whatever appears in your life. Look for and find the value in people and events, including the lessons to be learned from your illness/healing.

Step 8: Get deep-tissue massage and/or bodywork, including prostate and inner muscle massage, to release tight muscles and stuck emotions, especially around the prostate.

Step 9: Find and practice gratitude for everything in your life.

Step 10: Develop an alternative standard medical treatment plan (mine was seed radiation). Visit the physician, clinic, and/or hospital to get all the preliminaries out of the way. Set a timetable for your program. Give yourself 90 days, six months, or a year to see definite improvement. If you don't feel that you have made solid progress within that time, then implement your alternative plan.

Decide on a "fall-back" plan for standard medical treatment.

Step 11: Consider adding therapies that will help you, such as:

- Microwater to speed things up.
- A hormone test and evaluation, plus natural supplements to balance any imbalances.

- Chelation to increase circulation (including erections) and/or to lower your blood pressure (if you have any heart or circulation problems).
- Growth hormones and/or live-cell therapy to jump-start your plan.

Step 12: Develop and practice an active tantric love life.

Step 13: Develop and commit to an exercise program that works for you, no matter how little exercise you may be capable of performing when you begin. Stay with your program, exercising at least three times a week. You'll be surprised at how quickly you become stronger and more fit.

Step 14: Adopt a total hygiene program to raise your albumin level (see Chapter 9).

Step 15: Continually reevaluate your plan, making changes and adjustments as necessary. Use standard medical tests such as the PSA and DRE to monitor your progress, and learn all you can from your physician (but don't let them do any invasive treatments or fill you with their fear).

■ ■ ■

If you find you're having difficulty getting your program started or sticking to it, consider checking into one of the many residential cancer clinics here in the United States or abroad. A short stay can be restful and very educational.

This is *your* plan. It's designed by you and for you, and you will continually alter it to suit your needs. Carefully consider the advice of the professionals assisting you, but always do your own research and make your own decisions.

Remember, only YOU can heal yourself. Know that you CAN do it. Like countless other men, I am living proof that prostate cancer can be healed in 90 days—without surgery, radiation, or drugs.

For the latest information on developments in prostate health, visit the Prostate Health Resource Website: www.prostate90.com

APPENDIX

HOW TO FIND THE RIGHT HEALERS AND PRODUCTS

ANTI-PARASITE PRODUCTS

For information on ordering PC-1-2-3 and all other fasting products, contact:

Art Bartunek at BCN

(888) 803-5333 or (323) 962-7370

For information on Awareness™ Products, contact:

Donna Larmée
(310) 577-1102

AROMATHERAPY

These organizations can provide information, materials, and/or referrals.

Lotus Light
P.O. Box 1008
Wilmot, WI 53170
(262) 889-8501

BIOLOGIC DENTISTS

A leading biologic dentist in America, Dr. Harold Ravins, is located at 12381 Wilshire Blvd., Suite 103, Los Angeles, California 90025, (310) 207-4617.

For other referrals and/or information:

American Academy of Biological Dentistry
P.O. Box 856
Carmel Valley, CA 93924
(831) 659-5385

Dental Amalgam Syndrome (DAMS)
P.O. Box 64397
Virginia Beach, VA 23467-4367
(800) 311-6265

Environmental Dental Association
9974 Scripps Ranch Blvd., #36
San Diego, CA 92131
(800) 388-8124

Foundation for Toxic-Free Dentistry
P.O. Box 608010
Orlando, FL 32860

Holistic Dental Association
(970) 259-1091

BIO-OLIGO SUPPLEMENTS

To purchase, contact:

Molecular Biologics
Benicia, CA 94510

BLOOD SPECIFICITY TESTING

To learn about the testing, contact:

Rockwood Natural Medicine Clinic
800 S.E. 181st Avenue
Gresham, OR 97233
(503) 667-1961

BODYWORK

In Southern California, Raya King is an excellent, innovative bodyworker trained in Hellerwork and prostate massage. She can be reached at (323) 936-6696.

For other referrals and/or information:

American Massage Therapy Association
820 Davis Street, #100
Evanston, IL 60201-4444
(312) 761-2682

American Polarity Therapy Association
P.O. Box 19858
Boulder, CO 80308
(303) 545-2080

The Aston Training Center
P.O. Box 3568
Incline Village, NV 89450
(775) 831-8228
(specializing in Aston patterning)

Hellerwork International
3435 M St.
Eureka, CA 95503
(707) 441-4949

International Rolf Institute
P.O. Box 1868
Boulder, CO 80306
(303) 449-5903
(specializing in Rolfing)

North American Society of Teachers of the Alexander Technique
(800) 473-0620

PROSTATE MASSAGE

High Island Health
P.O. Box 55427
Houston, TX 77255
(713) 721-3611
(When ordering this product, please mention Prostate Health Resources as your referral.)

BTA

Michael Galitzer, M.D.
12381 Wilshire Blvd., Suite 102
Los Angeles, CA 90025
(310) 820-6042

For other referrals and/or information:

Biological Technologies International
Rob Greenberg
(520) 474-4181

CANCER CLINICS

Refer to current and past issues of *Alternative Medicine Digest*. The bimonthly magazine inspects and reports on clinics in each issue. These clinics can change rapidly, so it is important to have current information.

Alternative Medicine Digest
(800) 333-HEAL
www.alternativemedicine.com

CHELATION THERAPY

For information and/or referrals, contact:

American College for Advancement in Medicine
23121 Verdugo Drive, #204
Laguna Hills, CA 92653
(949) 583-7666

COLON THERAPY

For information and/or referrals, contact:

International Association for Colon Therapy
2051 Hilltop Drive, #A-11
Redding, CA 96022
(210) 366-2888
www.i-act.org

Wood Hygiene Institute
P.O. Box 420580
Kissimmee, FL 34742
(407) 933-0009

DETOXIFICATION (INCLUDING HEAVY METALS)

Dental Amalgam Syndrome (DAMS)
P.O. Box 64397
Virginia Beach, VA 23467-4367
(800) 311-6265

Hans Gruenn, M.D.
Culver City, CA
(800) 966-9194

EMOTIONAL BLOCKS, CLEARING

These practitioners and organizations may be helpful:

American Psychological Association
750 First Street NE
Washington, D.C. 20002
(202) 336-5700

Center for Cognitive Therapy
Science Center, Room 754
3600 Market Street
Philadelphia, PA 19104
(215) 898-4100

EMDR Institute (Clinician Referrals)
http://www.emdr.com
(512) 451-4777

National Association of Social Workers
750 First Street NE, #700
Washington, D.C. 20002
(202) 408-8600

The NLP Center of New York
(800) 422-8657

ENVIRONMENTAL MEDICINE

For information, books, and/or referrals, contact:

Human Ecology Action League
P.O. Box 29629
Atlanta, GA 30359
(404) 248-1898
(404) 248-0162 (fax)

Immuno Labs
1620 W. Oakland Park Blvd., #300
Ft. Lauderdale, FL 33311
(800) 231-9197

Natural Lifestyles Wholesale
P.O. Box 10332
Asheville, NC 28806
(828) 665-2820
(800) 958-2276

HANSI

For information and to purchase, contact:

(HANSI) World Health Advanced Technologies
1941 Northgate Blvd.
Sarasota, FL 34234

HOMEOPATHY

For information and referrals:

Michael Galitzer, M.D.
12381 Wilshire Blvd., Suite 102
Los Angeles, CA 90025
(310) 820 6042

National Center for Homeopathy
801 N. Fairfax, #306
Alexandria, VA 22314
(703) 548-7790
www.homeopathic.org

HORMONE BALANCING

Jonathan Wright, M.D.
Tahoma Clinic Dispensary
515 W. Harrison
Kent, WA 98302
(253) 850-5661
(253) 854-4900

HYGIENE PRODUCTS

Dr. Kenneth Seaton's hygiene products are available from:

High-Performance Hygiene
24000 Mercantile Road, Suite 7
Cleveland, OH 44122
(888) 262-5700 (*toll-free*)

HYPERTHERMIA

For information on hyperthermia, contact:

Bastyr College
14500 Juanita Dr. NE
Kenmore, WA 98028
(425) 823-1300

LAZARIS

Lazaris's books and tapes, as well as information about his seminars, are available from:

Concept: Synergy
P.O. Box 691867
Orlando, FL 32869
online: www.lazaris.com

(407) 876-4973 (information)
(800) 678-2356 (orders)

LIVE CELL THERAPY

International Clinic of Biologic Regeneration
(800) 826-5366

MAGNETIC FIELD THERAPY

For information, contact:

Bio-Electro Magnetics Institute
2490 W. Moana Lane
Reno, NV 89509
(775) 827-9099

Enviro-Tech Products
17171 S.E. 29th Street
Choctaw, OK 73020
(405) 390-3499

MEDITATION & RELAXATION

For information, workshops, materials, and referrals, contact:

Institute of Noetic Sciences
P.O. Box 909
Sausalito, CA 94966
(415) 331-5650

Institute of Transpersonal Psychology
744 San Antonio Rd., #15
Palo Alto, CA 94303
(650) 493-4430

Maharishi International University
1000 N. Fourth Street
Fairfield, IA 52557
(515) 472-7000
(specializing in transcendental meditation)

Stress Reduction Clinic
University of Massachusetts Memorial
Medical Center
55 Lake Avenue N.
Worcester, MA 01655
(508) 856-2656

MICROWATER

The Microwater devices discussed in Chapter 6 are available by calling Universal Water at (714) 526-7917. For local distributors, call (800) 456-4520. The process of producing Microwater is being constantly refined. Dr. Dennis Higgins of Newport, California, is intimately involved with the refinement and improvement of Microwater units, making them more cost-effective in the process. He believes that less expensive, more effective units will soon be available from Japan. Units currently available for home or office use sell for around $1,000.

NEURAL THERAPY

For referrals to practitioners of this science, contact:

The American Academy of Neural Therapy
1468 S. Saint Francis Drive
Sante FE, NM 87501
(505) 988-3086

NUTRITIONAL & ENZYME THERAPY

For information, contact:

American College of Advancement in Medicine
P.O. Box 3427
Laguna Hills, CA 92654
(714) 583-7666

American College of Nutrition
722 Robert E. Lee Drive
Wilmington, NC 28480
(919) 452-1222

Center for Science in the Public Interest
1875 Connecticut Avenue NW, #300
Washington, D.C. 20009
(202) 332-9110 ext. 384

Lia Lee, Ph.D.
2852 Williamette Street, #397
Eugene, OR 97405
(503) 746-7621
(for information on doctors using enzyme therapy)

NESS
2903 N.W. Platte Road
Riverside, MO 64150
(800) 637-7893

OXYGEN THERAPY

To learn more about this therapy, contact:

The American College of Hyperbaric Medicine
Ocean Medical Center
4001 Ocean Drive #105
Lauderdale-by-the-Sea, FL 33308
(305) 771-4000

ECH2O2 Newsletter
9845 N.E. Second Avenue
Miami, FL 33138
(305) 758-8710

International Ozone Association
31 Strawberry Hill Avenue
Stamford, CT 06902
(203) 348-3542

Medical Society for Ozone Therapy
Klagen Furtestrasse 4
D. 7000 Stuttgart 30
Germany

SUPPORT AND INFORMATION GROUPS

There are numerous cancer support and information groups in major cities, and at least one in many smaller cities. Many, such as the National Institute of Cancer and PAACT, serve people nationwide. You may want to begin by contacting one of the following organizations (particularly PAACT, which focuses solely on prostate cancer).

American Foundation for Urologic Disease
300 W. Pratt St., Suite 401
Baltimore, MD 21201
(800) 242-2383

Provides information on prostate and other urologic dis eases, and acts as a clearinghouse for more than 200 prostate cancer support groups.

CancerFax®
(301) 402-5874

Provides cancer information from the National Cancer Institute's Physician Data Query (PDQ) system. Call the above number from a fax machine, and then key in the appropriate information when prompted to request information.

Cancer Information Service (CIS)
(800) 4-CANCER or (800) 422-6237

Provides up-to-date information on cancer to patients and their families, health professionals, and the general public. CIS is sponsored by the National Cancer Institute.

National Cancer Institute
Office of Cancer Communication
Building 31, Room 10A24
9000 Rockville Pike
Bethesda, MD 20892
(800) 4-CANCER

The National Coalition for Cancer Survivorship (NCCS)
(301) 650-9127

The largest network of individuals and independent organizations interested in cancer support, advocacy, and survivorship. The organization emphasizes maintaining a full life while dealing with cancer.

Patient Advocates for Advanced Cancer Treatments (PAACT)
1143 Parmelee NW
Grand Rapids, MI 49504
(616) 453-1477

The organization's sole interest is prostate cancer. It offers the latest information on treatment with drugs and surgery, and particularly combination hormonal therapy, via its newsletter, CANCER COMMUNICATION, and through other books and pamphlets. Membership is inexpensive, and free to anyone with financial hardship.

US TOO
300 W. Pratt St., Suite 401
Baltimore, MD 21201
(800) 808-7866
(708) 323-1002

Offers information and counseling for prostate cancer survivors and their families. It also has more than 200 support groups in the U.S. and Canada.

The Wellness Community
2716 Ocean Park Blvd., Suite 1040
Santa Monica, CA 90405-5211
(310) 314-2555

The largest organization of its kind in the U.S., it offers free education and psychological support. Call the Santa Monica office to get the phone number of a branch near you.

VISUALIZATION (BOOKS AND TAPES)

The Academy for Guided Imagery
P.O. Box 2070
Mill Valley, CA 94941
(800) 726-2070

VIT-RA-TOX (COLON CLEANSE PRODUCTS)

(800) 544-8147

YOGA

International Association of Yoga Therapists
109 Hillside Avenue
Mill Valley, CA 94941
(415) 383-4587

Yoga Journal
2054 University Avenue
Berkeley, CA 94704
(510) 841-9200
(Publishes an annual directory of yoga instructors.)

P. 109 PC Spes 888-803-533
CHINESE HERB FORMULA

RECOMMENDED READING

Knowledge is your best weapon against disease. Read all you can, whether the material discusses alternative or traditional Western approaches to prostate cancer. Here are some books and magazine articles to get you started.

Adler, J. The killer we don't discuss. *Newsweek* 12/27/93, p. 40(2).

Alternative Medicine (bimonthly magazine), *Alternative Medicine Digest* and *Alternative Medicine: The Definitive Guide*, (800) 333-HEAL, (800) 515-HEAL, www.alternativemedicine.com.

Assessing need for repeated biopsies. *USA Today* (magazine) 2/93, p. 13(1).

Bowers, J. Adieu, old pal. *American Health* 10/92, p. 62(2).

Brennan, Barbara Ann. *Hands of Light.* New York: Bantam Books, 1988.

Burroughs, Stanley. *The Master Cleanser.* Auburn, California: Burroughs Books, 1976. (*The complete description of the Master Cleanser fast.*)

Cancer Facts. Published periodically by the National Cancer Institute. Available through their web site: http://www.nci.nih.gov/.

Carey, B. The prostate predicament. *Health* 5–6/94, p. 101(4).

Carlson, Robert. The other prostate problem: New drugs and procedures to reduce an enlarged gland and relieve symptoms. *American Health*, 10/92, p. 59.

Cunningham, Chet. *Your Prostate: What Every Man Over 40 Needs to Know… Now!* United Research Publishers, 1990.

Dittman, R. Jr. Help for the disease men fear most. *Readers' Digest* 12/92, p. 209(6).

Does sex help the prostate? *Consumer Reports* 11/93, p. 743(1).

Dunn, D. Prostate cancer: How to thwart a killer. *Business Week* 3/16/92, p. 132(2).

Galitzer, Michael. *Clinical Bioenergetics.* Los Angeles: International Academy of Modern Bioenergetics, 1994. (*A brief, readable introduction to the science of bioenergetics.*) www.ahealth.com/ahi/

Garnick, Marc. The dilemmas of prostate cancer. *Scientific American*, 4/94, p. 72.

Gerber, Richard. *Vibrational Medicine.* Sante Fe, New Mexico: Bear & Company, 1988.

Gorman C. The private pain of prostate cancer. *Time*, 10/5/92, p. 77(2).

Grove, Andy. Taking on prostate cancer. *Fortune* 5/13/96, p. 55. (*An excellent discussion of prostate cancer and the pros and cons of traditional treatments.*)

High (34.9%) retreatment of radical prostectomy patients. *Alternative Medicine Digest* #17, 3–4/97, p. 99.

Jensen, Bernard and Bell, Sylvia. *Tissue Cleansing Through Bowel Management.* Escondido, California: Bernard Jensen, 1981.

Laliberte, R. The prostate debate. *Men's Health* 12/93, p. 65(5).

Lax, E. Is your husband dying of embarrassment? The truth about prostate cancer. *Family Circle* 7/20/93, p. 57(4).

Lend the gland a hand: Exercise lowers risk for prostate cancer. *Prevention* 8/92, p. 10(2).

Lymph dysfunction and its role in prostate cancer. *Explore!* 11/3/95.

Mann, Charles. The prostate cancer dilemma. *Atlantic Monthly*, 11/93, p. 102.

Meinig, George. *Root Canal Cover-Up*. Ojai, California: Bion Publishing, 1996.

Mobilizing for early prostate cancer detection. *Saturday Evening Post*, 9–10/92, p. 56(2).

Mowrey, Daniel. To kiss a cobra: The prostate, man's worst friend. *Let's Live*, 8/93, p. 16.

Muir, Charles and Caroline. *Tantra: The Art of Conscious Loving*. San Francisco: Mercury House, 1989.

Walter, Richard. *Options. The Alternative Cancer Therapy Book*. New York: Avery Publishing Group, 1993.

Prostate cancer: Conspiracy of silence. *U.S. News and World Report* 5/11/92, p. 68(2).

Prostate puzzle. *Consumer Reports*, 7/93, p. 459.

Prostate health resources website: www.prostate90.com

Rous, Stephen. *The Prostate Book*. New York: W. W. Norton & Company, 1994. (*Written by a very traditional Western physician, this book explains surgery and radiation.*)

Seaton, Kenneth. *Life, Health and Longevity*. Huntington, West Virginia: Kenneth Seaton, 1994. (*An in-depth look at hygiene and albumin.*)

Steinner, David. *Diet for a Poisoned Planet*. New York: Ballantine Books, 1990.

Thornton, J. Pharm aid: Ten new medicines you should know about. *Men's Health* 10/90, p. 73(5).

Walker, Norman. *Colon Health: The Key to a Vibrant Life*. Prescott, Arizona: Norwalk Press, 1979.

What if it's cancer? *Consumer Reports* 7/93, p. 463(3).

INDEX

tate cancer, but now it would soon be adopted any way as the gold standard for diagnosing the disease. When I wrote the letter, I received dozens of irate letters from urologists, oncologists, and others saying I was misleading readers. I can assure you that wasn't the case. Since that time, thousands of men have undoubtedly had unnecessary biopsies or removal of their prostate glands, and as a result suffered hormone problems, distress, anxiety, sexual dysfunction, and even an early death.

Dr. Thomas Stamey of Stanford University, one of the strongest advocates of PSA testing initially, recently spoke of its shortcomings at the American Urological Association conference.

Dr. Stamey now says that PSA is no longer a useful or reliable marker for detecting prostate cancer. Very often it is simply a sign of an enlarged prostate gland, which happens to be common in the large majority of elderly men.

His findings were based on his own experience, plus his careful evaluation of the medical records of 1,317 men who had radical prostatectomies during the past 20 years. His lab at Stanford re-examined every prostate that had been removed since 1983 and compared the size of the cancer with the blood PSA levels. In the early years, prostate screening was not longer has a relationship to prostate cancer. Because we all develop the cancer, we're now removing prostates from men whose cancer is so small that they do not need the procedure. We're finding all these little cancers that are never going to be a danger to the patient. *In smaller cancers, the PSA test is not relevant anymore; you might as well biopsy a man because he has blue eyes."*

PSA is a glycoprotein that is secreted by normal prostate glands. Its blood levels will increase if the gland enlarges, even if due to a non-cancerous condition. Many doctors fail to explain this adequately to their patients but instead insist on a biopsy. Until a better, more reliable test is available, Dr. Stamey recommends that patients and doctors rely on a digital rectal exam (i.e., a lubricated, gloved finger) and a thorough history to monitor prostate health.

I thought I received a lot of irate letters and calls after my article in 1992. I can only imagine the flak Dr. Stamey is receiving. It takes a lot of courage for him to release this information and to honestly state that, "I removed a few hundred prostates that I wish I hadn't." If there was more of such honesty in medical research today, a lot less suffering would take place and a lot more healing could take place.

Most people (the public and doctors alike) still think that probiotics may be beneficial for food-type allergies, but they fail to make the connection between beneficial bacterial flora in the bowel and airborne allergens and pathogens. As Professor Huffnagle correctly pointed out, "everything you inhale, you also swallow."

If you suffer from allergies, either from food *or airborne pollutants,* make sure you re-establish your gut flora with fermented foods and probiotics. In many cases, this alone will solve the problem. I have no doubt that keeping the flora in the intestinal tract intact can be the difference between life and death in many situations. It probably explains why some people are able to survive while others perish when exposed to various biological agents, flu viruses, bacteria, and other pathogens. Antibiotics are not harmless remedies to be used indiscriminately.

PSA Is a Pretty Silly Argument

SAN FRANCISCO, CALIFORNIA—In the August 1992 issue (Vol. 4, No. 14), I wrote about a new test for prostate cancer called the PSA test (prostate specific antigen). If you have a copy of that issue I would ask that you pull it out and read it again now.

such a widespread or popular procedure. When the screening began, there were obviously more cancers detected and the PSA values appeared to be more relevant. Dr. Stamey found that 15 to 20 years ago PSA was related to prostate cancer about 60 percent of the time, but during the most recent 5-year period (1999 through 2003) an elevated PSA level related to cancer only 2 percent of the time. This means that 98 percent of the time an elevated PSA level today is only related to prostate size, benign enlargement of the prostate. Regardless of this fact, an elevated PSA has now become the main reason for prostate biopsy in this country.

The public has the misperception that if you have an elevated PSA level you have prostate cancer. Prostate cancer is being over-diagnosed and over-treated because of this misconception. Rather surprisingly, Dr. Stamey presented his findings about the same time revised guidelines were issued concerning PSA levels and biopsies. New guidelines by the National Comprehensive Cancer Network call for starting PSA prostate screening tests at age 40 and performing a biopsy if the PSA level exceeds 2.5 ng/mL. The previous recommendations were age 50 and PSA level of over 4 ng/mL before a bi

ABOUT THE AUTHOR

W. Lawrence Clapp, Ph.D., J.D., author, practicing attorney, corporate CEO, public figure, and real estate developer, was chief executive officer of an international real estate conglomerate, developing hundreds of homes and commercial projects in Hawaii, California, Samoa, the Philippines, and France. He was co-founder of the Bank of Honolulu, trustee of the Hawaii School for Girls, and chaired several public organizations in Hawaii, including the Honolulu Public Transit Authority.

He earned his J.D. degree at the University of Michigan Law School in 1963. His Ph.D., earned at Galien University in London in 1996, was based on the six years of research and writing of this book, in Hawaii; England; San Francisco; Boulder, Colorado; and Santa Monica.

During seven years of intensive research, he studied under several medical doctors, biological dentists, and alternative healers, developing expertise in cleansing, nutritional healing, pH balancing, herbology, homeopathy, bodywork, and energetic and spiritual healing. Combining the best of these healing arts, he developed this successful treatment program (with which he healed himself) for prostate cancer.

Dr. Clapp is co-author of *Awaken the Healer Within* (Prime Books, 1992), which focuses on the emotional aspects of healing, and he coaches men suffering from prostate problems, including cancer. The carefully tailored version of the plan he gives to each has helped them deal with these life-threatening ailments.

Website: **www.Prostate90.com**

For a free copy of

10 Steps to a Healthy Prostate,

fill out the form below and mail to:

Larry Clapp, Ph.D.
Ten Steps
1431 Ocean Ave. #1611
Santa Monica, CA 90401

Name ____________________

Address ____________________

City ______________ State ________ Zip Code __________

Country ______________

E-Mail ______________

Your Age ______________

Comments ____________________

____

____

____

____

____

____

We hope you enjoyed this Hay House book. If you would like to receive a free catalog featuring additional Hay House books and products, or if you would like information about the Hay Foundation, please write or call:

Hay House, Inc.
P.O. Box 5100
Carlsbad, CA 92018-5100

(760) 431-7695 or **(800) 654-5126**
(760) 431-6948 (fax) or **(800) 650-5115 (fax)**

Please visit the Hay House Website at:
www.hayhouse.com

Please visit the Prostate Health Resources Website at:
www.prostate90.com